World Monetary Units

World Monetary Units

An Historical Dictionary,
Country by Country

Howard M. Berlin

McFarland & Company, Inc., Publishers
Jefferson, North Carolina, and London

LIBRARY OF CONGRESS CATALOGUING-IN-PUBLICATION DATA

Berlin, Howard M.
World monetary units : an historical dictionary,
country by counry / Howard M. Berlin.
p.   cm.
Includes bibliographical references and index.

ISBN 0-7864-2080-4 (illustrated case binding : 50# alkaline paper) ∞

1. Money—Dictionaries. 2. Money—History. I. Title.
HG216.B465   2006   332.4'03—dc22   2005025416

British Library cataloguing data are available

Cover photograph © 2005 Photospin

Manufactured in the United States of America

*McFarland & Company, Inc., Publishers
Box 611, Jefferson, North Carolina 28640
www.mcfarlandpub.com*

Table of Contents

Preface 1

How to Use This Book 3

"For one cent, you can get one penny's worth."
— Chinese proverb

Preface

Money has always fascinated me. My interest probably was sparked when I started collecting coins and world stamps when I was about 10 years old. I was inquisitive about the strange monetary units on the stamps, coins and paper money — the only ones I knew about were dollars, pounds, francs, and pesos. I discovered that the familiar dollar sign ($) was used by other countries for units other than the dollar. I wondered about the origin of the denominations of many of the world's currencies, even the well-known ones like the ruble, franc, or peso. I wondered why the British pound was called a *pound*. Why was it divided into the awkward units of shillings, pence, and farthings? Why did it have a fancy looking letter L (£) as its symbol?

I soon found that I was not alone in my curiosity, and also that finding answers is not easy. For some units, a good English dictionary provides the answers. Foreign language dictionaries provide additional clues. The Internet can be a helpful resource, although errors and contradictions are prevalent. One good starting point is Adrian Room's helpful book *Dictionary of Coin Names*. As informative as Room's book is, however, it is nearly two decades old, and the world has changed quite a bit since then. Even this book will eventually need revision, but I have to draw the line somewhere.

This work is really several books in one, and I have tried to make it different from all others. It includes information about what monetary units have been used in 203 countries and four confederations, how their names changed over the years, and how they are divided into smaller units. Each country or confederation's entry typically covers the last 100 to 150 years. Many of the monetary units can best be understood in the context of the political history, geography, and languages of a country, and for these reasons, each country's history is briefly narrated. In many cases a former colony, after gaining independence, adopted the monetary system of its colonial ruler, while other countries made a clean break with their colonial past.

One area in which this book will prove helpful is orthography, as it provides the proper spelling of the monetary units, including their plural forms. Some plurals simply follow the conventional rules of English — the addition of the letter s; for others, the singular and plural form are either very different or exactly the same. When a language (such as Arabic, Hindi, or Russian) does not use the Latin alphabet, the transliteration of names into English does have its variations, such as ruble vs. rouble. In an effort to provide guidance to researchers, writers, and editors, I have attempted what I hope will be useful and reliable standardization of spellings employed by the central bank of each country if letters of the Latin alphabet are used for its language. For countries with non–Latin alphabets (e.g., Russia, India, Saudi Arabia, Israel), I normally have used the spelling found most often in major financial, numismatic, and philatelic sources.

At the end of this work is a glossary of more than 250 monetary units. Most of the entries give the unit's etymology, or origin of its name. The names chosen for monetary units often include, but are not limited to, names based on geography (afghani, lwei), animals (leone, quetzal), important people (balboa, sucre), units of weight (shekel, pound), synonyms for "weight" (peso, tael), royalty (korona, riyal), objects (escudo, kreuzer), bits and pieces (cent, paisa), size (grosz, gourde), shape (yen, yuan), and intrinsic metallic properties (guilder, ngultrum).

An introductory chapter explains how the information in this book is arranged, the conventions used for spelling and foreign language words, and the monetary symbols and abbreviations employed. This introduction is followed by monetary information (history, chronology, and orthography for singular and plural forms) for each country and confederation, alphabetized from Afghanistan to Zimbabwe. The book concludes with five appendices: Foreign Language Number Systems; Families of Monetary Units; Monetary Abbreviations and Symbols; ISO-4217 Currency Codes; and Central Banks.

The writing of nonfiction is rarely done in a vacuum, and I have called on many people to provide assistance in areas where I lacked the required knowledge and expertise. I would like to acknowledge the help provided by the following individuals: Hasan Avlar, Phil Doudar, Ulrich Greve, Armen Hovsepian, Dr. Irina Knyazeva, Dr. Juri Kopolovič, Dr. Juan José Marcos, Archana Sharma, Ken Weaverling, and Orhan Zorer. Knowledgeable assistance and clarifications were also provided by either the central bank or the embassy of the following countries: Australia, Cyprus, Czech Republic, Denmark, Estonia, Hungary, Latvia, Lithuania, Malta, Serbia and Montenegro, Slovakia, Slovenia, Suriname, and Switzerland.

Howard M. Berlin
Wilmington, Delaware

How to Use This Book

This book contains information on the monetary systems of 203 countries and four confederations, arranged in alphabetical order from Afghanistan to Zimbabwe.

Immediately following each country or confederation's name is its current three-letter ISO-4217 abbreviation for the country's major monetary unit. This code is now often used instead of any conventional symbols or abbreviations. For example, the code for the U.S. dollar is USD, so 10 dollars would often be written as either USD 10 or 10 USD instead of $10. A summary of all the three-letter ISO codes is given in Appendix D.

Following the country name and ISO abbreviation is a brief history of the country and the changes in its monetary system.

Next in each entry comes a chronology, that is, a table of monetary units giving dates of use, in reverse chronological order, of the major and equivalent minor units. In many instances, the dates are approximate and periods often overlap, such as when two monetary units (like the euro) were in force during a transition period.

A typical chronology looks like this:

Year	Denomination	Equivalent
1999–present	euro	100 euro-cent
1861–2002	Finnish markka	100 pennia (*penniä*)
1809–1861	Russian ruble	100 kopecks

For each denomination, the generally accepted English-language spelling is given. If the foreign spelling is different from the English and is often encountered, it follows in parentheses. In most cases, the spellings are given without diacriticals if the unit name is used by two or more countries, because the usage of diacriticals varies from country to country. If there are several divisions for the same unit, these are listed with the highest unit first (e.g., pounds, then shillings, then pence), as illustrated below:

Year	Denomination	Equivalent
1970–present	dalasi	100 butut
1964–1970	Gambian pound	20 shillings
	shilling	12 pence
–1964	West African pound	20 shillings
	shilling	12 pence

3

Finally in the entry comes a table showing orthography and number, which summarizes the commonly accepted English-language spelling of singular and plural forms of the monetary units for that country and is arranged alphabetically by its singular spelling. In many cases, the singular and plural forms are the same, especially if the word is of non–English origin (e.g., yen). For some names, the plural can be correctly spelled with or without a final s (e.g., anna or annas) and these are noted with an asterisk (*). Alternate English spellings follow in parentheses; foreign-language equivalents are italicized (e.g., *livres* for pound) and are placed within parentheses following the English unit.

When there is a known symbol or abbreviation for a given unit, an example is given that illustrates its use in conjunction with an amount —1, if the symbol or abbreviation is singular, and usually 10 if the symbol or abbreviation is either restricted to the plural or can be used with any amount (e.g., Re1 or Rs10). For some countries, the amount and monetary abbreviation can be written in either order (e.g., 10NP or NP10). As a general practice, there is no space between the amount and the monetary symbol (e.g., 10¢, £10) but often there is no set rule regarding the insertion of a space.

Singular	Plural	Known Abbreviations and Symbols	Examples
centime	centimes	c	10c
piastre	piastres	P غ ق	10P 10P50 غ١٠ ق١٠
pound (*livre*)	pounds (*livres*)	L£ L.L. ل.ل.	L£10 L.L. 10 ل.ل١٠.

It is not uncommon for several countries to use the same monetary unit but with different symbols or abbreviations. In many cases, especially on coins and postage stamps, the abbreviations and symbols for the same country may be rendered in a variety of styles.

Monetary units are often rendered in both lower-case and upper-case letters, or in some combination. For example, the symbol or abbreviation for the French franc may appear in any of these ways:

f   F   FR   fr   Fr

Sometimes a period may be included, as for the rupee:

Rs.   Rs

Some abbreviations may have one or more letters underlined, as for the centime:

Cen   cen

Some letters may be raised:

C^{es} C^{ES} C$_{ES}$ C^{ES}

The convention used in this book is that unless an underline, dot, or period (e.g., c, ċ, or c.) is required as the official abbreviation or symbol, it is omitted. In addition, abbreviations and symbols are generally rendered as lower-case, although there will be exceptions (e.g., KD, for the Kuwaiti dinar).

WORLD MONETARY UNITS

Afghanistan (AFA)

In 1919 Afghanistan gained its independence from Great Britain's control of its foreign affairs. Because of its location and control by Great Britain, its monetary system closely followed that of British India with its rupees and paise. The habibi, equal to 30 rupees, was named after Habibullah Khan, an Afghan emir who ruled from 1901 to 1919. In 1925 the monetary system was reformed with the introduction of the afghani, divisible into 100 puls.

Although Afghanistan primarily uses the Latin alphabet for its abbreviations, it also uses letters from the Pashtu alphabet for certain monetary units, such as the letter *pe* (پ) as the abbreviation for pul (پول) when combined with the Persian numerals shown below:

0	1	2	3	4	5	6	7	8	9	10	50	100	500	1000
٠	١	٢	٣	۴	۵	۶	٧	٨	٩	١٠	۵٠	١٠٠	۵٠٠	١٠٠٠

CHRONOLOGY

Year	Denomination	Equivalent
2002–present	new afghani	100 puls
1925–2002	afghani	100 puls
–1925	rupee	100 paise
	tilla	10 rupees
	habibi	30 rupees

ORTHOGRAPHY AND NUMBER

Singular	Plural	Known Abbreviations and Symbols	Examples
afghani	afghanis	Af Afg Afs	1 Af 10 Afs
paisa	paise		
pul	puls	P Ps پ	10P 10 Ps ١٠پ
rupee	rupees	R Rs	1R 10Rs

7

Albania (ALL)

Until 1912, Albania was part of the Ottoman Empire, and its monetary system consisted of the Ottoman lira, which was divisible into non-decimal units such as altilik, beshlik, yuzluk and the like. A monetary reform in 1881 greatly simplified the system, leaving the piastre, divisible into 40 para. From independence in 1912 until 1925 Albania did not have an independent monetary system of its own. It relied on French francs, Italian liras, and Greek drachmas — monies of the Latin Monetary Union — in addition to Austrian kronen.

In 1925 Albania introduced the franga, a derivative of the franc. The franga, formally known as the franga ari, was divisible into 100 qindarka — derived from the Albanian word *njëqind*, meaning "one hundred." The current monetary unit, the lek, is derived from the abbreviation of the Albanian spelling of Alexander the Great; it replaced the franga as the standard monetary unit in 1946 at an exchange of five lek for one franga. Although the English singular and plural forms for the lek are the same, the spelling of the Albanian-language plural for lek is either lekë or leku, depending on the number it is associated with.

CHRONOLOGY

Year	Denomination	Equivalent
1946–present	lek	100 qindarka
1925–1946	franga	100 qindarka
1881–1912	piastre	40 para

ORTHOGRAPHY AND NUMBER

Singular	Plural	Known Abbreviations and Symbols	Examples
franga	franga	Fr	10 Fr
lek	lek	L	L10
para	para(s)*		
piastre	piastres		
qindar	qindarka	q qd qind	10q 10 qind

*Optional final s.

Algeria (DZD)

Algeria was part of the Franc Zone following its annexation by France in 1830 as a French colony. In 1959, inflation required the issuance of the nouveau (new) franc, equal to 100 old francs, and divisible into 100 centimes. Although it gained independence in 1962, Algeria continued the use of the nouveau franc until 1964, when the franc was replaced with the dinar—the Arabic form of the ancient Roman denarius.

The Arabic letters *dal-nun* (دن) together form the abbreviation for dinar (دينار), which is sometimes used with the Arabic-language numerals below:

0	1	2	3	4	5	6	7	8	9	10	50	100	500	1000
٠	١	٢	٣	٤	٥	٦	٧	٨	٩	١٠	٥٠	١٠٠	٥٠٠	١٠٠٠

CHRONOLOGY

Year	Denomination	Equivalent
1964–present	Algerian dinar	100 centimes
1959–1964	new (*nouveau*) franc	100 centimes
1848–1959	franc	100 centimes

ORTHOGRAPHY AND NUMBER

Singular	Plural	Known Abbreviations and Symbols	Examples
centime	centimes	c cme	10c 10 cme
dinar	dinars	DA دن	10 DA ١٠دن
franc	francs	F Fr	10F 10Fr
new franc (*nouveau franc*)	new francs (*nouveaux francs*)	NF	10 NF

Andorra
(EUR; replaced former codes ESP and FRF)

Andorra is situated in the Pyrenees Mountains, bordered on the north and east by France and on the south and west by Spain. For 715 years—until 1993—it was ruled jointly by the leader of France and Spain's Catalan Bishop of Urgel. Andorra's monetary system then reflected this dual governance, with the French franc and Spanish peseta serving as legal tender in their respective administrative areas. Even though Andorran voters approved their first constitution in 1993, which transferred power to the "parliamentary coprincipality" of Andorra, the dual monetary system continued until 2002, when France and Spain both joined the Eurozone and adopted the euro. *See also* **European Union.**

CHRONOLOGY

Year	Denomination	Equivalent
1999–present	euro	100 euro-cent
–2002	Spanish peseta	100 centimos
	French franc	100 centimes

ORTHOGRAPHY AND NUMBER

Singular	Plural	Known Abbreviations and Symbols	Examples
centime	centimes	c	10c
centimo	centimos	c cts cents	10 cts
euro	euro	€	10€
euro-cent	euro-cent	€	0.10€
franc	francs	F	10F 5F10
peseta (*pesseta*)	pesetas (*pessetes*)	pta ptas pts	10 pta 10 pts

Angola (AOA)

Angola was first established as a Portuguese colony in 1575; its status was upgraded to an overseas province in 1951. During much of its colonial period the monetary system was the same as Portugal's, using the milréis and the centavo. In 1911, the milréis was replaced at par with the escudo. In 1926, the Portuguese replaced the escudo at par with the angolar. At the same time the macuta, a local coin, was also introduced; it equaled five centavos. The escudo was reintroduced in 1958.

Although Angola gained its independence in 1975, it continued to use the escudo until 1977. In that year it was replaced by the kwanza, divisible into 100 lwei (also spelled lwee, lweys for the plural). These names were taken from two rivers — the Kwanza (also found spelled Cuanza), one of the country's main rivers, and the Lwei, a tributary of the Kwanza. Since the introduction of the kwanza, high inflation has caused several changes. The novo, or new kwanza replaced the kwanza at par in 1990; in 1995 the kwanza reajustado, equal to 1,000 novo kwanzas, was introduced; in 1999 a newer kwanza was introduced, equal to one million kwanzas reajustados. Continuing inflation has now made use of the lwei no longer practical.

The dollar sign ($) is used both as the symbol for the escudo and as a decimal point between escudos and the smaller centavos. As an example, 10$50 equals 10.50 escudos. It should be noted that the abbreviation Ag is for one angolar, while Ags is the plural abbreviation.

CHRONOLOGY

Year	Denomination	Equivalent
1999–present	kwanza	100 lwei
1995–1999	kwanza reajustado	100 lwei
1990–1995	novo kwanza	100 lwei
1977–1990	kwanza	100 lwei
1958–1977	Portuguese escudo	100 centavos
1926–1958	angolar	100 centavos
1911–1926	Portuguese escudo	100 centavos
–1911	Portuguese milréis	1,000 réis

ORTHOGRAPHY AND NUMBER

Singular	Plural	Known Abbreviations and Symbols	Examples
angolar	angolares	Ag Ags	1 Ag 10 Ags
centavo	centavos	c cts	10c
escudo	escudos	E ESC $	10E 10$50
kwanza	kwanzas	Kz	Kz10
kwanza reajustado	kwanzas reajustados	KZr	KZr 10
lwei	lwei	lw	10 lw
new kwanza	new kwanzas	NKZ	NKZ10
réis	réis	R	10R

Anguilla (XCD)

Anguilla has a long history of being part of the British Empire and the Sterling Zone. In 1935 it changed its monetary system from the imperial LSD (pounds/shillings/pence) system to one based on the British West Indies dollar of the Eastern Caribbean Currency Authority. In 1965, the Eastern Caribbean Central Bank succeeded the Eastern Caribbean Currency Authority and replaced the West Indies dollar with the East Caribbean dollar. *See also* **East Caribbean States.**

CHRONOLOGY

Year	Denomination	Equivalent
1965–present	East Caribbean dollar	100 cents
1935–1965	British West Indies dollar	100 cents
1825–1935	pound sterling	20 shillings
	shilling	12 pence
	penny	4 farthings

ORTHOGRAPHY AND NUMBER

Singular	Plural	Known Abbreviations and Symbols	Examples
cent	cents	c ¢	10c
dollar	dollars	$ EC$	$10 EC$10
farthing	farthings	d	¼d ½d
penny	pence	d	10d
pound	pounds	£ (or £)	£10
shilling	shillings	/	10/-

Antigua and Barbuda (XCD)

Antigua was once part of the British Empire, which included the dependencies of Redona and Barbuda, and was a member of the Sterling Zone. In 1935 it changed its monetary system from the imperial LSD system to one based on the British West Indies dollar of the Eastern Caribbean Currency Authority. In 1965, the Eastern Caribbean Central Bank succeeded the Eastern Caribbean Currency Authority and replaced the West Indies dollar with the East Caribbean dollar. When the country gained independence from Great Britain in 1981, it adopted the name of Antigua and Barbuda. *See also* **East Caribbean States**.

CHRONOLOGY

Year	Denomination	Equivalent
1965–present	East Caribbean dollar	100 cents
1935–1965	British West Indies dollar	100 cents
1825–1935	pound sterling	20 shillings
	shilling	12 pence
	penny	4 farthings

ORTHOGRAPHY AND NUMBER

Singular	Plural	Known Abbreviations and Symbols	Examples
cent	cents	c ¢	10c 10¢
dollar	dollars	$ EC$	$10 EC$10
farthing	farthings	d	¼d ½d
penny	pence	d	10d
pound	pounds	£ (or ₤)	£10
shilling	shillings	s /	10s 10/-

Argentina (ARS; replaced ARA in 1992)

After obtaining its independence from Spain in 1816, Argentina continued to use its former ruler's monetary system of reales, escudos, and pesos along with a coin of its own — the sol, named in honor of the country's discoverer, the Spanish navigator Juan Diaz de Solis (ca. 1470–1516). Inflation frequently changed Argentina's monetary system, as was the case in most South American countries. In 1970 the peso was revalued at the rate of 100 to 1; in 1983 the peso argentino — not to be confused with the argentino, the name for an older 10-peso gold coin — replaced the peso at an exchange of 10,000 pesos for one peso argentino. The year 1985 saw the introduction of the austral, from a Spanish adjective meaning "southern"— primarily referring to the southern hemisphere. The austral was exchanged for 1,000 pesos; in 1992 the peso was reintroduced as the new peso, in exchange for 10,000 australes.

CHRONOLOGY

Year	Denomination	Equivalent
1992–present	new peso	100 centavos
1985–1992	austral	100 centavos
1983–1985	peso argentino	100 centavos
1970–1983	new peso	100 centavos
ca. 1850–1970	peso	100 centavos
–ca. 1850	escudo	16 reales
	sol, real	100 centavos

ORTHOGRAPHY AND NUMBER

Singular	Plural	Known Abbreviations and Symbols	Examples
austral	australes	₳	₳10
centavo	centavos	c	10c
escudo	escudos	E	10E
peso	pesos	$ $a	$10
peso argentino	pesos argentinos	$a	$a10
real	reales	R Ra Rs	10R 10 Rs
sol	soles	S	10S

Armenia (AMD)

From 1922 to until its secession and independence in 1991, Armenia was part of the USSR (Union of Soviet Socialist Republics) and used its monetary system of rubles and kopecks. Following its independence Armenia continued the use of the Russian ruble until 1993, when it reformed its own system and introduced the dram, at an exchange of 200 drams per ruble. The dram is divided into 100 lumas; because of inflation, the luma is no longer used in daily commerce, such as for coins or stamps.

The transliteration of Armenian into English is not always a simple matter, and there are often variations in spelling. The monetary units, with their Armenian spellings, are:

dram	ԴՐԱՄ
luma	ԼՈՒՄԱ
ruble	ՌՈՒԲԼԻ

CHRONOLOGY

Year	Denomination	Equivalent
1993–present	dram	100 lumas
1922–1993	Russian ruble	100 kopecks

ORTHOGRAPHY AND NUMBER

Singular	Plural	Known Abbreviations and Symbols	Examples
dram	drams	AMD	10 AMD
kopeck	kopecks	к	10к
luma	lumas		
ruble	rubles	R Ռ Ռ-Բ Ռ-Բ-Լ	10R 10Ռ 10Ռ-Բ-Լ

Aruba (AWG)

Aruba's monetary system of guilders, from the Dutch *gulden*, meaning "golden," reflects the island's long association with the Netherlands. Aruba was established as a Dutch colony in 1634, spent a brief period under British control from 1805 to 1816, and has been part of the Netherlands Antilles since 1848. The Dutch replaced the coins of Spain and Portugal in the 1700s with the gulden, also known as the florin. In 1825, a monetary reform redefined the gulden as a decimalized system and divided it into 100 cents.

Aruba became a self-governing region of the Netherlands in 1986, and it replaced the Netherlands Antilles guilder with the Aruban florin at an exchange of 98 Aruban florins for every 100 guilders. The florin and guilder are used interchangeably.

CHRONOLOGY

Year	Denomination	Equivalent
1986–present	Aruban florin	100 cents
1825–1986	Netherlands Antilles guilder (*gulden*)	100 cents

ORTHOGRAPHY AND NUMBER

Singular	Plural	Known Abbreviations and Symbols	Examples
cent	cents	c ct ¢	10c 10ct 10¢
florin	florins	f Afl Naf	10f Naf10 Afl10
guilder (*gulden*)	guilders (*gulden*)	G	10G

Australia (AUD)

Australia was for many years part of the Sterling Zone, and even though it gained independence from Great Britain in 1901, it continued to use the imperial LSD system of pounds, shillings, and pence. It replaced the pound sterling at par with the Australian pound in 1909; like its predecessor, the Australian pound was divisible into 20 shillings and 240 pence. This system continued until 1966, when monetary reforms put the country on a decimalized system by replacing each pound with two Australian dollars, divisible into 100 cents. The Australian dollar is also used by the following Australian island group dependencies: Ashmore, Cartier, Christmas, Heard, Keeling-Cocos, McDonald, and Norfolk. In addition, the independent nations of Kiribati, Nauru, and Tuvalu use the Australian dollar as legal tender.

CHRONOLOGY

Year	Denomination	Equivalent
1966–present	Australian dollar	100 cents
1909–1966	Australian pound	20 shillings
	shilling	12 pence
–1909	pound sterling	20 shillings
	shilling	12 pence
	penny	4 farthings

ORTHOGRAPHY AND NUMBER

Singular	Plural	Known Abbreviations and Symbols	Examples
cent	cents	c ¢	10c 10¢
dollar	dollars	$ A$	$10 A$10
farthing	farthings	d	¼d ½d
penny	pence	d	10d
pound	pounds	£ (or £)	£10
shilling	shillings	s /	10s 10/-

Austria (EUR; replaced ATS in 1999)

Present-day Austria was once part of the Holy Roman Empire, which as far back as the early 1600s had three concurrent monetary systems. The area consisting of Bavaria, Franconia, the Rhineland, Swabia, and Austria used the gulden, equal to 60 kreuzer, or 240 pfennig. The area around Hamburg used the mark, divisible into 16 schillings, with 12 pfennig to a schilling. The third region, in northern Germany, used the thaler, equal to 30 groschen.

Eventually the diverse monetary systems were combined and decimalized, making the gulden equal to 100 kreuzer, meaning "cross." In 1892, Austria-Hungary adopted the gold standard and replaced the gulden with the krone, German for "crown," which was also called a "corona," its Latin equivalent. The krone was divisible into 100 heller, named after the town now known as Schwäbisch Hall.

Following Austria's independence after World War I, a 1924 monetary reform introduced the schilling, divided into 100 groschen. Because of post-war inflation, one schilling replaced 10,000 kronen. The schilling was intended to be similar to the English shilling except in its spelling. Groschen is a German diminutive variant of the French gros and the Italian grosso — meaning "large."

Between 1938 and 1945, Austria was under German control, and its monetary system was based on the German reichmark. Following Germany's defeat in World War II, the schilling was restored and remained in use until 2002. Austria joined the Eurozone in 1999 and adopted the euro, phasing out the schilling over the next three years. *See also* **European Union**.

CHRONOLOGY

Year	Denomination	Equivalent
1999–present	euro	100 euro-cent
1945–2002	schilling	100 groschen
1938–1945	reichmark	100 pfennig
1924–1938	schilling	100 groschen
1892–1924	krone	100 heller
1857–1892	gulden	100 kreuzer
–1857	gulden	60 kreuzer

ORTHOGRAPHY AND NUMBER

Singular	Plural	Known Abbreviations and Symbols	Examples
corona	coronas	COR	10 COR
euro	euro	€	10€
euro-cent	euro-cent	€	0.10€
florin	florins	fl	10 fl
groschen	groschen	g	10g
gulden	gulden		
heller	heller		
kreuzer	kreuzer	Kr	10Kr
krone	kronen	K kr	10K 10kr
schilling	schilling(s)*	S	S10

*Optional final s.

Azerbaijan (AZM)

From 1920 to until its secession and independence in 1991, Azerbaijan was a part of the Soviet Union and used its monetary system of rubles and kopecks. Following its independence, Azerbaijan briefly continued use of the Russian ruble. In 1992 it reformed its system and introduced the manat (also spelled man'at), equal to 10 rubles, and divisible into 100 qapik (also qepiq). According to Islamic lore, Manat was the daughter of Allah. The name is also that of a female deity worshipped in pre-Islamic Arabia who was considered to be the goddess of fate and destiny.

The ruble is written in Azeri as "manat" (مناث), the colloquial Georgian-language equivalent of the maneti (მანეთი) for the Russian ruble, and is the same as the monetary unit of Turkmenistan.

CHRONOLOGY

Year	Denomination	Equivalent
1993–present	Azerbaijani manat	100 qapik
1922–1993	Russian ruble	100 kopecks

ORTHOGRAPHY AND NUMBER

Singular	Plural	Known Abbreviations and Symbols	Examples
kopeck	kopecks	k cop коп	10 k 10 cop 10 коп
manat	manat	M MAN	10M 10 MAN
qapik (*qəpik*)	qapik (*qəpik*)	q	10q
ruble	rubles	RBL руб	10 RBL 10 руб

The Bahamas (BSD)

Because the Bahamas was a British colony from 1783 until its independence in 1973, it was also part of the Sterling Zone. It used the imperial LSD system of pounds, shillings, and pence until 1964, when monetary reforms put the country on a decimalized system, making the Bahamian dollar equal to 100 cents.

CHRONOLOGY

Year	Denomination	Equivalent
1966–present	Bahamian dollar	100 cents
1936–1966	Bahamian pound	20 shillings
	shilling	12 pence

Year	Denomination	Equivalent
–1936	pound sterling	20 shillings
	shilling	12 pence
	penny	4 farthings

ORTHOGRAPHY AND NUMBER

Singular	Plural	Known Abbreviations and Symbols	Examples
cent	cents	c	10c
dollar	dollars	$ B$	$10 B$10
farthing	farthings	d	¼d ½d
penny	pence	d	10d
pound	pounds	£ (or £)	£10
shilling	shillings	/	10/-

Bahrain (BHD)

Although the al-Khalifa family has ruled the country since 1783 as a hereditary emirate, Bahrain was a British protectorate from about 1880 until its independence in 1971. However, it had no monetary system of its own. Because of the British influence and its proximity to the Indian subcontinent, Bahrain used the established rupees, anna, and pies of India as its legal tender. In 1959 a special currency unit, the Persian Gulf rupee, officially known as the "external rupee," was issued. It was equal to 100 naye paise. In 1965 the rupee was replaced with the Bahraini dinar, the Arabic form of the ancient Roman denarius. Ten Persian Gulf rupees were replaced by one dinar, divisible into 1,000 fils.

It should be noted that the abbreviations A and R are for one anna and one rupee respectively, while As and Rs are the corresponding plural abbreviations.

CHRONOLOGY

Year	Denomination	Equivalent
1965–present	Bahraini dinar	1,000 fils
1959–1965	Persian Gulf rupee	100 naye paise
–1959	rupee	16 anna
	anna	12 pies

ORTHOGRAPHY AND NUMBER

Singular	Plural	Known Abbreviations and Symbols	Examples
anna	anna(s)*	A As	1A 10As
dinar	dinars	BD	BD 10

Singular	Plural	Known Abbreviations and Symbols	Examples
fils	fils		
naya paisa	naye paise	NP	NP 10
pie	pies		
rupee	rupees	R Rs	1R 10Rs

*Optional final s.

Bangladesh (BDT)

Bangladesh was part of British India from 1756 to 1947, and its monetary system was based on the Indian rupee. When it achieved independence in 1947 as Pakistan, it occupied the country's eastern province of East Bengal, and in 1955 it became known as East Pakistan. The Indian rupee was replaced in 1948 by the Pakistani rupee, which was divisible into 100 paise (also called pice) instead of 16 anna and 64 pice.

Pakistan's eastern province seceded in 1971 and renamed itself Bangladesh — Bangla for "Bengal nation." In the following year it replaced the rupee at par with the taka (a word taken from the Sanskrit *tanka*, meaning "coin"), divisible into 100 paisa (or *poishas*).

Although the Latin alphabet is primarily used for its monetary abbreviations, Bangladesh also uses Bangla-language abbreviations for taka (৳) and paisa (প) when combined with the Bangla numerals shown below:

0	1	2	3	4	5	6	7	8	9	10	50	100	500	1000
০	১	২	৩	৪	৫	৬	৭	৮	৯	১০	৫০	১০০	৫০০	১০০০

It should be noted that the abbreviations A and R are for one anna and one rupee respectively, while As and Rs are the corresponding plural abbreviations.

CHRONOLOGY

Year	Denomination	Equivalent
1972–present	taka	100 paisas (*poishas*)
1948–1972	Pakistani rupee	100 paise (*pice*)
ca. 1850–1948	Indian rupee	16 anna
	anna	4 pice
	pice	3 pies

ORTHOGRAPHY AND NUMBER

Singular	Plural	Known Abbreviations and Symbols	Examples
anna	anna(s)*	A As	1A 10As
paisa (*poisha*)	paisa(s)* (*poishas*)	P প	P10 10P ১০প

Singular	Plural	Known Abbreviations and Symbols	Examples
pice	pice		
pie	pies		
rupee	rupees	R Rs	R1 Rs10
taka	taka	TA Tk ৳	TA10 Tk10 ৳10 ৳১০

*Optional final s.

Barbados (BBD)

Barbados was part of the Sterling Zone since it was established as a British colony in 1663. In 1935, a monetary reform changed the imperial LSD system to a decimalized one based on the British West Indies dollar of the Eastern Caribbean Currency Authority. Just prior to Barbados' independence in 1966, the Eastern Caribbean Central Bank succeeded the Eastern Caribbean Currency Authority and replaced the West Indies dollar with the East Caribbean dollar. In 1973, Barbados withdrew from the union and changed its system to that based on the Barbados dollar. *See also* **East Caribbean States**.

CHRONOLOGY

Year	Denomination	Equivalent
1973–present	Barbados dollar	100 cents
1965–1973	East Caribbean dollar	100 cents
1935–1965	British West Indies dollar	100 cents
–1935	pound sterling	20 shillings
	shilling	12 pence
	penny	4 farthings

ORTHOGRAPHY AND NUMBER

Singular	Plural	Known Abbreviations and Symbols	Examples
cent	cents	c	10c
dollar	dollars	$ Bds$	$10 Bds$10
farthing	farthings	d	¼d ½d
penny	pence	d	10d
pound	pounds	£ (or ₤)	£10
shilling	shillings	/	10/-

Belarus (BYB; replaced BYR in 2000)

Belarus is a former Soviet republic that was known as Byelorussia, or White Russia, when it joined the USSR in 1922 and adopted the Russian monetary systems of rubles and kopecks. Following independence in 1991, the monetary system was reformed, with the Belarusian ruble, or rublei (Belorusian: рублёў), replacing the Russian ruble at par. The rublei, which was divisible into 100 kapeek, suffered from inflation and was replaced with a newer ruble in 1994 on a 10–to-1 exchange. In 2000, a newer ruble issue replaced 1,000 rubles of the 1994 issue.

CHRONOLOGY

Year	Denomination	Equivalent
1992–present	Belarusian ruble	100 kapeek
1922–1992	Russian ruble	100 kopecks

ORTHOGRAPHY AND NUMBER

Singular	Plural	Known Abbreviations and Symbols	Examples
kapeek	kapeek		
kopeck	kopecks	коп	10 коп
ruble	rubles	руб	10 руб

Belgium (EUR; replaced BEF in 1999)

Prior to gaining its independence in 1830 from the Netherlands, Belgium at various times had been under the rule of Spain, Austria, and France. When under Spain, Belgium's monetary system consisted of sols, ducatons, reals, and liards, among others. Austrian control brought thalers and guldens (florins), while France instituted the French franc in 1795. Napoleon's defeat at Waterloo in 1815 reunited Belgium with the Netherlands. The Dutch guilder, or *gulden*, divisible into 20 stivers or 320 pennings, replaced the franc. *See also* **The Netherlands**.

When Belgium gained its independence, the Belgian franc, divided into 100 centimes, replaced the Dutch guilder at par as its monetary unit. The Flemish or German spelling *frank* is also encountered, but to a lesser degree. The letter F, besides serving as an abbreviation for the franc, is sometimes used in place of a decimal point between francs and the smaller centimes. In 1999 Belgium joined the European Union and adopted the euro, which became its sole legal tender in 2002. *See also* **European Union**.

CHRONOLOGY

Year	Denomination	Equivalent
1999–present	euro	100 euro-cent
1830–2002	Belgian franc (*frank*)	100 centimes
1815–1830	Dutch guilder (*gulden*)	20 stivers (*stuivers*)

ORTHOGRAPHY AND NUMBER

Singular	Plural	Known Abbreviations and Symbols	Examples
centime	centimes	c cen ces cent	10c 10 cen
euro	euro	€	10€
euro-cent	euro-cent	€	0.10€
franc (or *frank*)	francs (or *franks*)	f F Fʀ BF	10f 10F 10Fʀ 5F10

Belize (BZD)

Belize, formerly known as British Honduras, was established as an independent British crown colony in 1862. The colony's monetary system was first based on the pound sterling, divisible into 20 shillings. In 1894 the pound was replaced with the British Honduran dollar, divisible into 100 cents. The U.S. dollar also circulated freely. The country's name was changed to Belize in 1973, whereupon the British Honduran dollar was renamed the Belizean dollar. Belize gained full independence in 1981.

CHRONOLOGY

Year	Denomination	Equivalent
1974–present	Belizean dollar	100 cents
1894–1973	British Honduran dollar	100 cents
–1894	pound sterling	20 shillings
	shilling	12 pence
	penny	4 farthings

ORTHOGRAPHY AND NUMBER

Singular	Plural	Known Abbreviations and Symbols	Examples
cents	cents	c	10c
dollar	dollars	$ Bz$	$10
farthing	farthings	d	¼d ½d
penny	pence	d	10d
pound	pounds	£ (or £)	£10
shilling	shillings	/	10/-

Benin (XOF)

Benin was originally known as Dahomey, a French West African colony established in 1894, which gained its independence in 1960. It is currently part of a confederation of West African states comprised of other former French colonies which use the CFA (Communauté Financière Africaine, or African Financial Community) franc, divided into 100 centimes (also spelled santimes). The country's name was changed from Dahomey to Benin in 1975. *See also* **West African States.**

CHRONOLOGY

Year	Denomination	Equivalent
1945–present	CFA franc	100 centimes
1901–1945	West African franc	100 centimes
ca. 1855–1901	French franc	100 centimes

ORTHOGRAPHY AND NUMBER

Singular	Plural	Known Abbreviations and Symbols	Examples
centime	centimes	c	10c
franc	francs	F	10F

Bermuda (BMD)

Bermuda has long been part of the British Empire. Originally established as a crown colony in 1684, it has been a self-governing dependency since 1968. Bermuda was part of the British Sterling Zone until 1970, when the monetary system was decimalized and the pound sterling replaced with the Bermudan dollar, divisible into 100 cents.

CHRONOLOGY

Year	Denomination	Equivalent
1970–present	Bermudan dollar	100 cents
ca. 1793–1970	pound sterling	20 shillings
	shilling	12 pence
	penny	4 farthings

ORTHOGRAPHY AND NUMBER

Singular	Plural	Known Abbreviations and Symbols	Examples
cent	cents	c ¢	10c 10¢
dollar	dollars	$ Bd$	$10 Bd$10
farthing	farthings	d	¼d ½d
penny	pence	d	10d
pound	pounds	£ (or £)	£10
shilling	shillings	/	10/-

Bhutan (BTN; replaced INR)

The kingdom of Bhutan was established in 1907. In 1949, India agreed to recognize Bhutan's sovereignty and gave a guarantee not to interfere in its internal affairs. Although local rulers had their own currency since the seventeenth century, Bhutan's monarchy also allowed the use as legal tender of India's non-decimal monetary system of the Indian rupee, which was divided into 16 anna and 64 paise.

Because India converted to a decimal monetary system in 1957, with its rupee now divided into 100 naye paise, Bhutan did also. In addition to the decimalized rupee, another unit, the sertum, was equal to 100 rupees.

In 1974, the Indian rupee was replaced at par with the ngultrum, a word derived from *ngul*, a Dzongkha-language word meaning "silver," and *trum*, a loanword possibly from the Hindi word *tramka*, meaning "money." The ngultrum, often referred to as the Bhutan rupee, is divided into 100 chetrum, which has been spelled chhetrum by the Royal Monetary Authority of Bhutan since 1979. The term chetrum is derived from the combination of the Tibetan or Burmese word *che*, meaning "half," and *trum*— "money." It should be noted that the abbreviations A and R (also Re and Rp) are for one anna and one rupee respectively, while As and Rs are the corresponding plural abbreviations.

CHRONOLOGY

Year	Denomination	Equivalent
1974–present	ngultrum	100 chetrum
	sertum	100 ngultrum
1957–1974	Indian rupee	100 naye paise
	sertum	100 rupees
1907–1957	Indian rupee	16 annas
	anna	4 paise

ORTHOGRAPHY AND NUMBER

Singular	Plural	Known Abbreviations and Symbols	Examples
anna	anna(s)*	A As	1A 10As
chetrum, chhetrum	chetrums, chhetrums	CH	10 CH
ngultrum	ngultrum(s)*	NU	10 NU
paisa	paise	P	10P
rupee	rupees	R Re Rp Rs	R1 Re1 Rp1 Rs10
sertum	sertum(s)*		

*Optional final s.

Bolivia (BOB)

After years as a dependency of the viceroyalty of Peru, Bolivia won its independence from Spain in 1825. Following independence, it continued the use of the Spanish escudo until about 1852, when it was replaced by the peso, divided into 8 soles. In 1863, monetary reforms instituted a decimalized system based on the boliviano, divisible into 100 centavos.

As a result of continuing inflation, in 1963 the boliviano was replaced by the peso boliviano at the exchange of 100 bolivianos for one peso boliviano. In 1987, the boliviano was restored at an exchange rate equal to one million pesos bolivianos.

CHRONOLOGY

Year	Denomination	Equivalent
1987–present	boliviano	100 centavos
1963–1987	peso boliviano	100 centavos
1863–1963	boliviano	100 centavos
ca. 1852–1863	peso	8 soles
ca. 1790–ca. 1852	escudo	16 reales

ORTHOGRAPHY AND NUMBER

Singular	Plural	Known Abbreviations and Symbols	Examples
boliviano	bolivianos	Bs $b	Bs10 $b10
centavo	centavos	c	10c
escudo	escudos	$	$10
real	reales	R	10R
sol	soles	S	S10

Bosnia-Herzegovina (BAM)

Bosnia-Herzegovina, often referred to simply as Bosnia, was part of the Ottoman Empire until 1878, when it became part of the Austro-Hungarian Empire. When it was part of the Ottoman Empire, its monetary system was based on the piastre, divided into 40 para. During Austro-Hungarian rule, the monetary system was based on the gulden, followed by the krone.

In 1918, after the end of World War I, Bosnia-Herzegovina, along with Croatia, Macedonia, Montenegro, Serbia, and Slovenia, united to form the Kingdom of the Serbs, Croats and Slovenes. At this time a diversity of currencies circulated throughout the new kingdom. The first reform aimed at creating a national monetary unit based it on the Austrian krone, divided into 100 heller. However, the krone was replaced in 1919 with the dinar used in Serbia, which was divided into 100 para and equal to four kronen. This new monetary system continued after the kingdom was renamed Yugoslavia in 1929.

During World War II, from 1941 to 1943, Germany occupied Yugoslavia; Bosnia-Herzegovina was made part of the independent state of Croatia under joint German and Italian control. The monetary system was based on the Croatian kuna, a Croatian word (also *kunitsa*— Russian: куница) for "marten," a mink-like animal; the kuna was divided into 100 banica. Following World War II, in 1945 Bosnia-Herzegovina was again made part of Yugoslavia. In 1992, Bosnia declared its independence from Yugoslavia, but it did not gain full independence until 1996. Also in 1992, the Yugoslav dinar was replaced at par with the Bosnian dinar. A monetary reform in 1995 replaced the Bosnian dinar with the convertible mark, divided into 100 convertible fenings.

CHRONOLOGY

Year	Denomination	Equivalent
1998–present	convertible mark (*marka*)	100 convertible fenings (*pfeniga*)
1992–1998	Bosnian dinar	100 para
1944–1992	Yugoslav dinar	100 para
1941–1944	Croatian kuna	100 banica
1919–1941	Serbian dinar	100 para
1900–1919	krone	100 heller

ORTHOGRAPHY AND NUMBER

Singular	Plural	Known Abbreviations and Symbols	Examples
banica	banica		
dinar	dinars	D	10 D
fening (*pfeniga*)	fenings (*pfeniga*)	KM	0.10 KM
heller	heller	X	
krone	kronen	K	

Singular	Plural	Known Abbreviations and Symbols	Examples
kuna	kuna	KN	10KN
mark (*marka*)	marks (*marka*)	KM	10 KM
para	para(s)*		

*Optional final s.

Botswana (BWP)

Botswana is a former British protectorate that was known as Bechuanaland from 1885 until its independence in 1966. Prior to 1920, Bechuanaland's monetary system was based on the pound sterling, often known as the pond, the Afrikaans equivalent. Because of its geopolitical association with South Africa, its monetary system was changed to the South African pound in 1920, and in 1961 to the South African rand. A monetary reform in 1976 replaced the pound with the pula, a native word meaning "rain" or "blessings." The pula is divisible into 100 thebe, a native word meaning "shield."

CHRONOLOGY

Year	Denomination	Equivalent
1976–present	Botswana pula	100 thebe
1961–1976	South African rand	100 cents
1920–1961	South African pound	20 shillings
	shilling	12 pence
ca. 1885–1920	pound sterling	20 shillings
	shilling	12 pence
	penny	4 farthings

ORTHOGRAPHY AND NUMBER

Singular	Plural	Known Abbreviations and Symbols	Examples
cent	cents	c	10c
farthing	farthings	d	¼d ½d
penny	pence	d	10d
pound	pounds	£ (or £)	£10
pula	pula	P	P10
rand	rand	R	R10
shilling	shillings	/	10/-
thebe	thebe	t	10t

Brazil (BRL; replaced BRR [cruzeiro real] in 1994, which in turn replaced BRE [cruzeiro] in 1993)

Although Brazil gained its independence from Portugal in 1822, it retained the milréis until 1942, long after Portugal replaced its own milréis with the escudo in 1911. Hyperinflation, all too common in Latin America, would require multiple monetary reforms for the remainder of the twentieth century, with monetary units that would be variations of previous names.

The first of many monetary reforms starting in 1942 replaced the milréis at par with the cruzeiro, which was divided into 100 centavos. The name cruzeiro is taken from *cruz*, a Portuguese word meaning "cross." In 1967 the cruzeiro novo, or new cruzeiro, replaced the older cruzeiro at an exchange of 1,000 to 1. Then came the cruzado, whose name is probably derived from the Portuguese *cruzar*, meaning "to cross" or "traverse," which replaced the cruzeiro novo in 1987 at a rate of 1,000 to 1. The cruzado then begat the cruzado novo in 1989, equal to 1,000 old cruzados. The cruzeiro was reinstated one year later at par with the cruzado novo.

In 1993 the cruzeiro real, equal to 1,000 cruzieros, was introduced, followed by the real in 1994; the real was equal to 2,750 cruzeiros reais. Brazil is one of the all-time hyperinflation leaders — it takes a staggering 2,750,000,000,000,000,000 réis issued before 1942 to equal a single real today.

The dollar sign ($) is often used as the symbol for the major unit of Brazil's money, and in some cases it also represents a decimal point followed by a multiplier of 1,000. As examples, 1$5 is equivalent to 1,500 réis, and 10$ is equivalent to 10,000 réis.

CHRONOLOGY

Year	Denomination	Equivalent
1994–present	real	100 centavos
1993–1994	cruzeiro real	100 centavos
1990–1993	cruzeiro	100 centavos
1989–1990	cruzado novo	100 centavos
1987–1989	cruzado	100 centavos
1967–1987	cruzeiro novo	100 centavos
1942–1967	cruzeiro	100 centavos
1846–1942	milréis	1,000 réis

ORTHOGRAPHY AND NUMBER

Singular	Plural	Known Abbreviations and Symbols	Examples
centavo	centavos	cts cents	10c 10 cents
cruzado	cruzados	Cz$	Cz$10
cruzeiro	cruzeiros	Cr$ ₵	Cr$10 ₵10
real	reais	R$	R$10
réis	réis	Rs	Rs10 1$5 10$

Brunei (BND)

Prior to its independence in 1984, Brunei was a former Malay state established as a British protectorate in 1888. The monetary system was based on the Straits Settlements dollar, divisible into 100 cents. In 1946, when the Straits Settlements were broken up, the Malayan dollar replaced the Straits Settlements dollar at par. The Malayan dollar was replaced in 1967 with the Brunei dollar, divisible into 100 cents.

The Brunei dollar is often referred to as the *ringgit*, a Malay word meaning "jagged," referring to the milled edge of the coin. The sen is the alternative name for cent, from the Japanese word meaning "coin."

CHRONOLOGY

Year	Denomination	Equivalent
1967–present	Brunei dollar (*ringgit*)	100 cents (*sen*)
1946–1967	Malayan dollar	100 cents
1888–1946	Straits Settlements dollar	100 cents

ORTHOGRAPHY AND NUMBER

Singular	Plural	Known Abbreviations and Symbols	Examples
cent	cents	c	10c
dollar	dollars	$	$10
ringgit	ringgit	$	$10
sen	sen	c	10c

Bulgaria (BGN; replaced BGL in 1999)

Once a province under Ottoman Turkish suzerainty, Bulgaria achieved independence in 1878 and briefly adopted a monetary system of francs and centimes. In 1880, when Bulgaria joined the Latin Monetary Union, the monetary unit was changed to the lev, meaning "lion." The lev is divided into 100 stotinki, derived from *sto* (Bulgarian: сто), meaning "one hundred." Although the Bulgarian-language plural is transliterated as *leva* (Bulgarian: лева), the English plural is generally taken as lev.

Bulgaria's monetary units, with their Cyrillic spellings, are:

Unit	Singular	Plural
lev	лев	лева
stotinka	стотинка	стотитнки

CHRONOLOGY

Year	Denomination	Equivalent
1880–present	lev	100 stotinki
1878–1880	franc	100 centimes

ORTHOGRAPHY AND NUMBER

Singular	Plural	Known Abbreviations and Symbols	Examples
centime	centimes	c	10c
franc	francs	Fʀ	10Fʀ
lev	lev (*leva*)	Lv л лв	10Lv 10лв
stotinka	stotinki	c ст стот sᴛ	10c 10cᴛ 10sᴛ

Burkina-Faso (XOF)

Present-day Burkina-Faso was established as a French protectorate in 1919. Beginning in the 1800s, the monetary system was based on the West African franc, although thalers were used. The colony was a member of the Franc Zone under the geographical area known as French West Africa. In 1947, this area was reconstituted as the separate territory of Upper Volta; it was renamed Burkina-Faso in 1984. The current monetary system is based on the Communauté Financière Africaine (African Financial Community, CFA) franc, a monetary union of former French colonies in Africa. *See also* **West African States**.

CHRONOLOGY

Year	Denomination	Equivalent
1945–present	CFA franc	100 centimes
1919–1945	West African franc	100 centimes

ORTHOGRAPHY AND NUMBER

Singular	Plural	Known Abbreviations and Symbols	Examples
centime	centimes	c	10c
franc	francs	F	10F

Burma (Myanmar) (MNK)

From 1886 until 1937, Burma was part of British India, and its monetary system was based on the Indian rupee, divided into 100 paise. Burma became a separate colony in 1937, but it was not until 1939 that the Indian rupee was replaced at par with the Burmese rupee. In 1952 the kyat, meaning "weight" or "coin," was introduced and divided into 100 pyas. The country was renamed Myanmar, a name which has not been universally accepted, in 1989 by its military authorities.

It should be noted that the abbreviations A and R are for one anna and one rupee respectively, while As and Rs are the corresponding plural abbreviations. Burmese-language abbreviations and symbols, such as those for the anna (ˋ), paisa (ᵇ), pya (ᵗ), and rupee (°), are generally used with the Burmese numerals below:

0	1	2	3	4	5	6	7	8	9	10	50	100	500	1000
၀	၁	၂	၃	၄	၅	၆	၇	၈	၉	၀၀	၅၀	၀၀၀	၅၀၀	၀၀၀၀

As examples: ၆ is 1 rupee, ၁ is 1 anna, and ၆ is 1 paisa.

Chronology

Year	Denomination	Equivalent
1952–present	kyat	100 pyas
1939–1952	Burmese rupee	16 anna
	anna	12 pies
1886–1939	Indian rupee	100 paise

Orthography and Number

Singular	Plural	Known Abbreviations and Symbols	Examples
anna	anna(s)*	A As ˋ	1A 10As ၆
kyat	kyat(s)*	K	K10
paisa	paise	Ps P$ ᵇ	10Ps ၆
pya	pyas	p ᵗ	10p ၀၀ᵗ
rupee	rupees	R Rs °	1R 10Rs ၆

*Optional final s.

Burundi (BIF)

Starting in 1884, present-day Burundi was part of the German East Africa protectorate, and its monetary system was the German East African (*Deutsch Ostafrika*) rupie. The rupie was divisible into 64 pesa, the German equivalent of the Indian paisa.

During World War I, Belgium occupied the territory, beginning in 1916. Belgium was mandated Ruanda-Urundi as a trust territory from the League of Nations in 1922, and later in 1946 from the United Nations. In 1962, the trusteeship terminated, and the territory was divided into the two independent states of Rwanda and Burundi. At the time of independence, the Rwanda-Urundi franc was on par with the Belgian franc. In 1964, Burundi introduced its own franc, divided into 100 centimes.

CHRONOLOGY

Year	Denomination	Equivalent
1964–present	Burundi franc	100 centimes
1916–1964	Ruanda-Urundi franc	100 centimes
1906–1917	German East African rupie	100 heller
–1906	German East African rupie	64 pesa

ORTHOGRAPHY AND NUMBER

Singular	Plural	Known Abbreviations and Symbols	Examples
centime	centimes	c	10c
franc	francs	F FBu	10F
heller	heller		
pesa	pesa		
rupie	rupien		

Cambodia (KHR)

At different times Cambodia was a vassal state of Siam (now Thailand) and of Vietnam; from 1841 to 1863 it was under their joint suzerainty. During the latter period its monetary system was based on the Thai tical, divisible into 8 fuang; the fuang was divided into 8 att. In 1863, when the French established Cambodia as a protectorate (it became part of French Indochina in 1887), the tical was replaced with a decimalized system based on the Indochinese piastre, divided into 100 centimes.

When France recognized Cambodia's independence in 1954, the Indochinese piastre was replaced at par with the Khmer riel, divided into 100 sen. However, after the country was taken over by the Khmer Rouge, there essentially was no monetary system (other than traditional bartering) from 1975 to 1979. The Khmer Rouge were defeated in 1979 by the Vietnamese, and the government instituted a monetary system based on the new riel, which is divided into 100 su or 10 kak.

Although the Latin alphabet is primarily used for monetary abbreviations, Cambodia also uses the Khmer-language abbreviation for riel (៛) when combined with the Khmer numerals shown at the top of the following page:

0	1	2	3	4	5	6	7	8	9	10	50	100	500	1000
០	១	២	៣	៤	៥	៦	៧	៨	៩	១០	៥០	១០០	៥០០	១០០០

The letter R is the abbreviation for riel and also serves as a decimal point. As an example, 1R50 equals 1.50 riels.

CHRONOLOGY

Year	Denomination	Equivalent
1975–present	new riel	10 kak
	kak	10 su
1954–1975	Khmer riel	100 sen
1863–1954	Indochinese piastre	100 cents
–1863	tical	8 fuang
	fuang	8 att

ORTHOGRAPHY AND NUMBER

Singular	Plural	Known Abbreviations and Symbols	Examples
att	att		
centime	centimes	c	10c
fuang	fuang		
kak	kak		
piastre	piastres		
riel	riel(s)*	R ៛	10R 1R50 ៛១០
sen	sen		
su	su		
tical	ticals		

*Optional final s.

Cameroon (XAF)

Cameroon was a German protectorate from 1884 until Germany's defeat in World War I. During the war, both British shillings and French francs were legal tender alongside the German mark. The League of Nations partitioned the protectorate into British and French mandates, which later became United Nations trust territories. In 1960, the larger eastern French Cameroon, a part of the Franc Zone, declared its independence. In 1961, the western British Cameroon was partitioned between Nigeria, which adopted the Nigerian pound with its shillings and pence, and the former French Cameroon, which used the West African franc. All parts were then united in 1962 as a single republic, with a monetary system based on the Communauté Financière Africaine (African Financial Community, CFA) franc, a monetary union of former French colonies in Africa. *See also* **Central African States.**

CHRONOLOGY

Year	Denomination	Equivalent
1962–present	CFA franc	100 centimes
1961–1962	Nigerian pound (British Cameroon)	20 shillings
	shilling	12 pence
1920–1962	West African franc	100 centimes
1916–1920	French franc	100 centimes
1915	pound sterling	20 shillings
	shilling	12 pence
1897–1918	German mark	100 pfennig

ORTHOGRAPHY AND NUMBER

Singular	Plural	Known Abbreviations and Symbols	Examples
centime	centimes	c	10c
franc	francs	F	10F
mark	marks	M	10M
penny	pence	d	10d
pfennig	pfennig	pf	10pf
pound	pounds	£ (British) N£ (Nigerian)	£10 N£10
shilling	shillings	s	10s

Canada (CAD)

Prior to 1857, the monetary system of the eastern Canadian provinces was based on the pound sterling, though there were French-based units in use, like the dernier, liard, sol, and livre. In 1857, ten years before its independence from Great Britain, Canada adopted the dollar, divisible into 100 cents, as its monetary system equal to the United States dollar.

CHRONOLOGY

Year	Denomination	Equivalent
1857–present	Canadian dollar	100 cents
–1857	pound sterling	20 shillings
	shilling	12 pence

ORTHOGRAPHY AND NUMBER

Singular	Plural	Known Abbreviations and Symbols	Examples
cent	cents	c ¢	10c 10¢
dollar	dollars	$ C$	$10 C$10

Singular	Plural	Known Abbreviations and Symbols	Examples
penny	pence	d	10d
pound	pounds	£ (or ₤)	£10
shilling	shillings	/	10/-

Cape Verde (CVE)

Cape Verde's monetary system of milréis and escudos has paralleled that of its former Portuguese ruler. The island was made a Portuguese colony in 1460, and in 1951 it was declared an overseas province. When it gained independence in 1975, Cape Verde retained the decimal escudo system. The dollar sign ($) is used both as the symbol for the escudo and as a decimal point between escudos and the smaller centavos. As an example, 1$50 equals 1.50 escudos.

CHRONOLOGY

Year	Denomination	Equivalent
1976–present	Cape Verde escudo	100 centavos
1911–1976	Portuguese escudo	100 centavos
–1911	Portuguese milréis	1,000 réis

ORTHOGRAPHY AND NUMBER

Singular	Plural	Known Abbreviations and Symbols	Examples
centavo	centavos	c $	$10
escudo	escudos	$	10$ 1$50
réis	réis	Rs	Rs10

Cayman Islands (KYD)

Until 1959, the Cayman Islands was a dependency of Jamaica, and it kept the Jamaican dollar until 1972. A monetary reform in 1972 replaced the Jamaican dollar at par with the Cayman Islands dollar.

CHRONOLOGY

Year	Denomination	Equivalent
1972–present	Cayman Islands dollar	100 cents
1969–1972	Jamaican dollar	100 cents

Year	Denomination	Equivalent
1840–1969	Jamaican pound	20 shillings
	shilling	12 pence
	penny	4 farthings

ORTHOGRAPHY AND NUMBER

Singular	Plural	Known Abbreviations and Symbols	Examples
cent	cents	c	10c
dollar	dollars	$ CI$	$10 CI$10
penny	pence	d	10d
pound	pounds	£ (or ₤)	£10
shilling	shillings	/	10/-

Central African Republic (XAF)

From the late nineteenth century until its independence in 1960, the Central African Republic was a French colony known as Ubangi-Chari. It was a member of the Franc Zone under the colonial federation of territories known as French Equatorial Africa. The current monetary system is based on the Communauté Financière Africaine (African Financial Community, CFA) franc, a monetary union of former French colonies in Africa. *See also* **Central African States**.

CHRONOLOGY

Year	Denomination	Equivalent
1960–present	CFA franc	100 centimes
–1960	franc	100 centimes

ORTHOGRAPHY AND NUMBER

Singular	Plural	Known Abbreviations and Symbols	Examples
centime	centimes	c	10c
franc	francs	F	10F

Central African States (XAF)

The Central African States is currently a confederation of Equatorial Guinea, a former Spanish colony, and five former French colonial possessions of the administrative unit known as French Equatorial Africa: Cameroon, Central African Republic, Chad, Congo (Brazzaville), and Gabon. Before their independence in 1960, the former French colonies' monetary systems were part of the Franc Zone.

The monetary system of the Central African States is based on the Communauté Financière Africaine (African Financial Community, CFA) franc, a monetary union almost solely of former French colonies in Africa. The CFA franc is guaranteed by the French treasury and pegged to the French franc, into which it is freely convertible. *See also* **West African States**.

CHRONOLOGY

Year	Denomination	Equivalent
1960–present	CFA franc	100 centimes

ORTHOGRAPHY AND NUMBER

Singular	Plural	Known Abbreviations and Symbols	Examples
centime	centimes	c	10c
franc	francs	F	10F

Chad (XAF)

From about 1910 until its independence in 1960, Chad was a French colony and a member of the Franc Zone under the colonial federation of regions known as French Equatorial Africa. The current monetary system is based on the Communauté Financière Africaine (African Financial Community, CFA) franc, a monetary union of former French colonies in Africa. *See also* **Central African States**.

CHRONOLOGY

Year	Denomination	Equivalent
1960–present	CFA franc	100 centimes
1900–1960	franc	100 centimes

ORTHOGRAPHY AND NUMBER

Singular	Plural	Known Abbreviations and Symbols	Examples
centime	centimes	c	10c
franc	francs	F	10F

Chile (CLP)

After years as a dependency of the viceroyalty of Peru, Chile won its independence from Spain in 1810. However, it retained the monetary system of escudos and reales of its colonial ruler. In 1851, the monetary system was decimalized, and the peso, divided into 100 centavos, replaced the escudo. In 1960, with high inflation, the peso was revalued, the newly created escudo equaled 1,000 pesos and was divided into 100 centesimos. Another revaluation in 1975 reinstalled the peso, equal to 1,000 escudos, as the major monetary unit.

CHRONOLOGY

Year	Denomination	Equivalent
1975–present	Chilean peso	100 centavos
1960–1975	Chilean escudo	100 centesimos
1851–1960	Chilean peso	100 centavos
–1851	Chilean escudo	2 pesos
	peso	8 reales

ORTHOGRAPHY AND NUMBER

Singular	Plural	Known Symbols and Abbreviations	Examples
centavo	centavos	cts	10cts
centesimo	centesimos	cts	10cts
escudo	escudos	E°	E°10
peso	pesos	$ Ch$	$10 Ch$10
real	reales	R Rs	10R 10 Rs

China (CNY)

For much of China's imperial history, its monetary units, such as the tael, cash, mace, and candareen were based on specific weights of silver. In the late nineteenth and early twentieth centuries, the "Chinese dollar," a silver-dollar-sized coin, was the popular English-language term for the yuan (圓). Also spelled yüan, it means "round," a "circle," i.e., a coin. The yuan is also the name of a river in southeast-central China, a tributary of the Yangtze as well as the name of a Mongol dynasty. The yuan was divided into 100 fen (分), or cents.

In 1949, following the revolution that drove the Nationalists to the nearby island of Taiwan, the monetary system was reformed to a more egalitarian one. The yuan was renamed the yuan renminbi, or "people's currency," and was divided into 10 jiao (角)

and 100 fen (also fyng). In Mandarin, the yuan is commonly called kuai ("piece"), jiao is also called mao, and the yuan simply goes by the term renminbi."

China primarily uses the numerals 0 through 9 with Chinese ideographs of its monetary units. However, older documents combine the units with the Chinese numbers shown below:

	0	1	2	3	4	5	6	7	8	9	10	50	100	500	1000
Official Form		壹	貳	叁	肆	伍	陸	柒	捌	玖	拾	拾伍	佰	佰伍	仟壹
Common Form	零	一	二	三	四	五	六	七	八	九	十	十五	百	百五	千

CHRONOLOGY

Year	Denomination	Equivalent
1949–present	yuan renminbi	10 jiao
	jiao	10 fen
1897–1949	yuan	100 fen
–1897	tael	10 mace
	mace	10 candareen

ORTHOGRAPHY AND NUMBER

Singular	Plural	Known Abbreviations and Symbols	Examples
candareen	candareens		
fen	fen	分	10分 分十
jiao	jiao	角	10角 角十
mace	mace		
tael	taels		
yuan	yuan	Y 圓	Y10 10圓 圓十

Colombia (COP)

After years as a Spanish colony, Colombia achieved its independence in 1819. It was then known as Grand Granada and retained the monetary system of its colonial ruler. Until 1847, the escudo was divisible into two pesos, and each peso was equal to 16 reales. In that year the peso was decimalized, being divided into 10 reales and 100 decimos. In 1853 the decimo was divided into 10 centavos. Twenty years later, the decimo was eliminated, and the peso was simply divided into 100 centavos.

CHRONOLOGY

Year	Denomination	Equivalent
1872–present	peso	100 centavos
1853–1872	peso	10 decimos
	decimo	10 centavos
1847–1853	peso	10 reales
	real	10 decimos
1819–1847	escudo	2 pesos
	peso	8 reales

ORTHOGRAPHY AND NUMBER

Singular	Plural	Known Abbreviations and Symbols	Examples
centavo	centavos	c cs cts cvs cent ctvs cvos ¢	10c 10 ctvs 10¢
decimo	decimos		
escudo	escudos	E	10E
peso	pesos	$	$10
real	reales	R	10R

Comoros (KMF)

As a former French protectorate established in 1886, and part of Madagascar (later the Malagasy Republic) since 1914, the Comoro islands were part of the Franc Zone. In 1975, following the Comoros' independence, monetary reforms replaced the CFA (Communauté Financière Africaine, or African Financial Community) franc with the Comorian franc, divisible into 100 centimes. Because the country is an Islamic republic, the centime is also spelled santime, as transliterated from its Arabic spelling (سنتيم).

CHRONOLOGY

Year	Denomination	Equivalent
1975–present	Comorian franc	100 centimes
1945–1975	CFA franc	100 centimes
1925–1945	Madagascar franc	100 centimes
ca. 1890–1925	French franc	100 centimes

ORTHOGRAPHY AND NUMBER

Singular	Plural	Known Abbreviations and Symbols	Examples
centime	centimes	c	10c
franc	francs	F CF	10F 10CF

Congo (Democratic Republic of) (CDF)

Before its independence from Belgium in 1960, the country was referred to as the Belgian Congo. Its monetary system was first based on the Belgian franc of its colonial ruler; in 1911 that was replaced at par by the Belgian Congo franc, divided into 100 centimes. It in turn was replaced by the Congolese franc, following independence.

In 1967, monetary reforms created a new unit, the likuta (plural, makuta), which is divided into 100 sengi. Likuta is derived from *kuta* ("stone") in the language of the Nupe, an ethnic group indigenous to several African countries. Later in 1967, the zaire (also zaïre), divided into 100 makuta, replaced the smaller likuta. The symbol K represents both the singular (likuta) and plural (makuta) forms.

Rampant inflation devalued the zaire several times, and in 1993 monetary reforms created the *nouveau zaïre*—"new zaire." Inflation continued, and the devalued new zaire was replaced in 1998 by the Congolese franc, equal to 50,000 new zaires. Because of inflation, it takes a staggering 300,000,000,000,000 Belgian Congo francs issued before 1911 to equal a single Congolese franc today.

The country has undergone several changes in both its name and capital city since independence. It has been known as the Democratic Republic of the Congo; Zaire (beginning in 1965), after an indigenous native word for "river," and once again (1999) the Congo Democratic Republic, with its capital at Kinshasa, the former Leopoldville. All of this is confusing when its western neighbor is the Congo Republic, a former French colony, with Brazzaville as its capital. Not only do the countries have similar names, both currently use the franc as their monetary unit — one is Congolese; one is CFA. *See also* **Congo-Brazzaville.**

CHRONOLOGY

Year	Denomination	Equivalent
1998–present	Congolese franc	100 centimes
1993–1998	new zaire (*nouveau zaïre*)	100 new makuta (*nouveaux makuta*)
1967–1993	zaire	100 makuta
1967	likuta	100 sengi
1960–1967	Congolese franc	100 centimes
1911–1960	Belgian Congo franc	100 centimes
–1911	Belgian franc	100 centimes

ORTHOGRAPHY AND NUMBER

Singular	Plural	Known Abbreviations and Symbols	Examples
centime	centimes	c ces	10c 10 ces
franc	francs	F Fr	10F 10Fr
likuta	makuta	K	1K 10K
new likuta	new makuta	NK	1NK 10NK

Singular	Plural	Known Abbreviations and Symbols	Examples
new zaire (*nouveau zaïre*)	new zaires (*nouveaux zaïres*)	NZ	10NZ
sengi	sengi	s	10s
zaire (*zaïre*)	zaires (*zaïres*)	Z	10Z

Congo–Brazzaville (Republic of) (XAF)

The territory first known as French Congo was renamed the Middle Congo in 1910, and it became a member of the Franc Zone under the colonial federation of regions known as French Equatorial Africa. The country gained independence in 1960, and the current monetary system is based on the Communauté Financière Africaine (African Financial Community, CFA) franc, a monetary union of former French colonies in Africa. This can be confusing when its eastern neighbor is the Democratic Republic of the Congo, a former Belgian colony previously known as Zaire. In addition to having similar names, both countries currently use the franc as their monetary unit — one is CFA, one is Congolese. *See also* **Central African States** and **Congo (Democratic Republic of)**.

The letter *F* is used both as the symbol for the franc and (sometimes) as a decimal point between francs and the smaller centimes. As an example, 5F10 equals 5.10 francs.

CHRONOLOGY

Year	Denomination	Equivalent
1960–present	CFA franc	100 centimes
–1960	franc	100 centimes

ORTHOGRAPHY AND NUMBER

Singular	Plural	Known Abbreviations and Symbols	Examples
centime	centimes	c	10c
franc	francs	F Fr	10F 5F10 10Fr

Costa Rica (CRC)

When Spanish rule ended in 1821, Costa Rica became a part of Mexico for two years. From 1824 until 1838 it was part of the United Provinces of Central America, a federation of states established after the various colonies declared their independence from Spain and Mexico. This federation included modern-day Costa Rica, El Salvador, Guatemala, Honduras, and Nicaragua. All used the escudo, divisible into 16 reales. In 1896 Costa Rica's monetary system was changed to a decimal system based on the colón, named in honor of Christopher Columbus (Spanish: Cristóbal Colón). El Salvador followed suit in 1919.

CHRONOLOGY

Year	Denomination	Equivalent
1896–present	colón	100 centimos
1838–1896	escudo (or peso)	100 centavos
1824–1838	Central American escudo	2 pesos
	peso	8 reales
–1824	Spanish escudo	2 pesos
	peso	8 reales

ORTHOGRAPHY AND NUMBER

Singular	Plural	Known Abbreviations and Symbols	Examples
centavo	centavos	Cˢ cto cts	10Cˢ 10 cto 10 cts
centimo	centimos	c cts ¢	10c 10 cts 10¢
colón	colónes	c CR ¢ ₡	¢10 10CR ₡10
escudo	escudos	E	E10
peso	pesos	$	$10
real	reales	R	10R

Croatia (HRK)

Croatia was part of the Ottoman Empire until 1878, and the monetary system was based on the piastre, divided into 40 para. After it became part of the Austro-Hungarian Empire, the monetary system was based on the gulden, followed by the krone in 1892.

In 1918, after the end of World War I, Croatia united with Bosnia-Herzegovina, Macedonia, Montenegro, Serbia, and Slovenia, to form the Kingdom of the Serbs, Croats and Slovenes. The first currency reform created a national monetary unit that was based on the Austrian krone, divided into 100 heller. However, it was replaced in 1919 by the dinar used in Serbia, which was divided into 100 para and equal to four kronen. This new monetary system continued after the kingdom was renamed Yugoslavia in 1929.

During World War II Croatia gained some measure of independence as the independent state of Croatia, but was under German and Italian control. The Croatian kuna, a Croatian word (also *kunitsa*—Russian: куница) for "marten," a mink-like animal, was divided into 100 banica. Following the war, in 1945 Croatia again became part of

Yugoslavia until its independence in 1991. From 1991 until 1993, the Croatian dinar replaced the Yugoslav dinar as a transitional currency. The kuna was reintroduced in 1993, replacing the dinar at an exchange of 1,000 dinars for one kuna. It was divided into 100 lipa, a word meaning "linden"—a lime tree.

Serbo-Croatian, the national Language of the former Yugoslavia, is bi-scriptal. When written with the Latin (or Roman) alphabet, it is Croatian; when the Cyrillic alphabet is used, it is Serbian. The Serbian abbreviations д and дин are for the dinar (динар), while п is for the para (пара). The corresponding Croatian abbreviations are D and DIN for dinar, and P for para.

CHRONOLOGY

Year	Denomination	Equivalent
1993–present	Croatian kuna	100 lipa
1991–1993	Croatian dinar	100 para
1945–1991	Yugoslav dinar	100 para
1941–1945	Croatian kuna	100 banica
1919–1941	Serbian dinar	100 para
1918–1919	Croatian krone	100 filler
1892–1918	Austrian krone	100 heller
1878–1892	Austrian gulden	100 kreuzer
–1878	Ottoman piastre	40 para

ORTHOGRAPHY AND NUMBER

Singular	Plural	Known Abbreviations and Symbols	Examples
banica	banica		
dinar	dinars	D DIN д дин	10D 10д 10 дин
filler	filler		
gulden	gulden		
heller	heller		
kreuzer	kreuzer	KR	10KR
krone	kronen	K	10K
kuna	kuna	KN	10KN
lipa	lipa	lp	10lp
para	para(s)*	P п	10P 10 п

*Optional final s.

Cuba (CUP)

Cuba was once part of the Spanish West Indies, and its monetary system was similar to that of its Spanish ruler. Prior to 1867, the system was based on the peso, which was divided into eight reales plata. In Spanish, *peso* means "weight," *real* means "royal," and *plata* means "silver." About 1867, Spain replaced that monetary system with a decimalized one, and the change was also carried out in Cuba. The new system was based on the peseta (the Spanish diminutive form of the peso), divisible into 100 centesimos.

Spain's defeat in the Spanish-American War transferred administrative control of Cuba to the United States at the start of 1899; it was declared a republic in 1902. Cuba kept the peseta until 1914, when it reinstituted the peso, now divided into 100 centavos.

CHRONOLOGY

Year	Denomination	Equivalent
1914–present	Cuban peso	100 centavos
1867–1914	peseta	100 centesimos
–1867	peso	8 reales plata

ORTHOGRAPHY AND NUMBER

Singular	Plural	Known Abbreviations and Symbols	Examples
centavo	centavos	c cent ¢	10c 10¢
centesimo	centesimos	cent	10 cent
peseta	pesetas		
peso	pesos	$	$10
real plata	reales plata	RL PTA	10 RL PTA

Cyprus (CYP)

Cyprus was once part of the Ottoman Empire. It was annexed by Great Britain in 1914, and became a crown colony in 1925. The monetary system was based on the Cyprus pound, equal to 20 shillings or 240 pence. The hoarding of banknotes in Cyprus during World War II, and the difficulty of receiving replacements from Great Britain, required the delivery from Palestine (the nearest territory under British rule) of £100,000 in £1 notes of the Palestine Currency Board. These were legal tender for a six-month period during 1942, until replacement Cyprus pound notes could arrive. When Cyprus gained its independence in 1960, the Cyprus pound was decimalized, divisible into 1,000 mills. In 1983 it was changed to be divisible into 100 cents.

In 1974 the Greek majority attempted to seize control of the government, despite constitutional guarantees for the Turkish minority. Turkey responded with military intervention and eventually controlled almost 40 percent of the island. The Turkish-held area declared itself the "Turkish Republic of Northern Cyprus" in 1983, but its existence is recognized only by Turkey. In this area the Turkish lira has been instituted as legal tender, but the Cyprus pound is also accepted.

In 2004 Cyprus joined the European Union, but it will not participate in the European Union's monetary system (Eurozone) and adopt the euro until about 2006. *See also* **European Union.**

CHRONOLOGY

Year	Denomination	Equivalent
1983–present	Cyprus pound	100 cents
1960–1983	Cyprus pound	1,000 mills
1914–1960	Cyprus pound	20 shillings
	shilling	12 pence

ORTHOGRAPHY AND NUMBER

Singular	Plural	Known Abbreviations and Symbols	Examples
cent	cents	c	10c
mill	mills		
penny	pence	d	10d
pound	pounds	£ (or £) £C	£10 £C10
shilling	shillings	/	10/-

Czech Republic (CZK; replaced CSK in 1993)

The former country of Czechoslovakia was established in 1918 as a union of the Czech and Slovak regions of the Austro-Hungarian Empire. The monetary system was based on the koruna, divided into 100 halers. The koruna is both the Czech and Slovak word for "crown," and the haler is related to the Austrian heller, whose name is from the town now known as Schwäbisch Hall.

In 1939, Germany partitioned the Czechoslovak regions of Moravia and Bohemia as a protectorate, while Slovakia was declared an independent state. The German reichmark (imperial mark), divided into 100 pfennig, replaced the koruna in Moravia and Bohemia. With Germany's defeat in 1945, Slovakia was reunited with Moravia and Bohemia as Czechoslovakia, and the monetary system was again based on the Czechoslovak koruna.

In 1993, Czechoslovakia peacefully divided itself into the Czech Republic and Slovakia. The Czechoslovak koruna was renamed the Czech koruna, divisible into 100 halers. In 2004, the Czech Republic joined the European Union, but it will not participate in the European Union's monetary system (Eurozone) and adopt the euro until about 2010.

The abbreviations Kč and Kčs (*koruna Československa*) were used in Czechoslovakia from 1918 to 1939 and from 1945 to 1993. With the formation of the Czech Republic in 1993, the abbreviation Kč (*korun Českých*) represents only the Czech koruna.

CHRONOLOGY

Year	Denomination	Equivalent
1993–present	Czech koruna	100 halers
1945–1993	Czechoslovak koruna	100 halers

Year	Denomination	Equivalent
1939–1945	German reichmark	100 pfennig
1918–1939	Czechoslovak koruna	100 halers

ORTHOGRAPHY AND NUMBER

Singular	Plural	Known Abbreviations and Symbols	Examples
haler	halers	h	10h
koruna	korun	K Kč Kčs	10K 10Kč 10Kčs
mark	marks	M RM	10 M 10 DM
pfennig	pfennig	pf	10 pf

Denmark (DKK)

Denmark's monetary system prior to 1873 was based on the rigsbank (national bank) daler, often simply called the rigsdaler, which was divided into 96 rigsbank skillings. The daler is a Danish variation of the German thaler, and is thought by many to be the origin of the word "dollar," while the skilling was a variation of the British shilling. In 1873 Denmark adopted the krone, divisible into 100 øre, and replaced the rigsdaler at par. The krone is also used in the Danish dependencies of Greenland and the Faröe Islands.

The year 1873 also marked the formation of the Scandinavian Monetary Union, which initially included only Denmark and Sweden; Norway joined in 1875. Norway shared Denmark's monetary system until 1814, and both Norwegian and Swedish coins were legal tender in Denmark until 1914.

The monetary units of these three countries are very similar: krone (Denmark and Norway) and krona (Sweden). The Icelandic króna, a derivative of the Danish krone, was introduced after the breakup of the Scandinavian Monetary Union and Iceland's independence from Denmark in 1918 (it attained full sovereignty in 1944). Whatever its spelling or language, the name means "crown." The øre, like the Swedish öre and the Icelandic eyrir, is derived from *aureus*, Latin for "gold."

CHRONOLOGY

Year	Denomination	Equivalent
1873–present	krone	100 øre
1813–1873	rigsdaler	96 rigsbank skilling

ORTHOGRAPHY AND NUMBER

Singular	Plural	Known Abbreviations and Symbols	Examples
daler	daler		
krone	kroner	kr Dkr	10kr Dkr10

Singular	Plural	Known Abbreviations and Symbols	Examples
øre	øre		
skilling	skillings	s sk RBS	10s 10sk 10 RBS

Djibouti (DJF)

The country now known as Djibouti had a long association with France and membership in the Franc Zone. In 1888, it was a colony called French Somaliland; in 1946 it became an overseas territory. As early as 1885, the French franc, Indian rupee, and Austro-Hungarian thaler were all legal tender in the colony — the latter two currencies until 1943. French Somaliland left the Franc Zone in 1949, when it tied its franc system to the U.S. dollar instead of the French franc. In 1967 French Somaliland was renamed the French Territory of the Afars and Issas. In 1977, it received independence and was renamed Djibouti.

CHRONOLOGY

Year	Denomination	Equivalent
1977–present	Djibouti franc	100 centimes
1949–1977	Afars and Issas franc	100 centimes
ca. 1885–1949	French franc	100 centimes

ORTHOGRAPHY AND NUMBER

Singular	Plural	Known Abbreviations and Symbols	Examples
centime	centimes	c	10c
franc	francs	F FD Fr	10F 10FD 10Fr

Dominica (XCD)

Great Britain acquired Dominica from France in 1763. In 1833 it was made part of the Leeward Islands dependency; it was attached to the Windward Islands group in 1940. Dominica attained full independence in 1978.

During much of this time Dominica was a member of the Sterling Zone, even though U.S. dollars were also accepted as legal tender. In 1935, the monetary system was changed from the imperial LSD system to a decimal system based on the British West Indies dollar of the Eastern Caribbean Currency Authority. In 1965, the Eastern Caribbean Central Bank succeeded the Eastern Caribbean Currency Authority and replaced the West Indies dollar with the East Caribbean dollar. *See also* **East Caribbean States**.

CHRONOLOGY

Year	Denomination	Equivalent
1965–present	East Caribbean dollar	100 cents
1935–1965	British West Indies dollar	100 cents
–1935	pound sterling	20 shillings
	shilling	12 pence

ORTHOGRAPHY AND NUMBER

Singular	Plural	Known Abbreviations and Symbols	Examples
cent	cents	c	10c
dollar	dollars	EC$ $	$10 EC$10
penny	pence	d	10d
pound	pounds	£ (or £)	£10
shilling	shillings	/	10/-

Dominican Republic (DOP)

In 1492 Christopher Columbus, seeking a sea route to India, discovered several islands in the Caribbean. One of these he called La Isla Española and claimed it for Spain. It would later be renamed Hispaniola. In 1697 the island was divided: Saint-Domingue, controlled by France, became Haiti in 1804; Santo Domingo, under Spanish control, became the Dominican Republic in 1821. During its turbulent history, it has been occupied by other countries numerous times; it gained independence for the last time in 1863.

Despite the fact that it had its own monetary system, most often based on the peso, currencies from other countries — Haitian gourdes, pounds sterling, and Spanish escudos — freely circulated. From 1897 until 1948, the United States dollar was also considered legal tender alongside the peso.

CHRONOLOGY

Year	Denomination	Equivalent
1885–present	Dominican Republic peso	100 centavos
1883–1885	franco	100 centimos
1880–1883	peso	100 centavos
–1880	peso	8 reales

ORTHOGRAPHY AND NUMBER

Singular	Plural	Known Abbreviations and Symbols	Examples
centavo	centavos	c cts ¢	10c 10¢
centimo	centimos		
franco	francos		
peso	pesos	$ RD$	$10 RD$10
real	reales	R Rs	10R 10 Rs

East Caribbean States (XCD)

The East Caribbean States is a confederation of eight of the countries that had once been part of the British Sterling Zone. The current confederation includes the former dependencies of Antigua and Barbuda, Dominica, Grenada, St. Kitts and Nevis, St. Lucia, and St. Vincent and the Grenadines, and the British overseas territories of Anguilla and Montserrat. Trinidad and Tobago, Barbados, and British Guiana (now Guyana) are no longer members. As an economic confederation, they share the same currency.

The British West Indies (BWI, often pronounced "bee-wee") dollar, divisible into 100 cents, was introduced in 1935. The British pound sterling was equal to 4.80 BWI dollars, and banknotes were issued by the local governments and commercial banks. In 1951, the Board of Commissioners of Currency, British Caribbean Territories (Eastern Group), became the sole note-issuing authority for these dependencies, issuing both notes and coins. Both British Guiana and Trinidad and Tobago withdrew from the British Caribbean Currency Board in 1962. In 1965 the BWI dollar was replaced by the East Caribbean dollar, which was controlled by the East Caribbean Currency Authority's bank in St. Kitts and Nevis. Barbados withdrew from the currency union in 1973. In 1983, the Eastern Caribbean Central Bank succeded the Eastern Caribbean Currency Authority.

CHRONOLOGY

Year	Denomination	Equivalent
1965–present	East Caribbean dollar	100 cents
1935–1965	British West Indies dollar	100 cents

ORTHOGRAPHY AND NUMBER

Singular	Plural	Known Abbreviations and Symbols	Examples
cent	cent	c	10c
dollar	dollars	$ EC$ BWI$	$10 EC$10 BWI$10

East Timor *see* Timor Lestep

Ecuador (USD; replaced ECS in 2000)

Even after gaining its independence from Spain in 1830, Ecuador continued to use the escudo, peso, and reales monetary system of its colonial ruler. In 1884 Ecuador adopted a decimal monetary system. The sucre, named after the South American liberator and general Antonio José de Sucre (1795–1830), replaced the peso; it was divisible into 100 centavos and 10 decimos. (Strangely enough, although Sucre is the judicial capital of Bolivia, that country has no monetary unit by that name.) In 2000 Ecuador adopted the United States dollar as its currency.

CHRONOLOGY

Year	Denomination	Equivalent
2000–present	United States dollar	100 cents
1884–2000	sucre	100 centavos, 10 decimos
1871–1884	peso	8 reales
1835–1871	Ecuadorian escudo	2 pesos
	peso	8 reales
–1835	Spanish escudo	2 pesos
	peso	8 reales

ORTHOGRAPHY AND NUMBER

Singular	Plural	Known Abbreviations and Symbols	Examples
centavo	centavos	c/. ¢ cts ctvs ctvos	c/.0.10
escudo	escudos	E	10E
peso	pesos	$	$10
real	reales	R Rs	10R 10 Rs
sucre	sucre	$ S/.	S/.10 S/.0.10

Egypt (EGP)

Except for a brief period from 1799 to 1801, when it was controlled by France, Egypt was part of the Ottoman Empire. This ended in 1882 when Great Britain seized control of the government. The monetary system of piastres, with one piastre equal to four para or 120 aspers, was the same as that of its Ottoman rulers until 1885. At that time Egypt adopted a gold standard, and Great Britain instituted a decimal monetary system based on the Egyptian pound, which was equal to 100 piastres (also called guerches) or 1,000 milliemes (also mills).

With the Ottoman Turks involved in World War I, the British made Egypt a protectorate in 1914. The country gained full independence in 1936. In 1953, the piastre was removed as a monetary unit, but was reinstated in 1982. In Egypt and many other parts of the Arabic-speaking world, the pound is frequently referred to by its Arabic equivalent —*junyah* (جنيه).

Egypt's modern monetary system primarily uses the Latin alphabet for its abbreviations, but it also frequently uses letters from the Arabic alphabet, such as *pe* (پ) as the abbreviation for para (پاره), *qaf* (ق) for piastre or guerche (قروشا), and *mim* (م) for mills or millieme (مليم), when combined with the Arabic-language numbers shown below:

0	1	2	3	4	5	6	7	8	9	10	50	100	500	1000
٠	١	٢	٣	٤	٥	٦	٧	٨	٩	١٠	٥٠	١٠٠	٥٠٠	١٠٠٠

Chronology

Year	Denomination	Equivalent
1982–present	Egyptian pound	100 piastres
	piastre	10 milliemes
1953–1982	Egyptian pound	1,000 milliemes
1885–1953	Egyptian pound	100 piastres
	piastre	10 milliemes
1834–1885	piastre	40 para

Orthography and Number

Singular	Plural	Known Abbreviations and Symbols	Examples
millieme	milliemes	M م	10M ١٠م
para	para(s)*	پ	١٠پ
piastre	piastres	P. P.T. ق	10P. 10P.T. ١٠ق
pound	pounds	LE £ £E	LE10 £10 £E10

*Optional final s.

El Salvador (USD; replaced SVC in 2003)

When Spanish rule ended in 1821, El Salvador became a part of Mexico, remaining under its control until 1823. From 1824 until 1841 it was part of the United Provinces of Central America, a federation of states which had declared their independence from Spain and Mexico. This federation comprised five states that are now Costa Rica, El Salvador, Guatemala, Honduras, and Nicaragua. Their currency was the escudo, divisible into 16 reales.

About 1870, the monetary system was reformed and replaced with a decimalized one based on the peso, divisible into 100 centavos. In 1919, the monetary system was changed again. The peso was replaced at par with the colón, named in honor of Christopher

Columbus (Spanish: Cristóbal Colón). Costa Rica had done the same in 1896. The U.S. dollar was made legal tender in El Salvador in 2001; use of the colón continued until 2003, when the dollar became the country's only legal tender.

CHRONOLOGY

Year	Denomination	Equivalent
2001–present	U.S. dollar	100 cents
1919–2003	colón	100 centavos
ca. 1870–1919	peso	100 centavos
1841–ca. 1870	escudo	8 reales
1824–1841	Central American escudo	2 pesos
	peso	8 reales
–1824	Spanish escudo	2 pesos
	peso	8 reales

ORTHOGRAPHY AND NUMBER

Singular	Plural	Known Abbreviations and Symbols	Examples
cent	cents	¢	10¢
centavo	centavos	c cts	10c 10 cts
colón	colónes	$ (old) ¢ ₡ (present)	$10 ¢10 ₡10
dollar	dollars	$	$10
escudo	escudos	E	10E
peso	pesos	$	$10
real	reales	R Rs	10R 10 Rs

Equatorial Guinea (XAF; replaced GQE in 1985)

Equatorial Guinea gained independence in 1968 after 190 years of Spanish rule. In 1969, the Guinea peseta of 100 centimos replaced the Spanish peseta at par. In 1973, the Guinea peseta was renamed the ekuele (plural, bipkwele), but its spelling was changed to epkwele in 1979. In 1985, Equatorial Guinea joined the African Financial Community (Communauté Financière Africaine) and adopted the CFA franc, one franc in exchange for four bipkwele. *See also* **Central African States.**

CHRONOLOGY

Year	Denomination	Equivalent
1985–present	CFA franc	100 centimes
1979–1985	epkwele Guineana	100 centimos
1973–1979	ekuele Guineana	100 centimos
1969–1973	Guinea peseta	100 centimos
–1969	Spanish peseta	100 centimos

ORTHOGRAPHY AND NUMBER

Singular	Plural	Known Abbreviations and Symbols	Examples
centime	centimes	c	10c
centimo	centimos	c cts cents	10c 10 cts
CFA franc	CFA francs	FCFA	10 FCFA
epkwele (ekuele before 1979)	bipkwele	BK	10BK
peseta	pesetas	pta ptas	10 ptas

Eritrea (ERN)

From 1557 until 1890, present-day Eritrea was a province of the Ottoman Empire under the administration of Egypt. In 1890, Eritrea became an Italian colony; it was united with Ethiopia and Italian Somalia as Italian East Africa in 1936. The monetary system there was based on the Italian East Africa lira, divisible into 100 centesimi, and at par with the Italian lira.

Great Britain liberated Ethiopia and Eritrea in 1941 and replaced the Italian East African lira with the East African shilling, divisible into 100 cents. The Ethiopian dollar, divisible into 100 cents, replaced the shilling in 1945 at an exchange of two shillings per dollar.

In 1952 Eritrea became an autonomous part of Ethiopia, but its autonomy was subsequently revoked and it became an Ethiopian province in 1962. In 1976, monetary reforms in Ethiopia replaced the dollar with the birr, named after an Amharic word for "silver." The birr was divisible into 100 cents, although santime, the Arabic equivalent of the French centime, is frequently used instead.

Eritrea gained its independence from Ethiopia in 1993 but continued the use of the birr until 1997 when a monetary reform introduced the nakfa, divisible into 100 cents. The nakfa is named after Nak'fa, a town in the Sahel Mountains which served as the home of the Eritrean People's Liberation Front during its civil war with Ethiopia.

Eritrea uses letters from the Latin, Amharic, and Arabic alphabets for abbreviations of certain monetary units. The Amharic letter *bet* (ብ) is the abbreviation for birr (ብር), and *sat* (ሳ) is the abbreviation for centime/santime (ሳንቲም). These are combined with either the Arabic numerals 0 through 9, or the Amharic numerals shown below:

1	2	3	4	5	6	7	8	9	10	50	100	500	1000
፩	፪	፫	፬	፭	፮	፯	፰	፱	፲	፶	፻	፭፻	፲፻

The Arabic letter *sin* (س) is the abbreviation for either cent (سنتات) or centime/santime (سنتيم), which is used with the following Arabic-language numerals:

0	1	2	3	4	5	6	7	8	9	10	50	100	500	1000
٠	١	٢	٣	٤	٥	٦	٧	٨	٩	١٠	٥٠	١٠٠	٥٠٠	١٠٠٠

CHRONOLOGY

Year	Denomination	Equivalent
1997–present	nakfa	100 cents
1976–1997	birr	100 cents
1945–1976	Ethiopian dollar	100 cents
1941–1945	East African shilling	100 cents
–1941	East African lira	100 centesimi

ORTHOGRAPHY AND NUMBER

Singular	Plural	Known Abbreviations and Symbols	Examples
birr	birr	·ቢ	10ቢ ፲ቢ
cent	cents	c ¢ ሳ س	10c 10¢ 10ሳ ፲ሳ س١٠
centesimo	centesimi	cent	10 cent
lira	lire	L.	L.10
nakfa	nakfa	Nfa	Nfa10

Estonia (EEK)

Prior to its independence in 1918, Estonia was long part of the Russian Empire. The monetary system was the Russian ruble, divided into 100 kopecks, although the Finnish markka, divided into 100 penni, also circulated. Germany occupied Estonia for the last nine months of World War I. From 1918 until 1928, the monetary system was the Estonian mark, divisible into 100 penni.

A monetary reform in 1928 saw the mark replaced by the kroon, meaning "crown," which was divided into 100 senti — a variation of cent. In 1940, Estonia and the other Baltic states of Latvia and Lithuania were forcibly occupied by the Soviet Union, which reinstituted the ruble and kopeck. Following the Soviet Union's breakup in 1990, Estonia declared its independence in 1992; the kroon, equal to 10 rubles, was again made the country's monetary unit. In 2004 Estonia joined the European Union, but it is not clear when it will participate in the European Union's monetary system (Eurozone) and adopt the euro.

CHRONOLOGY

Year	Denomination	Equivalent
1992–present	kroon	100 senti
1940–1992	Russian ruble	100 kopecks
1928–1940	kroon	100 senti
1918–1928	Estonian mark	100 penni
–1918	Russian ruble	100 kopecks

ORTHOGRAPHY AND NUMBER

Singular	Plural	Known Abbreviations and Symbols	Examples
kopeck	kopecks	к коп	10 к 10 коп
kroon	krooni	kr	10kr
mark	marka	m mk	10m 10mk
penni	penni	P PEN	10 P 10 PEN
ruble	rubles	руб	10 руб
sent	senti	s	10s

Ethiopia (ETB)

Until the twentieth century, present-day Ethiopia was an independent country known as Abyssinia. Its monetary system primarily rested on the Maria Theresa thaler, equal to 16 piastres (colloquially called guerches). In 1894 the thaler was replaced by the dollar, also known as the Menelik dollar, named after Emperor Menelik II. In 1928, the dollar was renamed the talari, an Amharic-language variation of thaler, which was divided into 16 mehalek.

Ethiopia was annexed by Italy in 1935 and was united with Eritrea and Italian Somalia in 1936 as Italian East Africa. The monetary system was then based on the Italian East Africa lira, divisible into 100 centesimi and at par with the Italian lira.

Great Britain liberated Italian East Africa in 1941 and replaced the East African lira with the East African shilling, divisible into 100 cents. The Ethiopian dollar, divisible into 100 cents, replaced the shilling in 1945 at an exchange of two shillings per dollar. A 1976 monetary reform renamed the dollar the birr — Amharic for "silver" — which was divisible into 100 cents (although *santime*, the Arabic-language equivalent of the French centime, is frequently used).

Ethiopia uses letters from the Amharic alphabet for abbreviations of certain monetary units. The Amharic letter *bet* (ብ) is the abbreviation used for birr (ብር), dollar, and thaler; *sat* (ሳ) for centime or santime (ሳንቲም); and *gimel* (ግ) for piastre or guerche (ግርሽ). These abbreviations are combined with either the numerals 0 through 9 or the Amharic numerals shown below:

1	2	3	4	5	6	7	8	9	10	50	100	500	1000
፩	፪	፫	፬	፭	፮	፯	፰	፱	፲	፶	፻	፭፻	፲፻

CHRONOLOGY

Year	Denomination	Equivalent
1976–present	birr	100 cents
1945–1976	Ethiopian dollar	100 cents
1941–1945	East African shilling	100 cents
1936–1941	thaler	100 centimes

Year	Denomination	Equivalent
1928–1936	thaler	16 mehalek
1894–1928	Menelik dollar (*talari*)	16 guerches (or *piastres*)

ORTHOGRAPHY AND NUMBER

Singular	Plural	Known Abbreviations and Symbols	Examples
birr	birr	Eth$ $Eth ብ	Eth$10 $10Eth ፲ብ
cent	cents	c ሳ	10c ፲ሳ
centime	centimes	c cmes	10c 10 cmes
dollar	dollars	$ E$	$10 E$10
piastre (*guerche*)	piastres (*guerches*)	ግ	፲ግ
shilling	shillings	/	10/
thaler	thalers		

European Union (EUR; replaced XEU in 1999)

The European Union (EU) is a European government confederation that replaced the European Community (EC). The EC in turn was established in 1957 as the European Economic Community (EEC), with Belgium, France, Italy, Luxembourg, the Netherlands, and West Germany as the six original members. By 1995, nine more countries were added: Austria, Denmark, Finland, Great Britain, Greece, Ireland, Portugal, Spain, and Sweden.

The European Currency Unit, or ECU — not to be confused with the ecu, a former French coin — was a composite basket of the currencies of the European Community member states and was used as the European Community's unit of account. Its purpose was to minimize fluctuations between member states' currencies and the ECU, which was also used in some international financial transactions. Over its lifespan, its composition and weighting were repeatedly adjusted as new member countries joined the EC.

On January 1, 1999, 14 of the 15 EC member countries (the exception being Greece) were admitted into the new European Union, and the ECU was replaced at par by an actual currency: the euro, which was divided into 100 euro-cents. The European System of Central Banks (ESCB)— composed of the European Central Bank (ECB) headquartered in Germany, and the central banks of the member states participating in the euro — was charged with the sole authority to set monetary policy. The individual countries would be responsible for the printing, minting and distribution of notes and coins, and the operation of the payment system among member countries.

Both Denmark and the United Kingdom were granted "derogations in protocols" to the Treaty on European Union. This meant they are not legally required to adopt the euro until their governments decide otherwise. On the other hand, Sweden was not granted a derogation by any protocol, and the Swedish government has also decided against adopting the euro.

Some countries not members of the EU, and colonial possessions whose currencies were the same as those of a member country, also adopted the euro. Among these are:

France: Andorra, French Guiana, Guadeloupe, Martinique, Mayotte, Réunion Island, and St. Pierre & Miquelon
Monaco
San Marino
Spain: Andorra
Vatican City

The notes and coins of the old currencies, however, continued to be used until new notes and coins were introduced on January 1, 2002. The old currencies continued as denominations of the euro until they ceased to be legal tender on February 28, 2002.

Greece, a former EC member whose economy originally did not meet the EU's criteria for membership, joined the EU in 2001. In 2004, ten additional countries were admitted: Cyprus, Czech Republic, Estonia, Hungary, Latvia, Lithuania, Malta, Poland, Slovakia, and Slovenia. However, none of these ten will officially convert to the euro for at least several years. The EU countries that have officially adopted and are using the euro as their legal tender are frequently referred to as either the "Eurozone" or "Euroland."

The official practice, as documented in the English-language version of the EU legislation, is to use the units "euro" and "euro-cent" as both singular and plural. However, the plural forms "euros" and "cents" are in everyday use. In the non–English-speaking countries that make up the majority of the EU, there is some variation in these basic terms. Although the plurals "euros" and "cents" are also officially used in Spanish and Portuguese, it is surprising that in France, where the government tries to prevent the addition of foreign words to its language, "cent" is the official term, but most people still use the older term — the centime.

Greece was also given an exception, as its alphabet is the only one of the Eurozone countries not composed solely of Latin characters. The euro was allowed to be rendered by its Greek equivalent (ΕΥΡΩ), while the euro-cent was allowed to be replaced with the singular Greek and plural forms for the lepto (ΛΕΠΤΟ, ΛΕΠΤΑ).

CHRONOLOGY

Year	Denomination	Equivalent
1999–present	euro	100 euro-cent
1957–1999	ECU	none

ORTHOGRAPHY AND NUMBER

Singular	Plural	Known Abbreviations and Symbols	Examples
euro	euro (euros)	€	€10 or 10€
euro-cent	euro-cent	€	€0.10 or 0.10€

Falkland Islands (FKP)

Although the Falkland Islands is a British colony, it is also claimed by Argentina, which calls it Islas Malvinas. Regardless of which country has sovereignty, its monetary system belongs to the Sterling Zone — originally based on the imperial system of pounds, shillings, and pence. When Great Britain decimalized its pound in 1971, the Falkland pound also was subdivided into 100 pence.

CHRONOLOGY

Year	Denomination	Equivalent
1971–present	Falkland pound	100 pence
–1971	Falkland pound	20 shillings
	shilling	12 pence

ORTHOGRAPHY AND NUMBER

Singular	Plural	Known Abbreviations and Symbols	Examples
penny	pence	d p (since 1971)	10d 10p
pound	pounds	£F	£F10
shilling	shillings	/	10/-

Fiji (FJD)

Prior to its establishment as a British crown colony in 1874, Fiji served as a port of call for many nations, and its monetary system was briefly based on the United States dollar. Once it was colonized by Britain, Fiji became part of the Sterling Zone, and the pound was legal tender. In 1917, the pound sterling was replaced by the Fijian pound. In 1969, one year before Fiji's independence, the pound was replaced with a decimalized system based on the Fijian dollar, divisible into 100 cents.

CHRONOLOGY

Year	Denomination	Equivalent
1969–present	Fijian dollar	100 cents
1917–1969	Fijian pound	20 shillings
	shilling	12 pence
1874–1917	pound sterling	20 shillings
	shilling	12 pence
ca. 1872–1874	United States dollar	100 cents

ORTHOGRAPHY AND NUMBER

Singular	Plural	Known Abbreviations and Symbols	Examples
cent	cents	c	10c
dollar	dollars	$ F$	$10 F$10
penny	pence	d	10d
pound	pounds	£ (or £)	£10
shilling	shillings	/	10/-

Finland (EUR; replaced FIM in 1999)

Finland was part of Sweden prior to 1809, and its monetary system was the Swedish riksdaler and skilling. From 1809 until its independence in 1917, Finland was a grand duchy of Czarist Russia, and its monetary system was first based on the Russian ruble, which was divisible into 100 kopecks.

However in 1860 Finland stopped using the ruble and instituted the markka. Divided into 100 penniä, it replaced the ruble at an exchange of four rubles for one markka (often called the Finnish mark or "finnmark"). The name markka, like its German counterpart, was based on a medieval unit of weight. Both the markka and the smaller penni are loanwords based on the same roots as the German mark and pfennig. In 1999 Finland joined the European Union and adopted the euro, which became its sole legal tender in 2002. *See also* **European Union**.

CHRONOLOGY

Year	Denomination	Equivalent
1999–present	euro	100 euro-cent
1860–2002	markka	100 penniä
1809–1860	Russian ruble	100 kopecks

ORTHOGRAPHY AND NUMBER

Singular	Plural	Known Abbreviations and Symbols	Examples
euro	euro	€	10 €
euro-cent	euro-cent	€	0.10 €
kopeck	kopecks	КОР коп	10 KOP 10 коп
markka	markkaa	M MK	10M 10MK
penni	pennia (*penniä*)	P PEN пен	10 P 10 PEN 10 пен
ruble	rubles	руб	10 руб

France (EUR; replaced FRF in 1999)

The origin of the franc as a monetary unit is attributed to a Latin inscription, *Francorum Rex* ("King of the Franks"), found on a 14th-century gold coin issued in the reign of King John II, also known as Jean le Bon ("John the Good"). However, it wasn't until 1795 that the franc, divided into 100 centimes, replaced the livre—French for "pound"—as France's major monetary unit.

Francophone countries around the world, and those having strong ties to France, such as Belgium, Switzerland, and Luxembourg, also adopted versions of the franc. In 1999 France joined the Eurozone and adopted the euro, which became its sole legal tender in 2002. *See also* **European Union.**

CHRONOLOGY

Year	Denomination	Equivalent
1999–present	euro	100 euro-cent
1795–2002	franc	100 centimes
–1795	livre	20 sous

ORTHOGRAPHY AND NUMBER

Singular	Plural	Known Abbreviations and Symbols	Examples
centime	centimes	c	10c
euro	euro	€	10€
euro-cent	euro-cent	€	0.10€
franc	francs	F Fr F	10Fr 10F
livre	livres		
sou	sous		

French Polynesia (XPF)

The current boundaries of the French overseas territory of French Polynesia were fixed in 1900, and its monetary system was made part of the Franc Zone. Since 1945, the monetary system has been based on the Communauté Financière Pacificienne (Pacific Financial Community), which issues the CFP franc, a monetary union of French Polynesia, New Caledonia, and Wallis & Futuna Islands — all French colonies in the Pacific. This union is similar to the CFA franc, the basis of the monetary system of many former French colonies in central and western Africa.

CHRONOLOGY

Year	Denomination	Equivalent
1945–present	CFP franc	100 centimes
1903–1945	French franc	100 centimes

ORTHOGRAPHY AND NUMBER

Singular	Plural	Known Abbreviations and Symbols	Examples
centime	centimes	c	10c
franc	francs	CFPF F	10F

Gabon (XAF)

France gained control over Gabon in 1839, and made it part of the French Congo in 1886. From 1910 until 1960 Gabon was part of an administrative area known as French Equatorial Africa, and a member of the Franc Zone. The current monetary system is based on the Communauté Financière Africaine (African Financial Community, CFA) franc, a monetary union of former French colonies in Africa. *See also* **Central African States**.

CHRONOLOGY

Year	Denomination	Equivalent
1960–present	CFA franc	100 centimes
1910–1960	franc	100 centimes

ORTHOGRAPHY AND NUMBER

Singular	Plural	Known Abbreviations and Symbols	Examples
centime	centimes	c	10c
franc	francs	CFA F	10F

The Gambia (GMD)

The Gambia was first established as a British crown colony in 1843, and it was a protectorate from 1894 until its independence in 1965. Originally its monetary system was the pound sterling, but that was replaced at par in 1913 with the West African pound. The West African pound was also used by other British territories, including the Gold Coast and British Togoland (both now part of Ghana), Nigeria, British Cameroon, and Sierra Leone.

In 1964, the Gambian pound replaced the colonial West African pound. It was in turn replaced in 1970 by a decimalized monetary system based on the dalasi (Arabic: دلس), also found spelled as dalasy, which is divisible into 100 butut.

CHRONOLOGY

Year	Denomination	Equivalent
1970–present	dalasi	100 butut
1964–1970	Gambian pound	20 shillings
	shilling	12 pence
1913–1964	West African pound	20 shillings
	shilling	12 pence
–1913	pound sterling	20 shillings
	shillings	12 pence
	penny	4 farthings

ORTHOGRAPHY AND NUMBER

Singular	Plural	Known Abbreviations and Symbols	Examples
butut	bututs	b	10b
dalasi	dalasis	D	D10
farthing	farthings	d	¼d ½d
penny	pence	d	10d
pound	pounds	£ (or £)	£10
shilling	shillings	s /	10s 10/-

Georgia (GEL)

From 1922 to until its secession and independence in 1991, Georgia was a Soviet republic and used the USSR's monetary system of rubles and kopecks. Following its independence, Georgia briefly continued use of the Russian ruble. In 1993 it reformed its system and introduced a transitional currency—the coupon or kuponi, replacing the ruble at par. Inflationary pressure resulted in the introduction of the lari, equal to one million kuponi and divisible into 100 tetri.

Georgia's monetary units, with their Georgian spellings, are:

kuponi	კუპონი
lari	ლარი
ruble	მანეთი
tetri	თეთრი

It is interesting to note that the Georgian abbreviation for the ruble, მან (for *maneti*—

ⴋⴀⴌⴄⴇⴈ), is a possible variant of *manat*, which is the monetary unit of both Azerbaijan and Turkmenistan.

Georgia uses letters from its Mkhedruli alphabet for the abbreviations of certain monetary units when combined with the Mkhedruli numerals shown below:

1	2	3	4	5	6	7	8	9	10	50	100	500	1000
ა	ბ	გ	ღ	ე	ვ	჻	ჰ	ⴑ	ⴍ	ⴂ	ⴃ	ⴅ	ⴆ

CHRONOLOGY

Year	Denomination	Equivalent
1995–present	lari	100 tetri
1993–1995	coupon	100 kopecks
1922–1993	Russian ruble	100 kopecks

ORTHOGRAPHY AND NUMBER

Singular	Plural	Known Abbreviations and Symbols	Examples
coupon	coupons	ⴀⴋⴌ	10 ⴀⴋⴌ
kopeck	kopecks	коп	10 коп
lari	lari		
ruble	rubles	руб ⴋⴀⴌ	10 руб ⴍ ⴋⴀⴌ
tetri	tetri		

Germany (EUR; replaced DEM [deutsche mark] in 1999, which replaced DDM [ostmark] in 1990)

When Germany was unified following the dissolution of the German confederation in 1867, it faced the task of replacing six separate monetary systems denominated in groschen, thalers, and gulden. Many attempts were made to consolidate the various systems, but the parochialism of the rulers of the many principalities and bishoprics hindered the process until the establishment of the German Reich in 1871.

However, it wasn't until 1873 that the reichmark (imperial mark) was introduced. The mark, whose name traces its origin to a Norse term from the third century for a unit of weight of precious metal, was used as a monetary unit by the Goths. The mark was divided into 100 pfennig, a German variant of the penny.

When Hitler annexed neighboring Austria in 1938, the reichmark became its official currency until 1945, when it was replaced by the schilling. Following World War II, tensions between the Soviet Union and the western allies — the United States, Great Britain, and France — resulted in Germany's being split into two nations, each with its own monetary system.

In 1948 East Germany instituted the ostmark ("East mark"), while West Germany established the deutsche mark ("German mark"); both were divided into 100 pfennig. In 1990, the two Germanys were reunited as one nation, and the monetary system was based on the stronger deutsche mark. In 1999 Germany joined the European Union and adopted the euro, which became its sole legal tender in 2002. *See also* **European Union.**

CHRONOLOGY

Year	Denomination	Equivalent
1999–present	euro	100 euro-cent
1990–1992	deutsche mark	100 pfennig
1948–1990 (West Germany)	deutsche mark	100 pfennig
1948–1990 (East Germany)	ostmark	100 pfennig
1873–1949	reichmark	100 pfennig

ORTHOGRAPHY

Singular	Plural	Known Abbreviations and Symbols	Examples
euro	euro	€	€10
euro-cent	euro-cent	€	€0.10
mark	marks	M DM RM	10 M 10 DM
pfennig	pfennig	pf ₰	10 pf 10₰

Ghana (GHC)

First established as a British crown colony in 1843, Ghana was originally known as the Gold Coast. It was part of the administrative area known as British West Africa, along with Nigeria, the Gambia, British Cameroon, and Sierra Leone. As a participant in the Sterling Zone, Ghana's monetary system was based first on the pound sterling and then on the colonial West African pound, both divisible into 20 shillings. In 1957, the colony merged with British Togoland and was renamed Ghana. In addition, the West African pound was replaced with the Ghana pound.

In 1960 Ghana became independent; in 1965, it replaced the imperial pound system with a decimalized system based on the cedi, equal to one-half the older pound and divisible into 100 pesewas. Cedi, sometimes also spelled "sedi," is a native word for "shell," referring to cowries — the shell money once common among the tribes of the coast. The pesewa is a native word for "penny," and is virtually worthless today because of inflation. It is no longer used in daily commerce, such as for coins or stamps.

CHRONOLOGY

Year	Denomination	Equivalent
1972–present	cedi	100 pesewas
1967–1972	new cedi	100 new pesewas
1965–1967	cedi	100 pesewas

Year	Denomination	Equivalent
1958–1965	Ghana pound	20 shillings
	shilling	12 pence
–1957	West African pound	20 shillings
	shilling	12 pence

ORTHOGRAPHY AND NUMBER

Singular	Plural	Known Abbreviations and Symbols	Examples
cedi	cedis	¢ C	C10 ¢10
new pesewa	new pesewas	NP	10NP
penny	pence	D	10D
pesewa	pesewas	P	10P
pound	pounds	£ (OR £)	£10
shilling	shillings	/	10/-

Gibraltar (GIP)

Gibraltar became the property of the Spanish crown in 1501. It was ceded in perpetuity to Great Britain in 1713 by the Treaty of Utrecht and was made a crown colony in 1830. From about 1880 to 1970, the monetary system was the pound sterling, although the Spanish peseta also saw use from 1889 to 1895. Great Britain decimalized its monetary system in 1971, and although the pound sterling was replaced with the Gibraltar pound, divisible into 100 pence, the pound sterling is still also legal tender.

CHRONOLOGY

Year	Denomination	Equivalent
1971–present	Gibraltar pound	100 pence
ca. 1880–1971	pound sterling	20 shillings
	shilling	12 pence
	penny	4 farthings
1889–1895	peseta	100 centimos

ORTHOGRAPHY AND NUMBER

Singular	Plural	Known Abbreviations and Symbols	Examples
centimo	centimos	c	10c
farthing	farthings	d	¼d ½d
penny	pence	d p (after 1971)	10d 10p
peseta	pesetas	pta ptas	10 pta
pound	pounds	£ £G (or £G)	£10 £G10
shilling	shillings	/	10/-

Great Britain (GBP)

The imperial monetary system of Great Britain has a long, rich history. Its system of pounds, shillings and pence, often referred to as the LSD system, was introduced as units of account well before the Norman conquest in 1066. In fact, the LSD system was also used in France, where it consisted of the livre, sol, and denier.

The pound, also referred to as pound sterling, was once a weight (Latin: *pondus*), and corresponded to the ancient Roman libra. The penny was originally equal to a pennyweight of silver — $1/240$ of a troy pound — so that a pound was equal to 240 pence.

When referring to coins, the term "penny" (plural, "pennies") is used: "there are three pennies on the table." When referring to the monetary unit, "pence" is the correct plural: "your change is three pence." The shilling, derived from the Roman solidus, is $1/20$ of a pound; there are 12 pence to a shilling, and 4 farthings to a penny. The pound is often referred to by its slang term, "quid" while the shilling is also called a "bob." In 1971, the pound was decimalized, being divided into 100 pence.

Besides the divisions between the pound, shilling, and penny, the British monetary system had other coin equivalents as follows:

guinea: 21 shillings
sovereign: 20 shillings
half sovereign: 10 shillings
crown: 5 shillings (but equal to 25 pence after decimalization)
half crown: 2½ shillings (two shillings and sixpence)
florin: 2 shillings, also known as a "two-bob bit."
groat: 4 pence
halfpenny: 2 farthings

The symbol for the pound is taken from the initial letter of *libra*, written using a cursive capital letter *L* having either a single cross stroke (£) or double cross strokes (₤) through it. Prior to Great Britain's change to a decimalized pound in 1971, the double-cross-stroke symbol (₤) was primarily used. This is also the symbol for the Italian lira. Since 1971, the single-cross-stroke symbol has been preferred, so that it is not apt to be confused with the Italian lira. In other countries where the pound is the monetary unit, the simple capital letter *L* is often used.

The letter *s* or the solidus (/) symbol, is used to represent shillings, while the letter *d* is the symbol for the penny/pence — derived from the initial letter of the ancient denarius. Since 1971, however, the letter *p* — pronounced "pea" — signifies pence. For example, an amount of 20 pence (20p) is spoken as "20 pea."

Under the imperial system, the solidus is used for amounts less than a pound, separating shillings and the smaller pence. For example, 2½ shillings (i.e., 2 shillings, 6 pence) is written 2/6 and is generally spoken as "two and six"; "shilling" is often omitted in everyday speech. When there are shillings with no pence, either a hyphen or an equals sign follows the solidus to represent zero pence. For example, both 10/- and 10/=

represent 10 shillings. It should be noted that the abbreviations g and gn are for one guinea, while gs and gns are the plural abbreviations.

CHRONOLOGY

Year	Denomination	Equivalent
1971–present	pound sterling	100 pence
9th century-1971	pound sterling	20 shillings
	shilling	12 pence
	penny	4 farthings

ORTHOGRAPHY

Singular	Plural	Known Abbreviations and Symbols	Examples
farthing	farthings	d	¼d ½d
guinea	guineas	g gn gns gs	1g 1gn 10gns 10gs
penny	pence	d p (after 1970)	10d 10p
pound	pounds	£ (or £)	£10 £10
shilling	shillings	/	10/-

Greece (EUR; replaced GRD in 2002)

After the once-powerful ancient city states had disappeared, Greece was made part of the Ottoman Empire; its monetary system was the Turkish piastre, divisible into 40 paras. In 1822, Greece gained its independence. The Turkish monetary system was replaced in 1828 by the phoenix, divisible into 100 lepta, from the Greek *leptos* (ΛΕΠΤΟΣ) — meaning "slim" or "thin." In 1833, the phoenix was replaced with one of Greece's ancient monetary units — the drachma, also divisible into 100 lepta. The origin of "drachma" is probably either the Greek *drach* (ΔΡΑΞ), meaning "handful," or *drattomai* (ΔΡΑΤΤΟΜΑΙ), "to grasp."

In 2001 Greece joined the Eurozone, adopting the euro, which became its sole legal tender in 2002. However, the official practice of the European Union is to use the units euro and euro-cent to represent both singular and plural amounts. Greece was given an exception, as its alphabet is the only one of the Eurozone countries not composed solely of Latin characters. The euro, singular and plural, was allowed to be rendered by its Greek equivalent (ΕΥΡΩ), while the euro-cent was allowed to be replaced with the Greek singular and plural forms for lepto (ΛΕΠΤΟ, ΛΕΠΤΑ). *See also* **European Union.**

CHRONOLOGY

Year	Denomination	Equivalent
2001–present	euro	100 euro-cent
1833–2002	drachma	100 lepta
1828–1833	phoenix	100 lepta

ORTHOGRAPHY AND NUMBER

Singular	Plural	Known Abbreviations and Symbols	Examples
drachma	drachmas	𝒟𝑝 δρ ΔΡ ΔΡΧ ΔΡΑΧ	𝒟𝑝10 δρ10 ΔΡ10
euro (ΕΥΡΩ)	euro (ΕΥΡΩ)	€	10€
euro-cent (ΛΕΠΤΟ)	euro-cent (ΛΕΠΤΑ)	€	0.10€
lepton	lepta	Λ ΛΕΠ	Λ10
phoenix	phoenix		

Grenada (XCD)

Grenada had been a French colony for almost one hundred years before it came under British control in 1762. Because it was part of the British Empire until its independence in 1974, Grenada was also part of the Sterling Zone. In 1935 it changed its monetary system from the imperial LSD system to one based on the decimalized British West Indies dollar of the Eastern Caribbean Currency Authority. In 1965, the Eastern Caribbean Central Bank succeeded the Eastern Caribbean Currency Authority and replaced the West Indies dollar with the East Caribbean dollar. *See also* **East Caribbean States.**

CHRONOLOGY

Year	Denomination	Equivalent
1965–present	East Caribbean dollar	100 cents
1935–1965	British West Indies dollar	100 cents
–1935	pound sterling	20 shillings
	shilling	12 pence
	penny	4 farthings

ORTHOGRAPHY AND NUMBER

Singular	Plural	Known Abbreviations and Symbols	Examples
cent	cents	c ¢	10c 10¢
dollar	dollars	$ EC$	$10 EC$10
farthing	farthings	d	¼d ½d
penny	pence	d	10d
pound	pounds	£ (or £)	£10
shilling	shillings	/	10/-

Guatemala (GTQ)

After Spanish rule ended in 1821, Guatemala was a part of Mexico until 1823. From 1824 until 1847 it was part of the United Provinces of Central America, a federation of states established after those former colonies had declared their independence from Spain and Mexico. This federation comprised five states that are now Costa Rica, El Salvador, Guatemala, Honduras, and Nicaragua. All used the escudo, divisible into 16 reales.

In 1870, the monetary system was reformed and replaced with a decimalized one based on a peso divisible into 100 centavos. In 1925, the peso was replaced with the quetzal, named after the country's national bird. In 2001, the United States dollar was made legal tender in Guatemala alongside the quetzal.

CHRONOLOGY

Year	Denomination	Equivalent
1925–present	quetzal	100 centavos de quetzal
1870–1925	Guatemalan peso	100 centavos
1847–1870	Guatemalan peso	8 reales
1824–1847	Central American escudo	2 pesos
	peso	8 reales
–1824	Spanish escudo	2 pesos
	peso	8 reales

ORTHOGRAPHY AND NUMBER

Singular	Plural	Known Abbreviations and Symbols	Examples
centavo	centavos	c ct cts ¢	10c 10ct 10¢
escudo	escudos	$	10$
peso	pesos	$	$10
quetzal	quetzals	Q.	Q.10
real	reales		

Guinea (GNF; replaced GNS in 1986)

Guinea was first established as a French colony in 1893, and gained its independence in 1958. The monetary system prior to 1972 was based on the Communauté Financière Africaine (African Financial Community, CFA) franc, a monetary union of former French colonies in Africa. Following independence, Guinea withdrew from the Franc Zone in 1960 and replaced the franc with the syli in 1972, at the exchange rate of 10 francs. The name syli is a native language (probably Susa) term for "elephant," and is divisible into 100 cauris. The name cauri (also cory, caury) refers to the cowrie shells that once served as a type of currency. In 1986, Guinea returned to the Franc Zone and again adopted use of the CFA franc. *See also* **West African States.**

CHRONOLOGY

Year	Denomination	Equivalent
1986–present	CFA franc	100 centimes
1972–1986	syli	100 cauris
1945–1972	CFA franc	100 centimes
1893–1945	franc	100 centimes

ORTHOGRAPHY AND NUMBER

Singular	Plural	Known Abbreviations and Symbols	Examples
cauri	cauris		
centime	centimes	c	10c
franc	francs	F FG	10F 10FG
syli	sylis	S Sy	10S 10Sy

Guinea-Bissau (XOF; replaced GWP in 1997)

Guinea-Bissau was first established as a colony known as Portuguese Guinea in 1879. As a colony, its monetary systems were the same milréis and escudos used by its Portuguese colonial ruler. Guinea-Bissau gained independence in 1974, and one year it later replaced the escudo with the peso. The pre–1991 symbol using the letter P serves as a decimal point between pesos and the smaller centavos. In addition, the dollar sign ($) is used both as the symbol for the escudo and as a decimal point between escudos and the smaller centavos. As an example, 10$50 equals 10.50 escudos.

In 1997, the country instituted monetary reforms and joined the Franc Zone. The new monetary system was based on the Communauté Financière Africaine (African Financial Community, CFA) franc, a monetary union of former French colonies in Africa. The CFA franc is divisible into 100 centimes.

CHRONOLOGY

Year	Denomination	Equivalent
1997–present	CFA franc	100 centimes
1975–1997	Guinea-Bissau peso	100 centavos
1911–1975	escudo	100 centavos
–1911	milréis	1,000 réis

ORTHOGRAPHY AND NUMBER

Singular	Plural	Known Abbreviations and Symbols	Examples
centavo	centavos	c	10c
centime	centimes	c	10c
escudo	escudos	$ ESC	10$ 10$50
franc	francs	F	10F
peso	pesos	P PG (after 1991)	10P 10P50 10PG
réis	réis	Rs	Rs10

Guyana (GYD)

By 1831, those parts of Guyana that were once under Dutch control had been ceded to Great Britain, forming British Guiana. In 1839, the British Guiana dollar, divided into 100 cents, replaced the Dutch monetary system of guilders and stivers. However, the pound sterling was also legal tender, and one dollar was equivalent to four shillings and two pence. In 1935, the dollar was changed to the British West Indies dollar of the Eastern Caribbean Currency Authority. In 1965, the British West Indies dollar was replaced at par with the Guyanese dollar. In 1966, when it gained its independence from Great Britain, the country's name was changed to Guyana. *See also* **East Caribbean States**.

CHRONOLOGY

Year	Denomination	Equivalent
1965–present	Guyanese dollar	100 cents
1935–1965	British West Indies dollar	100 cents
ca. 1839–1935	dollar	100 cents
-ca. 1839	guilder	20 stivers

ORTHOGRAPHY AND NUMBER

Singular	Plural	Known Abbreviations and Symbols	Examples
cent	cents	c ¢	10c 10¢
dollar	dollars	$ G$	$10
guilder (*gulden*)	guilders (*gulden*)	G Gi	10G 10Gi
stiver (*stuiver*)	stivers (*stuivers*)	S St	10S 10St

Haiti (HTG; USD)

In 1492 Christopher Columbus, seeking a sea route to India, discovered several islands in the Caribbean. One of these he called La Isla Española and claimed it for Spain. Later renamed Hispaniola, it would be divided in half in 1697. Saint-Domingue, controlled by France, became Haiti in 1804; Santo Domingo, under Spanish control, became the Dominican Republic in 1821.

In 1814, a silver gourde replaced several currencies that had been in use in both sections of the island. The gourde's value has since declined greatly. The U.S. dollar is now also legal tender in Haiti.

CHRONOLOGY

Year	Denomination	Equivalent
1814–present	gourde	100 centimes

ORTHOGRAPHY AND NUMBER

Singular	Plural	Known Abbreviations and Symbols	Examples
centime	centimes	c ct cts cent	10c 10 cent
gourde	gourde	G	10G

Honduras (HNL)

When Spanish rule ended in 1821, Honduras became a part of Mexico. From 1824 to 1838, it was part of the United Provinces of Central America, a federation of former colonies which had declared their independence from Spain and Mexico. This federation comprised the five modern countries of Costa Rica, El Salvador, Guatemala, Honduras, and Nicaragua. All used the escudo, divisible into 16 reales.

Following independence, Honduras continued to use the monetary system of reales and pesos until about 1880, when the peso was decimalized and divided into 100 centavos. In 1926, the lempira, named in honor of Lempira (1497–1537), the Lenca Indian chief who fought against the first Spanish colonists, replaced the Honduran peso.

CHRONOLOGY

Year	Denomination	Equivalent
1926–present	lempira	100 centavos
ca. 1880–1926	peso	100 centavos
1838–1880	peso	8 reales

Year	Denomination	Equivalent
1824–1838	Central American escudo	2 pesos
	peso	8 reales
–1824	Spanish escudo	2 pesos
	peso	8 reales

ORTHOGRAPHY AND NUMBER

Singular	Plural	Known Abbreviations and Symbols	Examples
centavo	centavos	c cts ctvs	10c 10 cts
escudo	escudos	$	10$
lempira	lempiras	L.	L.10
peso	pesos	$	$10
real	reales	R Rs	10R 10 Rs

Hong Kong (HKD)

When China ceded Hong Kong to Great Britain in 1842, the colony's monetary system was a mix of foreign currencies including the British pound. In 1895, the crown colony adopted the Hong Kong dollar, which was divided into 100 cents. Even after Great Britain returned Hong Kong to China in 1997, the Chinese recognized the power of Hong Kong's economy in international trade and declared Hong Kong a special administrative region. As a result, it retained the dollar as its monetary system instead of adopting China's yuan renminbi.

CHRONOLOGY

Year	Denomination	Equivalent
1895–present	Hong Kong dollar	100 cents

ORTHOGRAPHY AND NUMBER

Singular	Plural	Known Abbreviations and Symbols	Examples
cent	cents	c ¢	10c 10¢
dollar	dollars	$ HK$	$10 HK$10

Hungary (HUF)

Present-day Hungary was once part of the Holy Roman Empire, which had several concurrent monetary systems as far back as the early 1600s. Eventually these diverse systems were combined and decimalized: the forint, equivalent to the florin or gulden, was divided into 100 kracjzár, the Hungarian equivalent of the Austrian kreuzer. The kracjzár was probably derived from the Polish *krzyż*—"cross."

In 1892, Austria-Hungary adopted the gold standard. The Austrian guilder was replaced with the krone, divided into 100 heller. The Hungarians replaced the forint with the korona, meaning "crown"; it was also called the "corona," its Latin equivalent. The korona was divisible into 100 filler (Hungarian: *fillér*), meaning "penny" or "mite."

Hungary gained its independence in 1918, and the korona was replaced in 1925 with the pengo (Hungarian: *pengő*), which is also spelled pengoe. It too was divided into 100 filler. After World War II, rising inflation forced the replacement of the pengo in 1946 with larger units having more zeros. The milpengo was equal to one million pengo; two weeks later, the bilpengo was equal to one million milpengo.

Inflation continued, one month later the forint was reintroduced, now replacing a staggering 400,000,000,000,000,000,000 pengo. As of 1999, the filler's value dropped to the point that it could no longer be used as a viable monetary unit for coins and stamps. In 2004, Hungary joined the European Union, but it will not participate in the European Union's monetary system (Eurozone) and adopt the euro until about 2007.

CHRONOLOGY

Year	Denomination	Equivalent
1946–present	forint	100 filler
1925–1946	pengo	100 filler
1892–1925	korona	100 filler
1857–1891	forint	100 krajczár

ORTHOGRAPHY AND NUMBER

Singular	Plural	Known Abbreviations and Symbols	Examples
filler (*fillér*)	filler (*fillér*)	f	10f
forint	forints (*forint*)	Ft	Ft10
korona	korona	KR	10KR
pengo (*pengő*)	pengo (*pengő*)	P	10P

Iceland (ISK)

Prior to 1918, Iceland was part of Denmark, and its monetary system prior to 1873 was based on the rigsbank (national bank) daler, divided into 96 rigsbank skillings. The year 1873 also marked the creation of the Scandinavian Monetary Union, which initially included only Denmark and Sweden; Norway joined in 1875.

The Icelandic króna, a derivative of the Danish krone, was introduced after the breakup of the Scandinavian Monetary Union and Iceland's independence from Denmark in 1918 (although it did not achieve full sovereignty until 1944). Whatever its spelling or language, the name means "crown." The króna was divided into 100 aurar — its name comes from the Latin *aureus* for gold, as do the Danish øre and Swedish öre.

CHRONOLOGY

Year	Denomination	Equivalent
1918–present	króna	100 aurar
1873–1918	Danish krone	100 øre
–1873	rigsbank daler	96 rigsbank skillings

ORTHOGRAPHY AND NUMBER

Singular	Plural	Known Abbreviations and Symbols	Examples
eyrir	aurar	A AUR	10A 10 AUR
daler	rigsdaler	RBS	10 RBS
króna	krónur	Kr	10Kr
skilling	skillings	Sk	10Sk

India (INR)

Before Britain established effective control in the mid–1750s, India had been largely under the rule of the Moghuls since 1526. The many regions and princely states of British India had their own monetary systems, some of which were based on the gold mohur. This chaotic situation was finally standardized by the British with the silver rupee, a name taken from the Sanskrit *rupaya*, meaning "silver." The rupee was divided into 16 anna — a word from the Hindi *ānā*, meaning "small." The rupee was also divided into 64 pice, the English form of paise — taken from either the Sanskrit word *padikaha* (पादिक:) or the Hindi *padik* (पादिक), meaning "quarter," as the pice (or paisa) was one-fourth of an anna.

After gaining its independence in 1947, India continued to use the rupee. However, a monetary reform in 1957 converted the rupee to a decimalized system, one that was divided into 100 naye paise (i.e., new pice). In 1964 the term "naya" was dropped, and the rupee was simply equal to 100 paise.

Because of the extent of Great Britain's colonial empire during the nineteenth and twentieth centuries, the rupee was used as the basis of the monetary systems of many countries in the Indian subcontinent, Persian Gulf, Middle East, and East Africa. The Indian rupee also generated variations like the rufiyaa (Maldives) and rupiah (Indonesia).

Because the two most important of India's 15 official languages are English and

Hindi, its monetary system uses both the Latin and Devanāgarī alphabets for its abbreviations. The Hindi forms आ for anna (आना), पा for pie, न प for naya paisa (नये पैसे), पै for paisa (पैसे), and रु for rupee (रुपया), are used either with the numerals 0 through 9 or with the Devanāgarī numerals shown below:

0	1	2	3	4	5	6	7	8	9	10	50	100	500	1000
०	१	२	३	४	५	६	७	८	९	१०	५०	१००	५००	१०००

It should be noted that the pice abbreviation P is singular and Ps is plural. For the anna, A is the singular abbreviation and As is the plural. Also, R , Re, and Rp are singular abbreviations for the rupee, while Rs is the plural abbreviation.

CHRONOLOGY

Year	Denomination	Equivalent
1964–present	Indian rupee	100 paise
1957–1964	Indian rupee	100 naya paise
ca. 1858–1957	Indian rupee	16 anna
	anna	4 pice (*paise*)
	pice (*paisa*)	3 pies

ORTHOGRAPHY AND NUMBER

Singular	Plural	Known Abbreviations and Symbols	Examples
anna	anna(s)*	A As आ	1A 10As 10आ १०आ
naya paisa	naye paise	NP न पै	10NP 10न पै १०न पै
pice (*paisa*)	pice (*paise*)	P पै	10P 10पै १०पै
pie	pies	P Ps पा	1P 10Ps 10पा १०पा
rupee	rupee(s)*	R Re Rp Rs रु	R1 Re1 Rp1 Rs10 १०रु

*Optional final s.

Indonesia (IDR)

Indonesia was known as the Netherlands East Indies after it was established as a Dutch colony in 1610. In 1817 the Netherlands Indies guilder replaced the Dutch guilder at par. The guilder, or *gulden*, was divisible into 30 stuivers and 120 duits until 1854, when the gulden was converted to a decimalized system and divided into 100 cents.

In 1945, following Japan's defeat in World War II, Indonesia declared its independence; however, it was not formally recognized until 1949. In 1950 the Netherlands Indies guilder was replaced with the Indonesian rupiah, divisible into 100 sen; the latter is no longer used.

CHRONOLOGY

Year	Denomination	Equivalent
1950–present	Indonesian rupiah	100 sen
1854–1950	Netherlands Indies guilder	100 cents
1817–1854	Netherlands Indies guilder	30 stuiver
	stuiver	4 duit
–1817	Dutch guilder	30 stuiver
	stuiver	4 duit

ORTHOGRAPHY

Singular	Plural	Known Abbreviations and Symbols	Examples
cent	cents	c ct	10c 10ct
guilder (*gulden*)	guilders (*gulden*)	G	10G
rupiah	rupiah	Rp	Rp10
sen	sen		

Iran (IRR)

Until 1935 Iran was known in the West by its English name — Persia. For over 400 years Iran's monetary system was based on the toman, divisible into 10,000 dinars, the Arabic form of the ancient Roman denarius. In 1825, the toman was also made divisible into 10 krans or 200 shahis. The shahi is derived from the Farsi (Persian) word *shah* (شاه), meaning "king."

The Pahlevi dynasty began in 1925, and a new monetary reform divided the toman into 1,000 dinars. In 1932, the rial, a spelling variation of the Saudi riyal, replaced the kran and the toman. The rial was divided into 100 dinars or 20 shahis. Even though the Pahlevi dynasty was overthrown and replaced with an Islamic republic in 1979, the Iranian rial, divisible into 100 dinars, was retained.

The Farsi numerals below:

0	1	2	3	4	5	6	7	8	9	10	50	100	500	1000
٠	١	٢	٣	۴	۵	۶	۷	۸	۹	١٠	۵٠	١٠٠	۵٠٠	١٠٠٠

are used in conjunction with the Farsi-language monetary units such as dinar (دينار), kran (تراه), and rial (ريال).

CHRONOLOGY

Year	Denomination	Equivalent
1979–present	Iranian rial	100 dinars
1932–1979	Iranian rial	20 shahis
	shahi	5 dinars

Year	Denomination	Equivalent
1925–1931	toman	10 krans
	kran	20 shahis
	shahi	5 dinars
1825–1925	toman	10 krans
	kran	20 shais
	shahi	50 dinars

ORTHOGRAPHY AND NUMBER

Singular	Plural	Known Abbreviations and Symbols	Examples
dinar	dinars	D drs	
rial	rials	R Rl Rls	10R 10Rls
shahi	shahis		
toman	tomans		

Iraq (IQD)

From 1831 to 1917, Iraq was part of the Ottoman Empire, and the basis for its monetary system was the Turkish pound (also called the lira), divisible into 100 piastres. In 1922 the British, who governed a number of post-World War I territories under mandates given by the League of Nations, took control of Iraq. Unlike the Palestine mandate, which had its own monetary system based on the Palestine pound, Iraq used both the Indian rupee, divided into 16 anna, and the Egyptian pound (frequently referred to by its Arabic name, *junyah* [جنيه]) as legal tender until the mandate's dissolution in 1932.

Upon independence, Iraq's monetary system was reformed and based on the dinar, the Arabic form of the ancient Roman denarius, which was at par with the pound sterling and divided into 1,000 fils. The dinar was also divided into 20 dirhams, equal to 50 fils.

Letters of the Arabic alphabet often serve as abbreviations for certain monetary units. The letter *feh* (ف) is the abbreviation for fils (فاس), and *mim* (م) stands for mills or millieme (مليم), when combined with the Arabic-language numerals shown below:

0	1	2	3	4	5	6	7	8	9	10	50	100	500	1000
.	١	٢	٣	٤	٥	٦	٧	٨	٩	١٠	٥٠	١٠٠	٥٠٠	١٠٠٠

CHRONOLOGY

Year	Denomination	Equivalent
1932–present	Iraqi dinar	1,000 fils
	dirham	50 fils
1922–1932	Indian rupee	16 anna
	Egyptian pound	100 piastres
	piastre	10 milliemes
–1922	Turkish pound (*lira*)	100 piastres

ORTHOGRAPHY AND NUMBER

Singular	Plural	Known Abbreviations and Symbols	Examples
anna	anna(s)*	An Ans	10An 10Ans
dinar	dinars		
dirham	dirhams		
fils	fils	ف	١٠ف 10ف
millieme	milliemes	M م	10M ١٠م
piastre	piastres		
pound (*lira*)	pounds (*liras*)	£	£10
rupee	rupee(s)*	R Rs	1R 10Rs

*Optional final s.

Ireland (EUR; replaced IEP in 1999)

Prior to the proclamation of the Irish Republic in 1919, all of Ireland was part of the United Kingdom and of the Sterling Zone, with its LSD system of pounds, shillings, and pence. Eight years later, after the lower 26 counties were granted independence as the Irish Free State, the Irish punt (Gaelic for "pound") replaced the pound sterling at par. However, the northern six counties, collectively known as Northern Ireland, still remain part of the United Kingdom and a member of the Sterling Zone.

Like Great Britain, Ireland converted its monetary system to a decimal system in 1971. The Irish punt was divided into 100 new pence also known as *pingine*. A crown, which formerly was equivalent to five shillings, now equaled 20 new pence, and a shilling was equal to five pence. In 1999 Ireland joined the Eurozone and adopted the euro, which became its sole legal tender in 2002. *See also* **European Union**.

CHRONOLOGY

Year	Denomination	Equivalent
1999–present	euro	euro-cent
1971–2002	Irish pound (*punt*)	100 new pence
	crown	20 new pence
	shilling	5 new pence

Year	Denomination	Equivalent
1927–1971	Irish pound (*punt*)	20 shillings
	shilling	12 pence
	penny	4 farthings
–1927	pound sterling	20 shillings
	shilling	12 pence
	penny	4 farthings

ORTHOGRAPHY AND NUMBER

Singular	Plural	Known Abbreviations and Symbols	Examples
euro	euro	€	€10
euro-cent	euro-cent	€	€0.10
farthing	farthings	d	¼d ½d
florin	florins		
new penny (*pingin*)	new pence (*pingine*)	P	10P
penny (*pingin*)	pence (*pingine*)	d (British) p (Irish)	10d 10p
pound (*punt*)	pounds (*punt*)	£ (or £) IR£	£10
shilling	shillings	s /	10s 10/-

Israel (ILS)

Until 1917, Israel, then known as Palestine, was part of the Ottoman Empire. Its monetary system mainly paralleled that of its Turkish rulers, and also used Egyptian piastres. After Turkey's defeat in World War I in 1917, Great Britain was given control of Palestine as a mandate by the League of Nations. The introduction in 1927 of the Palestine pound, at par with the pound sterling and divisible into 1,000 mils, replaced a variety of foreign currencies that were in use.

In 1948 the mandate ended and the state of Israel was established. The Israeli pound, also divisible into 1,000 mils, replaced the mandate's Palestine pound. The plural of mil is either "mils" or its Hebrew equivalent, milim. In 1949, the Israeli pound was replaced with the lira, divisible into 1,000 prutot. In 1960 another monetary reform divided the pound, this time into 100 agorot, meaning "small coin" in Hebrew. It should be noted that prior to 1980, pounds and lira, the Hebrew equivalent, were used interchangeably.

From 1980 to 1985 the lira was replaced by one of the best-known biblical monies — the shekel, at an exchange of 10 pounds (or lira) to the shekel. The shekel takes its name from the Hebrew *shakal* (שקל), "to weigh." Owing to inflation, the shekel was revalued in 1985, giving rise to the new Israel shekel (*shekel khadash* in Hebrew), equal to 1,000 old shekels.

The transliteration of Hebrew into English is not always a simple matter, and there are often variations in spelling. "Shekel" is the preferred spelling in the United States, but sheqel and sheqal are also encountered. This last spelling is the official spelling of the Bank of Israel, owing to its Hebrew spelling (שקל) and pronunciation. The English plural form is usually written as shekels, sheqels, or sheqals, but the transliterated Hebrew plural, shekalim (שקלים) is sometimes used. Both the singular and plural forms use the Hebrew letter *shin* (ש) for their Hebrew abbreviation. Israeli monetary units with their primary Hebrew spellings are as follows:

Singular		Plural	
agora	אגורה	agorot	אגורות
lira	לירה	lirot	לירות
mil	מיל	milim	מילים
pruta	פרוטה	prutot	פרוטות
shekel khadash	שקל חדש	shekalim khadashim	שקלים חדשים

CHRONOLOGY

Year	Denomination	Equivalent
1985–present	new Israel shekel	100 new agorot
1980–1985	shekel	100 agorot
1960–1980	Israeli pound (or *lira*)	100 agorot
1949–1960	Israeli lira	1,000 prutot
1948–1949	Israeli pound	1,000 mils
1927–1948	Palestine pound	1,000 mils

ORTHOGRAPHY AND NUMBER

Singular	Plural	Known Abbreviations and Symbols	Examples
agora	agorot	אג	10אג
mil	mils (*milim*)		
new Israel shekel	new Israel shekels (*shekalim khadashim*)	NIS ש״ח שׁ	10NIS ש״ח10 שׁ10
pound (*lira*)	pounds (*lirot*)	IL £	IL10 £10
pruta	prutot		
shekel	shekels (*shekalim*)	IS ש	IS10 ש10

Italy (EUR; replaced ITL in 1999)

One of the world's best-known monetary units, the lira has been part of Italian life since the seventh century. The name lira was taken from the Latin *libra*, meaning pound—a weight. By the 1800s, there were many Italian states with their own monetary systems, many of them dividing the lira into soldi and denari. Among many other names used were grosso, dopplo, scudo, ducato, and capilloni.

Italy was unified in 1861, and its modern monetary system was then based on the lira, divisible into 100 centesimi. The lira was also legal tender in San Marino and Vatican City. In 1999 Italy joined the Eurozone, adopting the euro, which became its sole legal tender in 2002. San Marino and Vatican City have also replaced the lira with the euro. *See also* **European Union**.

Like Great Britain, Italy also uses a cursive capital letter *L* as a symbol, but it is written using double cross strokes (£) through it, while the current British pound symbol has a single cross stroke.

CHRONOLOGY

Year	Denomination	Equivalent
1999–present	euro	euro-cent
1862–2002	Italian lira	100 centesimi

ORTHOGRAPHY AND NUMBER

Singular	Plural	Known Abbreviations and Symbols	Examples
centesimo	centesimi	c. cmi cts cent	c.10 cmi 10 10 cts cent 10
euro	euro	€	€10
euro-cent	euro-cent	€	€0.10
lira	lire	L. Lit. £	L.10 £10

Ivory Coast (XOF)

The Ivory Coast, also known by its French name, Côte d'Ivoire, was originally established as a French colony in 1893. Until 1960 it was a member of the Franc Zone under the geographical area known as French West Africa. It is currently part of a confederation of West African states which use the CFA (Communauté Financière Africaine, or African Financial Community) franc, divided into 100 centimes.

CHRONOLOGY

Year	Denomination	Equivalent
1960–present	CFA franc	100 centimes
–1960	franc	100 centimes

ORTHOGRAPHY AND NUMBER

Singular	Plural	Known Abbreviations and Symbols	Examples
centime	centimes	c	10c
franc	francs	F Fr	10F 10Fr

Jamaica (JMD)

As a British colony, Jamaica was part of the British Sterling Zone as early as 1840, and it adopted the Jamaican pound, divided into 20 shillings. The colony gained its independence in 1962, but it wasn't until 1969 that Jamaica reformed its monetary system. It then replaced the imperial system with a decimalized one based on the Jamaican dollar, at a rate of two dollars for every pound.

CHRONOLOGY

Year	Denomination	Equivalent
1969–present	Jamaican dollar	100 cents
1840–1969	Jamaican pound	20 shillings
	shilling	12 pence
	penny	4 farthings

ORTHOGRAPHY AND NUMBER

Singular	Plural	Known Abbreviations and Symbols	Examples
cent	cents	c ¢	10¢
dollar	dollars	$	$10
farthing	farthings	d	¼d ½d
penny	pence	d	10d
pound	pounds	£ (or £)	£10
shilling	shillings	s /	10s 10/-

Japan (JPY)

During much of the feudal shogun period, Japan had a monetary system that was primarily based on specified weights of gold and silver. In 1871, the Meiji restoration government instituted the New Coinage Act, and it formally adopted the yen in 1872 at par with the U.S. gold dollar. The yen (pronounced "en" in Japanese) is the Japanese-language equivalent of the Chinese yuan, meaning "round" or "circle." In Japanese, the ideograph for the yen (円) is an abbreviation for the Chinese yuan (圓). Even though the yen is divided into 100 sen and 1,000 rin, the two smaller units are worthless, and have not been used in daily commerce, such as for coins, since 1954.

CHRONOLOGY

Year	Denomination	Equivalent
1871–present	yen	100 sen
	sen	10 rin

ORTHOGRAPHY AND NUMBER

Singular	Plural	Known Abbreviations and Symbols	Examples
rin	rin	厘	10 厘
sen	sen	Sn 銭	10 銭
yen	yen	¥ 円	¥10 10 円

Jordan (JOD)

For almost 400 years prior to 1918, present-day Jordan was part of the Turkish Ottoman Empire. After the war, Jordan, along with Palestine (present-day Israel), was awarded to Britain as a mandate by the League of Nations. In 1922 the British divided the mandate into two parts, designating all lands west of the Jordan River as Palestine and those east of the river as Transjordan. From 1918 until 1930, Transjordan's monetary system was based on the piastre, sometimes called by its colloquial name, qirsh, which was divided into 1,000 milliemes.

The monetary system was then changed by the British authorities to the Palestine pound, known in Arabic as *junyah* (جنيه), which had been the legal tender in Palestine since 1927. Although it became independent in 1946, Transjordan (whose name was changed to Jordan in 1949) continued to use the Palestine pound until 1950, when it was demonetized. The pound was then replaced at par by the Jordanian dinar, the Arabic form of the ancient Roman denarius, divided into 1,000 fils. Besides the dinar there were also the dirham, equal to 100 fils, and the qirsh, equal to 10 fils. It should be noted that the singular form of fil on Jordanian coins has variously used and omitted the final *s*. A 1993 monetary reform divided the dinar into 100 piastres.

Jordan often uses the Latin-alphabet abbreviation JD (often pronounced as "jay-dee") for the Jordanian dinar with the numerals 0 through 9, but Jordan's Arabic monetary units below:

dinar	دينار	millieme	مليم
dirham	دراهم	piastre	قروش
fils	فاس	qirsh	غروش
mil	مل		

are also used in conjunction with the following Arabic-language numerals:

0	1	2	3	4	5	6	7	8	9	10	50	100	500	1000
٠	١	٢	٣	٤	٥	٦	٧	٨	٩	١٠	٥٠	١٠٠	٥٠٠	١٠٠٠

CHRONOLOGY

Year	Denomination	Equivalent
1993–present	Jordanian dinar	100 piastres
1950–1993	Jordanian dinar	1,000 fils
	dirham	100 fils
	qirsh	10 fils
1930–1950	Palestine pound	1,000 mils
1918–1930	piastre	1,000 milliemes

ORTHOGRAPHY AND NUMBER

Singular	Plural	Known Abbreviations and Symbols	Examples
dinar	dinars	JD	JD10
dirham	dirhams		
fil(s)*	fils		
mil	mils		
millieme	milliemes		
piastre	piastres		
pound	pounds	£P (or £P)	£P10 (or £P10)

*Optional final s.

Kazakhstan (KZT)

From 1918 until its secession and independence in 1991, Kazakhstan was a part of the Soviet Union and used the Soviet monetary system of rubles and kopecks. Like most of the former Soviet republics, following independence Kazakhstan briefly continued the use of the Russian ruble. In 1993 it reformed its monetary system and introduced the tenge, divided into 100 tiyn. The tenge is the same as the monetary unit of Tajikistan and of both the former emirate of Bukhara and khanate of Khira (a.k.a. Kwarezm)—the last two now part of Uzbekistan. Because of inflation, the tiyn quickly lost value and is no longer used. Tiyn-denominated banknotes and coins were withdrawn almost as soon as they were issued.

The transliteration of both Kazakh and Russian into English is not always a simple matter, and one often finds variations in English spellings such as tenge and tange, and tyjyn, tiyin, and tiyn—the last spelling being the one used by the national bank. Kazakhstan's monetary units, with their Cyrillic spellings, are:

Unit	Singular	Plural
kopeck	копейк	копейки
ruble	рубль	рублвй, рубля*
tenge	теңге	теңге
tiyn	тиын	тиын

*Russian plural form is grammatically dependent

CHRONOLOGY

Year	Denomination	Equivalent
1993–present	tenge	100 tiyn
1918–1993	Russian ruble	100 kopecks

ORTHOGRAPHY AND NUMBER

Singular	Plural	Known Abbreviations and Symbols	Examples
kopeck	kopecks	к коп	10к 10 коп
ruble	rubles	руб	10 руб
tenge	tenge		
tiyn	tiyn		

Kenya (KES)

Kenya was once a British protectorate, and with Uganda, Zanzibar, and Tanganyika formed an administrative area known as British East Africa. Because of the British influence and its proximity to the Indian subcontinent, its monetary system was based on India's rupee. The rupee was divided into 16 anna until 1906, when it was replaced with the East African rupee, equal to 100 cents.

The rupee was replaced in 1920 with the florin, equal to two shillings and divisible into 100 cents. The following year the florin was replaced by the shilling. One year after Kenya's independence in 1966, the East African shilling was replaced at par with the Kenyan shilling, which is also known by its Swahili name, *shilingi*.

CHRONOLOGY

Year	Denomination	Equivalent
1967–present	Kenyan shilling	100 cents
1921–1967	East African shilling	100 cents
1920–1921	East African florin	2 shillings, 100 cents
1906–1920	East African rupee	100 cents
–1906	Indian rupee	16 anna
	anna	4 pice

ORTHOGRAPHY AND NUMBER

Singular	Plural	Known Abbreviations and Symbols	Examples
anna	anna(s)*	A	10A
cent	cents	c	10c
florin	florins		
pice	pice		

Singular	Plural	Known Abbreviations and Symbols	Examples
rupee	rupees	Rs	Rs10
shilling	shillings	Kshs Shs S /	10/- 10S

*Optional final s.

Kiribati (AUD)

In 1892, Great Britain annexed the Gilbert Islands as a protectorate, and in 1916 the group became part of the Gilbert and Ellice Islands colony. Its monetary system was based on the Australian pound until 1966, when the decimalized Australian dollar replaced the pound. In 1976 the Ellice Islands seceded from the colony and were renamed Tuvalu. In 1979 the Gilbert Islands were given complete independence by Great Britain, and the country was renamed Kiribati.

CHRONOLOGY

Year	Denomination	Equivalent
1966–present	Australian dollar	100 cents
1892–1966	Australian pound	20 shillings
	shilling	12 pence

ORTHOGRAPHY AND NUMBER

Singular	Plural	Known Abbreviations and Symbols	Examples
cent	cents	c	10¢
dollar	dollars	$	$10
penny	pence	d	10d
pound	pounds	£ (or £)	£10
shilling	shillings	/	10/-

Korea (North and South)
(KPW North Korea; KRW South Korea)

Korea is an ancient country which, at one time or another, has been conquered by the Mongols, China, and Japan. The monetary system generally was that imposed by the current ruling nation, but the won, like the Chinese yuan (which means "round"), has long survived its conquerors. Even when Japan controlled Korea — from 1907 until 1945 — the won, divided into 100 chon, was still used alongside the Japanese yen.

In 1948, Korea was split in two, divided by the 38th parallel, and separate monetary systems were introduced; however their names remained the same. South Korea retained the won, but because of increasing inflation replaced it in 1953 with the hwan (환), equal to 100 won. Continued inflation required another monetary reform in 1962, in which the hwan was replaced with the new won, at an exchange of 10 hwan. Because it is virtually worthless today, the chon is no longer used.

In 1948 North Korea introduced the "people's won," but it was eventually replaced in 1959 by the won, also divisible into 100 chon, and equal to 100 people's won.

The transliteration of Korean into English is not always a simple matter, and there are often variations in spelling of its monetary units. Chon (전) is sometimes found with alternative spellings such as cheun, jun, and jeon, while won (원) is sometimes found spelled weun. The Korean ideographs for its monetary units are combined with either the numerals 0 through 9 or the Korean numerals shown below:

1	2	3	4	5	6	7	8	9	10	50	100	500	1000
일	이	삼	사	오	육	칠	팔	구	십	오십	백	오백	천

CHRONOLOGY—NORTH KOREA

Year	Denomination	Equivalent
1959–present	won	100 chon
1948–1959 (now North Korea)	people's won	100 chon
–1948 (as unified Korea)	won	100 chon

CHRONOLOGY—SOUTH KOREA

Year	Denomination	Equivalent
1962–present	new won	100 chon
1953-1962	hwan	100 chon
1948–1953 (now South Korea)	won	100 chon
–1948 (as unified Korea)	won	100 chon

ORTHOGRAPHY AND NUMBER

Singular	Plural	Known Abbreviations and Symbols	Examples
chon (cheun, jeon, jun)	chon (cheun, jeon, jun)	Cn 전	10 Cn 십전
hwan	hwan	환	십환
won	won	₩ Wn 원	10₩ 10Wn 십원

Kuwait (KWD)

Kuwait was a British protectorate from 1899 until its independence in 1961. Until 1959, its monetary system used the Indian rupee, divided into 16 anna, a system which was commonly used in other parts of the British Empire in the Middle East and the Indian subcontinent. A 1959 monetary reform replaced the rupee with the Persian Gulf rupee, divided into 100 naye ("new") paise, which was also used by several of the shiekdoms that now comprise the United Arab Emirates. When Kuwait became independent in 1961, the dinar, the Arabic form of the ancient Roman denarius, replaced the rupee at par with the pound sterling; it was divisible into 1,000 fils.

Although Kuwait primarily uses the Latin alphabet for its monetary abbreviations, it also uses the Arabic-language numerals shown below:

0	1	2	3	4	5	6	7	8	9	10	50	100	500	1000
٠	١	٢	٣	٤	٥	٦	٧	٨	٩	١٠	٥٠	١٠٠	٥٠٠	١٠٠٠

with the Arabic spelling of dinar (دينار) and fils (فاس). It should be noted that the abbreviation R is for one rupee, while Rs is the plural abbreviation.

CHRONOLOGY

Year	Denomination	Equivalent
1961–present	Kuwaiti dinar	1,000 fils
1959–1961	Persian Gulf rupee	100 naye paise
1899–1959	Indian rupee	16 anna

ORTHOGRAPHY AND NUMBER

Singular	Plural	Known Abbreviations and Symbols	Examples
anna	anna(s)*	A	10A
dinar	dinars	KD	KD 10
fils	fils		
naya paisa	naye paise	NP	10NP
paisa	paise	Ps	10Ps
rupee	rupees	R Rs	R1 Rs10

*Optional final s.

Kyrgyzstan (KGS)

Beginning about 1876, Kyrgyzstan, then known as both Kirghiz and Kirghizia, was part of czarist Russia. In 1926, it was proclaimed the Kirghiz Soviet Socialist Republic, and its monetary system was based on the ruble and kopeck.

Like most of the former Soviet republics, Kyrgyzstan continued the use of the Russian ruble following its independence in 1991. In 1993, when it reformed its monetary system, the ruble was replaced with the som, at an exchange rate of 200 rubles. The som was divisible into 100 tiyn.

The transliteration of both the Kyrgyz and Russian languages into English is not always a simple matter and one often finds variations in spelling for the monetary units such as tyjyn (the spelling used by the national bank), tiyin, and tiyn. Kyrgyzstan's monetary units, with their Cyrillic spellings, are:

Unit	Singular	Plural
kopeck	копейк	копейки
ruble	рубль	рублей, рубля*
som	сом	сом
tyjyn	тыйын	тыйын

*Russian plural form is grammatically dependent

Chronology

Year	Denomination	Equivalent
1993–present	som	100 tyjyn
–1993	Russian ruble	100 kopeks

Orthography and Number

Singular	Plural	Known Abbreviations and Symbols	Examples
kopeck	kopecks	к коп	10к 10 коп
ruble	rubles	руб	10 руб
som	som	с	10с
tyjyn	tyjyn	т	10т

Laos (LAK)

Prior to the French colonization of most of modern-day Laos in 1893, the country was part of Thailand, and its monetary system was based on the Thai tical. During Laos' years as a French colony and as part of French Indochina, the tical was replaced with the Indochinese piastre, divisible into 100 centimes. Although Laos declared its independence in 1953, it was not recognized by France until 1954. The Indochinese piastre was still used until 1955, when it was replaced at par with the kip, divided into 100 at (also spelled att). In 1976, the kip was replaced with the liberation kip at an exchange rate of 20 kips. Another monetary reform in 1979 exchanged 100 liberation kips for one new kip.

The Latin alphabet is primarily used for monetary abbreviations, but Laos also uses the Khmer-language abbreviation ກ for kip (ກີບ) when combined with the Khmer numerals shown below:

0	1	2	3	4	5	6	7	8	9	10	50	100	500	1000
໐	໑	໒	໓	໔	໕	໖	໗	໘	໙	໑໐	໕໐	໑໐໐	໕໐໐	໑໐໐໐

Under French rule, the dollar sign ($) was used as a symbol for the piastre, and also served as a decimal point separating the piastre from the smaller centimes.

CHRONOLOGY

Year	Denomination	Equivalent
1979–present	new kip	100 at
1976–1979	liberation kip	100 at
1955–1976	kip	100 at
1893–1955	Indochinese piastre	100 centimes

ORTHOGRAPHY AND NUMBER

Singular	Plural	Known Abbreviations and Symbols	Examples
at (or att)	at (or att)		
centime	centimes	cents $	0$10
kip	kip	K Ꝁ KN ₭	10K 10Ꝁ ໑໐₭
piastre	piastres	$	10$

Latvia (LVL)

Following the partitions of Poland in the 1790s, much of present-day Latvia was part of czarist Russia until 1917. After it proclaimed itself a republic in 1918, the country was controlled for a brief period by Russian Bolsheviks. They instituted the Latvian ruble (or rublis), which was divided into 100 kapeikas, the Latvian equivalent of the Russian kopeck. In 1920, the Bolsheviks were driven out, and in 1922 Latvia instituted a new monetary system based on the lat, equivalent to 50 Latvian rubles. The lat, an obvious shortening of the country's name, was divided into 100 santims, the Latvian equivalent of the French centime.

The Soviet Union, which promised in a 1920 treaty it would respect Latvia's sovereignty, nonetheless annexed Latvia in 1940 as a Soviet republic; the Russian ruble then replaced the rublis. Upon the breakup of the Soviet Union in 1991, Latvia seceded and once again replaced the ruble with the Latvian rublis and kapeika. This change, however, would be brief, for the rublis was again replaced with the lat in 1993.

Latvia joined the European Union in 2004, but it will not participate in the European Union's monetary system (Eurozone) and adopt the euro until about 2008. *See also* **European Union**.

The Latvian plural form of its monetary units depends on the number the unit is associated with. The plural of lat can be either lati or latu; either rubli or rublu for rubles; and either santimi or santimu for santims.

CHRONOLOGY

Year	Denomination	Equivalent
1993–present	lat	100 santims
1992–1993	Latvian ruble	100 kapeikas

Year	Denomination	Equivalent
1940–1992	Russian ruble	100 kopecks
1922–1941	lat	100 santims
1919–1922	Latvian ruble	100 kapeikas
–1919	Russian ruble	100 kopecks

ORTHOGRAPHY AND NUMBER

Singular	Plural	Known Abbreviations and Symbols	Examples
kapeika	kapeikas	KAP	10 KAP
kopeck	kopecks	коп	10 коп
lat	lats	Ls	Ls 10
ruble	rubles	руб	10 руб
rublis	rubli	RUB RBL	10 RUB
santim	santims	s sant	10s 10 sant

Lebanon (LBP)

Lebanon was a province of the Ottoman Empire prior to World War I, and it used the Turkish monetary system of the piastre (or guerche), divided into 40 para. From the war's end until the League of Nations granted France control of Lebanon and Syria as mandates in 1920, Egyptian pounds were used. Under the French mandate, the monetary system of both Lebanon and Syria was the Lebanese-Syrian pound, equal to 20 French francs and divisible into 100 centimes. Separate currencies were created in 1948 for the two countries, independent since 1943. The Lebanese pound, also called *livre* in French, replaced the piastre; in Syria, the Syrian pound replaced the piastre.

Lebanon's modern monetary system primarily uses the Latin alphabet for its monetary abbreviations, such as the letter P (piastre), which once also served as the decimal separator between piastres and centimes. Letters of the Arabic alphabet are also frequently used, such as either *qaf* (ق) or the older *ghain* (غ) as abbreviations for piastre/guerche (قروش), or a pair of *lams* (ل.ل.) to represent the Arabic equivalent of "Lebanese livres," when combined with the Arabic-language numbers shown below:

0	1	2	3	4	5	6	7	8	9	10	50	100	500	1000
٠	١	٢	٣	٤	٥	٦	٧	٨	٩	١٠	٥٠	١٠٠	٥٠٠	١٠٠٠

CHRONOLOGY

Year	Denomination	Equivalent
1948–present	Lebanese pound	100 piastres
1920–1948	Lebanese-Syrian pound	100 centimes
1918–1920	Egyptian pound	1,000 milliemes
–1917	Ottoman piastre	40 para

ORTHOGRAPHY AND NUMBER

Singular	Plural	Known Abbreviations and Symbols	Examples
centime	centimes	c	10c
para	para(s)*		
piastre	piastres	P غ ق	10P 10P50 غ ۱۰ ق ۱۰
pound (*livre*)	pounds (*livres*)	L£ L.L. ل.ل.	L£10 L.L. 10 ل.ل. ۱۰

*Optional final s.

Lesotho (LSL; replaced ZAR in 1980)

Lesotho was originally known as Basutoland, a British protectorate established in 1866 which became independent in 1966. Because it is completely encircled by South Africa, Basutoland was highly dependent on that country for virtually everything, including its monetary system. Prior to 1920, the pound sterling was used; in that year it was replaced at par with the South African pound.

In 1961, when South Africa became a republic, the pound was replaced by a decimalized system based on the South African rand; two rand equaled one pound. A 1980 reform of the monetary system ended Lesotho's dependence on the rand, and gave it a monetary system of its own. The rand was replaced with the loti, divisible into 100 lisente (also spelled licente).

CHRONOLOGY

Year	Denomination	Equivalent
1980–present	loti	100 lisente
1961–1980	South African rand	100 cents
1920–1961	South African pound	20 shillings
	shilling	12 pence
–1920	pound sterling	20 shillings
	shilling	12 pence

ORTHOGRAPHY AND NUMBER

Singular	Plural	Known Abbreviations and Symbols	Examples
cent	cents	c	10c
loti	maloti	M	M1 M10
penny	pence	d	10d
pound	pounds	£ (or ₤)	£10
rand	rand	R	R10
sente	lisente	s	10s
shilling	shillings	s /	10s 10/-

Liberia (LRD)

Once known as the "Grain Coast," Liberia was originally established as the Cape Mesurado Colony by freed American slaves in 1821, after a similar attempt had failed in Sierra Leone in 1815. Eventually the colony was renamed Liberia and was granted independence in 1847.

The U.S. dollar long served as its monetary system, but the West African pound and the pound sterling also circulated there. In 1944, monetary reforms led to the creation of the Liberian dollar, divisible into 100 cents. The U.S. dollar served as the sole source of paper money from 1880 until 2001, when Liberia began issuing its own banknotes. However, the U.S. dollar is still legal tender in Liberia.

CHRONOLOGY

Year	Denomination	Equivalent
1944–present	Liberian dollar	100 cents
1847–1944	pound sterling and	
	West African pound	20 shillings
	shillings	12 pence

ORTHOGRAPHY AND NUMBER

Singular	Plural	Known Abbreviations and Symbols	Examples
cent	cents	c ct cts ¢	10c 10ct 10¢
dollar	dollars	$	$10
pound	pounds	£ (or £)	£10
shilling	shillings	/	10/-

Libya (LYD)

Prior to 1912, when parts of present-day Libya were ceded to Italy, Libya was a part of the Ottoman Empire. Its monetary system was then based on the Turkish lira, divided into 100 piastres and 4,000 paras. Italy fully unified the country by 1934, and Libya's monetary system was then based on the Italian lira, divisible into 100 centesimi. After the fall of Tripoli in 1943, the country was placed under the joint control of Great Britain and France. The monetary system under this joint control was a combination of Egyptian pounds and Algerian francs.

When Libya gained its independence in 1951, the Libyan pound, divided into 100 piastres, replaced the currencies imposed by Great Britain and France. In 1971 the

Libyan dinar, the Arabic form of the ancient Roman denarius, replaced the pound at par; it was divided into 1,000 dirhams.

Although Libya primarily uses the Latin alphabet for its abbreviations, it also uses letters of the Arabic alphabet, such as *mim* (م) for mills or millieme (مليم), or the Arabic equivalent of dinar (دينار) and dirham (دراهم), when combined with the Arabic-language numerals shown below:

0	1	2	3	4	5	6	7	8	9	10	50	100	500	1000
٠	١	٢	٣	٤	٥	٦	٧	٨	٩	١٠	٥٠	١٠٠	٥٠٠	١٠٠٠

CHRONOLOGY

Year	Denomination	Equivalent
1971–present	Libyan dinar	1,000 dirhams
1951–1971	Libyan pound	100 piastres
	piastre	10 milliemes
1943–1951	Egyptian pound	100 piastres
	franc	100 centimes
1912–1943	Italian lira	100 centesimi
–1912	Turkish lira	100 piastres
	piastre	40 para

ORTHOGRAPHY AND NUMBER

Singular	Plural	Known Abbreviations and Symbols	Examples
centesimo	centesimi	c cent	10c 10 cent
dinar	dinars	LD	
dirham	dirhams		
lira (Turkish)	liras		
lira (Italian)	lire	L £	
millieme	milliemes	m م	10m م١٠
para	para(s)*	ب	ب١٠
piastre	piastres	p	
pound	pounds	£L	£L10

*Optional final s.

Liechtenstein (CHF)

Liechtenstein was created in 1719 as a principality. It was part of the German Confederation until 1866, but then became an independent principality externally administered by Austria-Hungary. During the later years of the Austro-Hungarian Empire and post-war Austria, Liechtenstein's currency was the krone, German for "crown," and the heller.

The krone's volatility following the war induced the principality to accept Swiss administration in 1921. Liechtenstein thus became a member of the Swiss Currency Area and adopted the Swiss franc, which is often spelled "frank" by its German-speaking inhabitants. The franc is divided into 100 rappen.

CHRONOLOGY

Year	Denomination	Equivalent
1921–present	Swiss franc	100 rappen
–1921	Austro-Hungarian krone	100 heller

ORTHOGRAPHY AND NUMBER

Singular	Plural	Known Abbreviations and Symbols	Examples
franc (*frank*)	francs (*franken*)	SFr Fr	10Fr
heller	heller	H	10H
krone	kronen	K	10K
rappen	rappen	Rp	10Rp

Lithuania (LTL)

Prior to the third partition of the Polish-Lithuanian commonwealth in 1795, when it became part of czarist Russia, Lithuania's monetary system was based on the Polish zloty. Under the czars, it was the ruble. From its independence in 1918 until 1922, Lithuania's monetary system was based on the auksinas, meaning "golden," which was divided into 100 skatiku (Lithuanian for "pennies"). In 1923 the litas, divided into 100 centu, replaced the auksinas.

In 1940 the Soviet Union annexed a number of independent Baltic states, including Lithuania, as Soviet republics; the Russian ruble then replaced the litas. With the breakup of the Soviet Union, Lithuania seceded in 1990. A year later it replaced the ruble temporarily with the talonas (Lithuanian for "coupon"), equal to 100 rubles. In 1993, the talonas was replaced with the litas and centu. In 2004, Lithuania joined the European Union, but it will not participate in the European Union's monetary system (Eurozone) and adopt the euro until about 2007. *See also* **European Union.**

The Lithuanian-language plural form for each monetary unit depends on the number it is associated with. The plural of centas can be either centai or centu; litai or litu for litas; and skatikai or skatiku for skatikas.

CHRONOLOGY

Year	Denomination	Equivalent
1993–present	litas	100 centu
1991–1993	talonas	none

Year	Denomination	Equivalent
1940–1991	Russian ruble	100 kopecks
1923–1940	litas	100 centu
1918–1923	auksinas	100 skatiku

ORTHOGRAPHY AND NUMBER

Singular	Plural	Known Abbreviations and Symbols	Examples
auksinas	auksinai		
centas	centu	c ct cnt cent	10c 10 cnt
kopeck	kopecks	к коп	10к 10 коп
litas	litu	L Lt Lit	10Lt
ruble	rubles	руб	10 руб
skatikas	skatiku	sk	10 sk
talonas	talonu		

Luxembourg (EUR; replaced LUF in 1999)

For almost 400 years Luxembourg was ruled by either France, Spain, or Austria. In 1815 Luxembourg was established as a grand duchy, ruled by the Netherlands and using its monetary system of guilders (*gulden*). From 1830 the grand duchy was involved in several political alliances, and was subsequently divided between Belgium and the Netherlands. It was part of the Prussian-controlled tariff union called the *Zollverein* from 1842 until 1867, when its future neutrality was guaranteed. During this period the Dutch guilder was replaced with the franc — also spelled "frang" by the duchy's Dutch residents — which was initially at par with both the Belgian and French francs.

During brief periods while under German control during World War I and World War II, the German reichmark was the legal tender, and the franc was called the frank, its German equivalent. Otherwise the franc remained the basis of Luxembourg's monetary system. In 1999 Luxembourg joined the Eurozone, adopting the euro, which became its sole legal tender in 2002. *See also* **European Union**.

CHRONOLOGY

Year	Denomination	Equivalent
1999–present	euro	100 euro-cent
1848–2002	Luxembourg franc	100 centimes
1815–1848	Dutch guilder (*gulden*)	100 cents

ORTHOGRAPHY AND NUMBER

Singular	Plural	Known Abbreviations and Symbols	Examples
centime	centimes	c ces cts cmes cent	10c
euro	euro	€	10€
euro-cent	euro-cent	€	0.10€
franc (*frank*)	francs (*franken*)	F Fr LuxF	10Fr
guilder (*gulden*)	guilders (*gulden*)	G	10G

Macao (MOP)

Macao, which was first established as a Portuguese colony in 1556, used the milréis as its monetary system prior to 1894. In that year a monetary reform replaced the milréis with the rupee, equal to 450 milréis and divisible into 78 avos. In 1901, the pataca — a possible corruption of an Arabic word for the Spanish peso — replaced the rupee, it was divided into 100 avos ("fractional parts").

When Portugal ceded Macao back to China in 1999, the Chinese — as they had with Hong Kong two years earlier — recognized Macao's strategic location and potential economic power in international trade. Consequently, China declared Macao a special administrative region, and Macao retained the pataca as its monetary system instead of adopting China's yuan renminbi.

CHRONOLOGY

Year	Denomination	Equivalent
1901–present	pataca	100 avos
1894–1901	rupee	78 avos
–1894	Portuguese milréis	1,000 réis

ORTHOGRAPHY AND NUMBER

Singular	Plural	Known Abbreviations and Symbols	Examples
avo	avos	A	10A
pataca	patacas	P pt ptc pts ptcs	10P 10 ptc
réis	réis	Rs	Rs10

Macedonia (MKD)

Macedonia was once part of the Ottoman Empire and used its monetary system, which was based on the piastre, divided into 40 para. From 1877 until the end of the

Second Balkan War in 1913, much of present-day Macedonia was divided between Greece, Bulgaria, and Serbia. The respective regions' currencies were the drachma, lev, and dinar. The dinar takes its name from the Arabic form of the ancient Roman denarius.

In 1918, after the end of World War I, Macedonia united with Bosnia-Herzegovina, Croatia, Montenegro, Serbia, and Slovenia to form the Kingdom of the Serbs, Croats and Slovenes. At this time a wide variety of currencies circulated throughout the new kingdom. The first reform aimed at creating a national monetary unit was based on the Austrian krone, divided into 100 heller. It was replaced in 1919 by the dinar used in Serbia, which was divided into 100 para and equal to four kronen. This new monetary system continued after the kingdom was renamed Yugoslavia in 1929. During World War II, Bulgaria, fighting with the Axis powers, annexed Macedonia and replaced the dinar with the Bulgarian lev.

In 1945, Macedonia was again made part of Yugoslavia, remaining so until its independence in 1991. The country is now known as the Former Yugoslav Republic of Macedonia (FYROM). In 1992, the Macedonian denar, divided into 100 deni, replaced the Yugoslav dinar at par. The dinar should not be confused with the denar: they are separate monetary units and have different English and Serbian/Macedonian spellings — dinar (динар) vs. denar (денар). Also, although the English plural of denar is generally taken as denars, the transliterated Macedonian plural denari (денари) is also used.

While Macedonia was part of Yugoslavia (1918 to 1991), abbreviations for monetary units used both the Latin alphabet, representing Croatian and Slovenian, and the Cyrillic alphabet, representing Serbian and Macedonian. The Cyrillic letters д and п respectively serve as the abbreviations for the dinar (денар) and para (пара).

CHRONOLOGY

Year	Denomination	Equivalent
1992–present	Macedonian denar	100 deni
1945–1992	Yugoslav dinar	100 para
1941–1944	Bulgarian lev	100 stotinki
1919–1992	Serbian dinar	100 para
1918–1919	krone	100 heller

ORTHOGRAPHY AND NUMBER

Singular	Plural	Known Abbreviations and Symbols	Examples
den	deni		
denar	denars		
dinar	dinars	D DIN д дин	10D 10д 10дин
heller	heller		
krone	kronen	Kr	10Kr
lev	lev	Lv л лв	10Lv 10л 10лв
para	para(s)*	P par п	10P 10 par 10п
stotinka	stotinki	с ст стот ST	10с 10ст 10ST

*Optional final s.

Madagascar (MGF)

Madagascar became a French colony in 1897 and was joined by the Comoro Islands in 1908. In 1925, the Madagascar franc, divided into 100 centimes, replaced the French franc. The Comoros became a separate French colony in 1945 and broke away from Madagascar in 1950. In 1945 Madagascar replaced the Madagascar franc with the CFA (Communauté Financière Africaine, or African Financial Community) franc, divided into 100 centimes. In 1958, Madagascar achieved autonomy and was renamed the Malagasy Republic, a name it kept until 1975, when its name was changed back to Madagascar.

CHRONOLOGY

Year	Denomination	Equivalent
1963–present	Madagascar franc	100 centimes
1945–1963	CFA franc	100 centimes
1925–1945	Madagascar franc	100 centimes
ca. 1890–1925	French franc	100 centimes

ORTHOGRAPHY AND NUMBER

Singular	Plural	Known Abbreviations and Symbols	Examples
centime	centimes	c	10c
franc	francs	F	10F

Malawi (MWK)

Malawi was known as Nyasaland when it was first established as a British protectorate. Later it was a partner in a federation with both Northern and Southern Rhodesia (which would become Zambia and Zimbabwe respectively). This was known as the Federation of Rhodesia and Nyasaland (or the Central African Federation) from 1953 until its dissolution in 1963. The monetary system of the federation was the Rhodesia and Nyasaland pound, which was divided into the same proportions of shillings and pence as the British pound sterling.

The Nyasaland protectorate gained independence in 1964 under its new name, Malawi. The new Malawi pound, equal to 20 shillings, replaced the Rhodesia and Nyasaland pound at par. In 1971 the country's monetary system was changed to a decimal system, replacing the Malawi pound with the kwacha, a Bantu word for "sunrise" or "dawn." The kwacha—also the monetary unit of Malawi's western neighbor Zambia—is divided into 100 tambala, a native word for "cockerel."

CHRONOLOGY

Year	Denomination	Equivalent
1971–present	Malawi kwacha	100 tambala
1964–1970	Malawi pound	20 shillings
1956–1964	Rhodesia and Nyasaland pound	20 shillings
	shilling	12 pence
1940–1956	Southern Rhodesia pound	20 shillings
	shilling	12 pence
–1940	pound sterling	20 shillings
	shilling	12 pence
	penny	4 farthings

ORTHOGRAPHY AND NUMBER

Singular	Plural	Known Abbreviations and Symbols	Examples
farthing	farthings	d	¼d ½d
kwacha	kwacha	K	K10
penny	pence	d	10d
pound	pounds	£ (or £)	£10
shilling	shillings	/	10/-
tambala	tambala	t	10t

Malaysia (MYR)

Prior to its independence in 1963, Malaysia was a former Malay state established as a British protectorate in 1888. The monetary system was based on the Straits Settlements dollar, divisible into 100 cents. In 1946, when the Straits Settlements were broken up, the Malayan dollar replaced the Straits Settlements dollar at par. In 1967, the Malayan dollar was replaced at par with the Malaysian dollar, divided into 100 cents. In 1976 the dollar was renamed the ringgit, a Malay word meaning "jagged," which probably refers to the milled edge of the coin and is still synonomous with "dollar." The ringgit is divided into 100 sen, from the Japanese word for "coin" (a variant of "cent").

CHRONOLOGY

Year	Denomination	Equivalent
1976–present	Malaysian ringgit	100 sen
1967–1976	Malaysian dollar	100 cents
1946–1967	Malayan dollar	100 cents
1888–1946	Straits Settlements dollar	100 cents

ORTHOGRAPHY AND NUMBER

Singular	Plural	Known Abbreviations and Symbols	Examples
cent	cents	c cts ¢	10c 10¢
dollar	dollars	$	$10
ringgit	ringgit	$ RM	RM10 $10
sen	sen	c ¢	10c 10¢

Maldives (MVR)

The Maldives came under British protection as part of Ceylon (now Sri Lanka) as early as 1796, and the islands were formally made a protectorate in 1887. The country gained independence in 1965. The Maldives' first monetary system was based on the Indian rupee, but it was divided into 100 cents instead of the customary 16 anna.

The Indian rupee was replaced with the Maldives rupee in 1947. However, a monetary reform in 1981 replaced the rupee with the rufiyaa, divided into 100 lari (also spelled laari). The larin takes its name from Laristan, a subdivision of the ancient Persian province of Fars.

CHRONOLOGY

Year	Denomination	Equivalent
1981–present	rufiyaa	100 lari
1947–1981	Maldives rupee	100 cents
1887–1951	Indian rupee	100 cents

ORTHOGRAPHY AND NUMBER

Singular	Plural	Known Abbreviations and Symbols	Examples
cent	cents	c	10c
larin	lari	L	10L
rufiyaa	rufiyah	R Rf	10R Rf10
rupee	rupees	Rs	Rs10

Mali (XOF)

The land of current-day Mali was once known as French Sudan. In 1904 it was incorporated into the French colony of Haut Sénégal-Niger (Upper Senegal-Niger). In 1920 it was again renamed French Sudan as a part of French West Africa, and its monetary system was based on the West African franc. In 1945, it was made part of a confederation of West African states with other former French colonies, all using the CFA (Communauté Financière Africaine, or African Financial Community) franc divided into 100 centimes.

In 1958 Mali achieved its independence as the Sudanese Republic, and in 1959 it merged with Senegal to form the Federation of Mali. The federation dissolved in 1960, and the Sudanese Republic renamed itself Mali. In 1962, Mali left the African Financial Community and issued its own franc at par with the CFA franc, but it reintroduced the CFA franc in 1969 after its own franc's value had dropped by half. *See also* **West African States**.

CHRONOLOGY

Year	Denomination	Equivalent
1969–present	CFA franc	100 centimes
1962–1969	Mali franc	100 centimes
1945–1962	CFA franc	100 centimes
1901–1945	West African franc	100 centimes
ca. 1880–1901	French franc	100 centimes

ORTHOGRAPHY AND NUMBER

Singular	Plural	Known Abbreviations and Symbols	Examples
centime	centimes	c	10c
franc	francs	F Fr Frs CFA F	10F

Malta (MTL)

From 1814 until its independence in 1964, Malta was a British crown colony; however, it was not until about 1886 that it was made part of the Sterling Zone. Prior to using British pounds, shillings, pence and farthings, the island had used Spanish and Italian coins. Although the pound sterling continued to serve as legal tender in Malta until 1949, the Maltese pound replaced the pound sterling in 1914 and was divided in the same manner — 20 shillings to the pound.

In 1972, the pound was decimalized and divided into 100 cents, each cent equal to 10 mils. In 1983 the Maltese pound was renamed the Maltese lira (plural, liri). In 2004, Malta joined the European Union, but it will be several years before it will participate in the European Union's monetary system (Eurozone) and adopt the euro. *See also* **European Union**.

Since 1990, the ċ symbol has been in common use. In addition, both cent symbols are used as a separator between cents and mils. The notation 10c5 equals 10 cents plus 5 mils — the same as 10.5 cents.

CHRONOLOGY

Year	Denomination	Equivalent
1983–present	Maltese lira	100 cents
	cent	10 mils
1972–1983	Maltese pound	100 cents
	cent	10 mils
1914–1972	Maltese pound	20 shillings
	shilling	12 pence
	penny	4 farthings
ca. 1886–1949	pound sterling	20 shillings
	shilling	12 pence
	penny	4 farthings

ORTHOGRAPHY AND NUMBER

Singular	Plural	Known Abbreviations and Symbols	Examples
cent	cents	c ċ	10c 10c5
farthing	farthings	d	¼d ½d
lira	liri	Lm £m	Lm10 £m10
mil	mils	m	10m
penny	pence	d	10d
pound	pounds	Lm £m	Lm10 £m10
shilling	shillings	s /	10s 10/-

Mauritania (MRO)

Mauritania was originally established as a French colony. Until its independence in 1960 it was a member of the Franc Zone under the geographical area known as French West Africa. After it became a republic in 1958, its monetary system was based on the Communauté Financière Africaine (African Financial Community, CFA) franc, a monetary union of former French colonies in Africa. A currency reform in 1973 replaced the CFA franc with the ouguiya, which was divided into five khoums (a division no longer used). *See also* **West African States**.

CHRONOLOGY

Year	Denomination	Equivalent
1973–present	ouguiya	5 khoums
1958–1973	CFA franc	100 centimes
–1958	franc	100 centimes

ORTHOGRAPHY AND NUMBER

Singular	Plural	Known Abbreviations and Symbols	Examples
centime	centimes	c	10c
franc	francs	F Fr	10F
khoums	khoums		
ouguiya	ouguiya	UM	10UM

Mauritius (MUR)

First colonized by the Dutch, who named it Ilha do Cerne, Mauritius was eventually abandoned by them and colonized by the French (as Île de France) in 1718. However, Great Britain captured the island in 1810 and made Mauritius a crown colony. The island gained independence in 1968.

While under French rule, the island's monetary system was that of the livre, divisible into 20 sols (French, *sous*). Following Britain's takeover, the monetary system was based on the pound sterling. About 1878, the pound sterling was replaced with the Indian rupee, divided into 100 cents, it was renamed the Mauritian rupee in 1934.

The abbreviation Re is used as the singular abbreviation for rupee; Rs is the plural abbreviation; and R is used for both. The Hindi form *ru* (रु) serves as the abbreviation for the rupee (रुपया, *rupiya*) and is used with the Hindi numerals below:

0	1	2	3	4	5	6	7	8	9	10	50	100	500	1000
०	१	२	३	४	५	६	७	८	९	१०	५०	१००	५००	१०००

CHRONOLOGY

Year	Denomination	Equivalent
1934–present	Mauritian rupee	100 cents
ca. 1878–1934	Indian rupee	100 cents
1810–ca. 1878	pound sterling	20 shillings
	shillings	12 pence

ORTHOGRAPHY AND NUMBER

Singular	Plural	Known Abbreviations and Symbols	Examples
cent	cents	c cs	10c 10cs
penny	pence	d	10d
pound	pounds	£ (or £)	£10
rupee	rupees	R Re Rs (रु)	R10 Re1 Rs10१०रु
shilling	shillings	/	10/-

Mexico (MXN; replaced MXP in 1993)

Although it won its independence from Spain in 1821, Mexico continued to use the monetary system of its colonial ruler—reales and centavos. In 1861, a monetary reform replaced the real with the peso, Spanish for "weight." Widespread inflation resulted in the 1993 introduction of the nuevo peso ("new peso"), equal to 1,000 of the pre–1993 pesos. This lasted until 1995, when the word "nuevo" was dropped from the name.

CHRONOLOGY

Year	Denomination	Equivalent
1995–present	peso	100 centavos
1993–1995	nuevo peso	100 centavos
1861–1993	peso	100 centavos
–1861	real	100 centavos

ORTHOGRAPHY AND NUMBER

Singular	Plural	Known Abbreviations and Symbols	Examples
centavo	centavos	c cs cts cent ctvs cents ¢	10c
peso	pesos	$	$10
real	reales	R Rs	10R 10 Rs

Micronesia (USD)

Present-day Micronesia was made a German protectorate in 1886 and became part of German New Guinea in 1906. The monetary system was that of the German mark, divided into 100 pfennig. In 1914 the islands were lost to Japan during World War I. They were captured by the United States in 1944 during World War II, and in 1947 they became part of the United Nations Trust Territory of the Pacific Islands. The territory was administered by the United States, and its monetary system was based on the United States dollar. In 1979, the islands gained autonomy and were renamed the Federated States of Micronesia; final independence came in 1990.

CHRONOLOGY

Year	Denomination	Equivalent
1944–present	U.S. dollar	100 cents
1914–1944	Japanese yen	100 sen
1899–1914	German mark	100 pfennig

ORTHOGRAPHY AND NUMBER

Singular	Plural	Known Abbreviations and Symbols	Examples
cent	cents	c ¢	10c 10¢
dollar	dollars	$	$10
mark	marks	m	10m
pfennig	pfennig	pf	10pf
sen	sen	Sn 銭	10 銭
yen	yen	¥ 円	¥10 10 円

Moldova (MDL)

Moldova, better known by its former Western name, Moldavia, was ruled by the Ottomans and Russians for much of the last 400 years. With its often-changing boundaries, the area known as Bessarabia merged with Romania in 1918 and adopted its monetary system based on the leu (plural, lei), meaning "lion," divisible into 100 bani.

After many years of being claimed by the Soviet Union, the Bessarabia territory was annexed by Russia in 1940. Except for a brief period while under German control, the area was again part of Romania. In 1944 Moldova was once more made a Soviet republic, and its monetary system again became the Russian ruble, divisible into 100 kopecks. In 1990 the republic changed its named from Moldavia to Moldova, and it seceded from the Soviet Union in 1991.

In 1992, Moldova based its monetary system on a transitional unit known as the "coupon," which was at par with the Russian ruble. The transition was completed in 1993, when the Moldovan leu replaced 1,000 coupons.

CHRONOLOGY

Year	Denomination	Equivalent
1993–present	Moldovan leu	100 bani
1992–1993	ruble coupon	
1944–1991	Russian ruble	100 kopecks
1941–1944	Romanian leu	100 bani
1940–1941	Russian ruble	100 kopecks
1918–1940	Romanian leu	100 bani
–1918	Russian ruble	100 kopecks

ORTHOGRAPHY AND NUMBER

Singular	Plural	Known Abbreviations and Symbols	Examples
ban	bani	b	10b
kopeck	kopecks	к коп	10 коп
leu	lei	L	10L
ruble	rubles	руб	10 руб

Monaco (EUR; replaced FRF in 1999)

Monaco is a principality that was long controlled by various Italian states, except for a brief period following the French Revolution. In 1861, Monaco's status as an independent state was restored, but once more under French guardianship. As a result, its monetary system is the same as France's: the French franc, divided into 100 centimes. However, in 1999 France joined the European Union and adopted the euro, which became its sole legal tender in 2002; Monaco followed suit. *See also* **European Union**.

CHRONOLOGY

Year	Denomination	Equivalent
1999–present	euro	100 euro-cent
1861–2002	French franc	100 centimes

ORTHOGRAPHY AND NUMBER

Singular	Plural	Known Abbreviations and Symbols	Examples
centime	centimes	c cme cme	10c
euro	euro	€	10€
euro-cent	euro-cent	€	0.10€
franc	francs	F Fc Fr Fcs Frs	10F

Mongolia (MNT)

A land once ruled by Genghis Khan, Mongolia was part of China until it declared its independence in 1911 under the protection of czarist Russia. However, it was annexed by China in 1920; in 1921 it again achieved independence. When it was part of China, the country's monetary system was that of the Chinese dollar, or yuan.

Following independence, Mongolia — often referred to as "Outer Mongolia" and not to be confused with "Inner Mongolia" — introduced the togrog, divisible into 100 mongo, in 1925. Togrog (the official English spelling used by the Bank of Mongolia) means "round," similar in meaning to the Chinese yuan. The term mongo is taken from the country's name and the Mongol Empire.

The transliteration of Mongolian into English is not always a simple matter, and there are often variations in spelling. The Mongolian monetary units, with their Cyrillic alphabet spellings and English spelling variants, are:

мөнгө   mongo, mungu, mung
төгрөг   togrog, tugrik, tughrik

Since 1937 Mongolian has been written using the Cyrillic alphabet; the Manchu-style alphabet is no longer in everyday use.

CHRONOLOGY

Year	Denomination	Equivalent
1925–present	togrog	100 mongo
–1925	Chinese dollar (*yuan*)	100 cents

ORTHOGRAPHY AND NUMBER

Singular	Plural	Known Abbreviations and Symbols	Examples
cent	cents		
mongo	mongo		10
togrog	togrog	Tg Tө Ŧ	10Tg 10Tө 10Ŧ
yuan	yuan		

Montserrat (XCD)

Montserrat has long been part of the British Empire and the Sterling Zone. In 1935 it changed its monetary system from the imperial LSD system to one based on the British West Indies dollar of the Eastern Caribbean Currency Authority. In 1965, the Eastern Caribbean Central Bank succeeded the Eastern Caribbean Currency Authority and replaced the West Indies dollar with the East Caribbean dollar. *See also* **East Caribbean States**.

CHRONOLOGY

Year	Denomination	Equivalent
1965–present	East Caribbean dollar	100 cents
1935–1965	British West Indies dollar	100 cents
–1935	pound sterling	20 shillings
	shilling	12 pence
	penny	4 farthings

ORTHOGRAPHY AND NUMBER

Singular	Plural	Known Abbreviations and Symbols	Examples
cent	cents	c ¢	10c 10¢
dollar	dollars	$ EC$	$10 EC$10
farthing	farthings	d	¼d ½d
penny	pence	d	10d
pound	pounds	£ (or £)	£10
shilling	shillings	s /	10s 10/-

Morocco (MAD)

After a turbulent history, Morocco was divided into French and Spanish protectorates in 1912. Prior to this partition, its monetary system was based on the rial hassani, named after Moulay-Hassan, the Moroccan king (Hassan I) who reformed Morocco's currency in 1881. The rial, whose name was borrowed from the Spanish real, meaning "royal," was divisible into 100 dirhams. Besides the rial, both the French franc and Spanish peseta circulated freely.

After the country's division, the rial was replaced with the Moroccan franc in the eastern French Sahara; the Spanish peseta, divided into 100 centimos, was the standard in Spanish Sahara. In 1957, the two protectorates gained their independence and were merged to create the Kingdom of Morocco. The Spanish peseta was replaced by 10 Moroccan francs. In 1959, the Moroccan dirham was introduced. The dirham, a name that is an Arabic version of the Greek drachma — meaning "handful" — is divided into 100 centimes. The name is also spelled santimes, as transliterated from the Arabic (سنتيم).

The Arabic letter *dal* (د), the abbreviation for dirham (درأهم), is sometimes used with the Arabic-language numerals below:

0	1	2	3	4	5	6	7	8	9	10	50	100	500	1000
.	١	٢	٣	٤	٥	٦	٧	٨	٩	١٠	٥٠	١٠٠	٥٠٠	١٠٠٠

CHRONOLOGY

Year	Denomination	Equivalent
1959–present	Moroccan dirham	100 centimes
1921–1959	Moroccan franc	100 centimes
1921–1957	Spanish peseta	100 centimos
–1921	rial	100 dirhams

ORTHOGRAPHY AND NUMBER

Singular	Plural	Known Abbreviations and Symbols	Examples
centime	centimes	c	10c
centimo	centimos	c cs cto cts ctms cents	10c 10 cs 10 cts

Singular	Plural	Known Abbreviations and Symbols	Examples
dirham	dirhams	DH ﺩ	10DH 10ﺩ
franc	francs	F	10F
peseta	pesetas	Pts	10 Pts
rial	rials		

Mozambique (MZM)

Mozambique was first established as a Portuguese colony in 1507. The monetary system was similar to that of its colonial ruler; in addition, the thaler, pound sterling, and Indian rupee were allowed to circulate. The milréis was replaced in 1907 by the Portuguese escudo, divisible into 100 centavos. Independence was granted in 1975, and the Portuguese escudo was replaced with an escudo divided into 100 centimos. A monetary reform in 1980 replaced the escudo with the metical, the Portuguese equivalent of the Arabic *miskal*—a one-time unit of weight.

The dollar sign ($) is used both as the symbol for the escudo and as a decimal point between escudos and the smaller centavos. The notation $10 represents 10 centavos and should not be confused with 10$, which equals 10 escudos. Another example is 10$50, which equals 10 escudos and 50 centavos.

CHRONOLOGY

Year	Denomination	Equivalent
1980–present	metical	100 centimos
1975–1980	Mozambique escudo	100 centimos
ca. 1907–1975	Portuguese escudo	100 centavos
1892–ca. 1907	Portuguese milréis	1,000 réis

ORTHOGRAPHY AND NUMBER

Singular	Plural	Known Abbreviations and Symbols	Examples
centavo	centavos	c cts	10c $10
centimo	centimos	ct	10ct
escudo	escudos	$	10$ 10
metical	meticais	MT	10 MT
réis	réis	Rs	Rs10

Myanmar *see* Burma

Namibia (NAD; replaced ZAR in 1993)

Namibia was a German protectorate called German South West Africa (Deutsch-Südwestafrika) from 1884 until 1915; its monetary system was then based on German paper marks. Following Germany's defeat in World War I, the region was transferred to South Africa as a mandate in 1920 by the League of Nations. The Southwest African pound replaced the mark, and the South African pound was also considered legal tender.

In 1946, Southwest Africa became a UN trust territory, which it remained until its independence in 1990. In 1961, monetary reforms replaced the imperial pound system with a decimalized system based on the rand, divisible into 100 cents. Although the rand was subsequently replaced at par by the Namibian dollar in 1993, the South African rand still serves as legal tender in Namibia.

CHRONOLOGY

Year	Denomination	Equivalent
1993–present	Namibian dollar	100 cents
1961–1993	South African rand	100 cents
1920–1961	Southwest African pound	20 shillings
	shilling	12 pence
	penny	4 farthings

ORTHOGRAPHY AND NUMBER

Singular	Plural	Known Abbreviations and Symbols	Examples
cent	cents	c	10c
dollar	dollars	N$	N$10
farthing	farthings	d	¼d ½d
penny	pence	d	10d
pound	pounds	£ (or ₤)	£10
rand	rand	R	R10
shilling	shillings	s /	10s 10/-

Nauru (AUD)

Nauru, formerly called Pleasant Island, is part of the Marshall Islands group. They became a German protectorate in 1886, and were made part of German New Guinea in 1906. The monetary system was then based on the New Guinea mark, divided into 100 pfennig. At the start of World War I, Germany lost the territory to Australian troops; the mark was replaced with the Australian pound.

In 1946, the United Nations granted Australia and New Zealand joint trusteeship over the territory. When Australia converted to a decimalized monetary system based on the Australian dollar in 1966, Pleasant Island followed suit, retaining the system even after its independence in 1968, when its name was changed to Nauru. The Australian dollar is also used by several Australian dependencies and the independent nations of Kiribati and Tuvalu.

CHRONOLOGY

Year	Denomination	Equivalent
1966–present	Australian dollar	100 cents
–1966	pound sterling	20 shillings
	shilling	12 pence
1966–1975	Australian dollar	100 cents
1914–1966	Australian pound	20 shillings
	shilling	12 pence
1906–1914	New Guinea mark	100 pfennig

ORTHOGRAPHY AND NUMBER

Singular	Plural	Known Abbreviations and Symbols	Examples
cent	cents	c ¢	10c 10¢
dollar	dollars	$	$10
mark	marks	m	10m
penny	pence	d	10d
pfennig	pfennig	pf	10pf
pound	pounds	£	£10
shilling	shillings	/	10/-

Nepal (NPR)

Once partitioned into three kingdoms, Nepal was unified in 1768, however, it became a de facto British protectorate in 1816. In the mid 19th century, Nepal's monetary system replaced the gold mohur with the Indian rupee, divisible into 16 anna and 64 paise. In 1961, a monetary reform decimalized the rupee, dividing it into 100 paise.

Nepal uses both the Latin and Devanāgarī alphabets for its monetary abbreviations. The Hindi forms आ for anna (आना), पै for paisa (पैसे), and रु for rupee (रुपया), are used with either the numerals 0 through 9 or the Devanāgarī numerals shown below:

0	1	2	3	4	5	6	7	8	9	10	50	100	500	1000
०	१	२	३	४	५	६	७	८	९	१०	५०	१००	५००	१०००

It should be noted that for the anna, A is the singular abbreviation and As is plural. Also, R , Re, and Rp are singular abbreviations for the rupee, while Rs is the plural abbreviation.

CHRONOLOGY

Year	Denomination	Equivalent
1961–present	rupee	100 paise
–1961	rupee	16 anna
	anna	4 paise

ORTHOGRAPHY AND NUMBER

Singular	Plural	Known Abbreviations and Symbols	Examples
anna	anna(s)*	A As आ	1A 10As 10आ १०आ
paisa	paise	P पै	10P 10पै १०पै
rupee	rupee(s)*	R Re Rp Rs रु	R1 Re1 Rp1 Rs10 १०रु

*Optional final s.

The Netherlands (EUR; replaced NLG in 1999)

Prior to its establishment as a kingdom in 1815, the Netherlands was under the successive rule of Austria, Spain, and France. The guilder, also known as the florin, had been in use as early as the fifteenthth century. The guilder is taken from the Dutch *gulden*, meaning "golden," and the florin is from a medieval coin known as the florenus. The rijksdaalder (national daalder), named after the thaler and a variant of the dollar, was equal to to 2½ guilders. The guilder was divisible into 20 stuivers, 40 grooten (English, groats), or 320 pennings. The penning, from the Dutch meaning "coin" or "medal," is a variant of the penny.

In addition to being divided into 16 pennings, the stuiver was also equal to four duits, a Dutch term meaning "small coin" (equivalent to the English doit). In 1875, the guilder was decimalized, divisible into 100 cents. In 1999, the Netherlands joined the Eurozone, adopting the euro, which became its sole legal tender in 2002. *See also* **European Union**.

CHRONOLOGY

Year	Denomination	Equivalent
2002–present	euro	euro-cent
1875–2002	guilder (*gulden*), or florin	100 cents
1815–1875	rijksdaalder	2½ guilders
	guilder (*gulden*), or florin	20 stivers
	stiver (*stuiver*)	16 pennings

ORTHOGRAPHY AND NUMBER

Singular	Plural	Known Abbreviations and Symbols	Examples
cent	cents	c ct cnt	10c 10ct 10cnt
euro	euro	€	€10
euro-cent	euro-cent	€	€0.10
florin	florins	f fl	10f 10fl
guilder (*gulden*)	guilders (*gulden*)	G Gi	10G 10Gi
penning	pennings (*penningen*)		
stiver (*stuiver*)	stivers (*stuivers*)	S St	10S 10St

Netherlands Antilles (ANG)

The Netherlands Antilles became a Dutch colony in 1634. The island group, together with Dutch Guiana (now Suriname), became known as the Dutch West Indies in 1828. Its monetary system was then the guilder (taken from the Dutch *gulden*, meaning "golden," and also known as the florin), which was divisible into 100 cents. With the exclusion of Dutch Guiana, the six islands of Aruba, Bonaire, Curaçao, Saba, St. Eustatius, and the southern half of St. Martin (known as St. Maarten; the northern half is French) were unified as the Dutch colony of Curaçao in 1848. The colony was renamed the Netherlands Antilles in 1948 and was declared an overseas member of the Netherlands with complete domestic autonomy in 1954. When Aruba gained its independence in 1986, it left the Netherlands Antilles.

CHRONOLOGY

Year	Denomination	Equivalent
1828–present	Netherlands Antilles guilder (*gulden*), or florin	100 cents

ORTHOGRAPHY AND NUMBER

Singular	Plural	Known Abbreviations and Symbols	Examples
cent	cents	c ct cts	10c 10ct 10cts
florin	florins	f Naf	10f Naf10
guilder (*gulden*)	guilders (*gulden*)	G Naf	10G NAf10

New Zealand (NZD)

Before New Zealand became a separate British colony from Australia in 1841, the pound sterling was widely used, in addition to other foreign coins. In 1897 the pound sterling was made the single legal tender; the New Zealand pound replaced it at par when New Zealand achieved dominion status in 1907. Nevertheless, the pound sterling continued to be considered legal tender until 1935.

A 1967 reform decimalized the monetary system, replacing the New Zealand pound with the New Zealand dollar (although the kiwi was once proposed as the new currency's name). The dollar, divided into 100 cents, is also used on Niue, Tokelau, Cook Islands, Pitcairn Island, and the Ross dependency.

CHRONOLOGY

Year	Denomination	Equivalent
1967–present	New Zealand dollar	100 cents
ca. 1855–1967	pound	20 shillings
	crown	5 shillings
	florin	2 shillings
	shilling	12 pence

ORTHOGRAPHY AND NUMBER

Singular	Plural	Known Abbreviations and Symbols	Examples
cent	cents	c	10c
crown	crowns		
dollar	dollars	NZ$ $	$10
penny	pence	d	10d
pound	pounds	£ (or ₤)	£10
shilling	shillings	/	10/-

Nicaragua (NIO)

After Spanish rule ended in 1821, Nicaragua was part of Mexico until 1823. From 1824 until 1838 it was part of the United Provinces of Central America, a federation of states which had declared their independence from Spain and Mexico. This federation comprised present-day Costa Rica, El Salvador, Guatemala, Honduras, and Nicaragua; all used the escudo, divisible into 16 reales. About 1862, the monetary system was changed to a decimalized one with the introduction of the Nicaraguan peso, divided into 100 centavos.

Inflation resulted in frequent changes in Nicaragua's monetary system, as was often the case with the countries of Central and South America. In 1912, a gold córdoba, named in honor of Hernández Gonzalo de Córdoba, a sixteenth-century governor of Nicaragua, replaced the peso at an exchange rate of 12½ pesos for one córdoba. Although it was relatively stable for much of the twentieth century, the córdoba's value eventually dropped substantially; in 1988, the new córdoba, or "Chanchero," replaced the córdoba at an exchange of 1,000 córdobas to one new córdoba. Even with monetary reforms, inflation continued; in 1990, the gold córdoba, or córdoba oro, replaced the new córdoba at a rate of one gold córdoba to five million new córdobas.

CHRONOLOGY

Year	Denomination	Equivalent
1990–present	córdoba oro	100 centavos
1988–1990	new córdoba	100 centavos
1912–1988	córdoba	100 centavos de córdoba
ca. 1862–ca. 1912	Nicaraguan peso	100 centavos
1838–ca. 1862	escudo	8 reales
1824–1838	Central American escudo	2 pesos
	peso	8 reales
–1824	Spanish escudo	2 pesos
	peso	8 reales

ORTHOGRAPHY AND NUMBER

Singular	Plural	Known Abbreviations and Symbols	Examples
centavo	centavos	c ct cts cent cvos ¢	10c 10cts 10¢
córdoba	córdobas	cs C$ ₡	cs10 C$10 ₡10
córdoba oro	córdobas oros	C$ ₡ C$o	C$10 ₡10 C$o10
peso	pesos	$	$10
real	reales	R Rs	10R 10 Rs

Niger (XOF)

Niger was an autonomous republic of the French community from 1922 until its independence in 1960. It is a member of the Franc Zone, and its current monetary system is based on the Communauté Financière Africaine (African Financial Community, CFA) franc, a monetary union of former French colonies in Africa. *See also* **West African States.**

CHRONOLOGY

Year	Denomination	Equivalent
1960–present	CFA franc	100 centimes
1922–1960	French franc	100 centimes

ORTHOGRAPHY AND NUMBER

Singular	Plural	Known Abbreviations and Symbols	Examples
centime	centimes	c	10c
franc	francs	F	10F

Nigeria (NGN)

The establishment of Nigeria as a British colony and protectorate was completed by 1914; the pound sterling served as its monetary system. The West African pound replaced the pound sterling at par in 1913. Even though Nigeria gained its independence in 1960, it wasn't until 1962 that the Nigerian pound replaced the West African pound at par. A monetary reform in 1973 introduced the naira, a name possibly based on that of the country. Equal to 10 former Nigerian shillings, the naira is divisible into 100 kobo, a native word for "copper."

CHRONOLOGY

Year	Denomination	Equivalent
1973–present	naira	100 kobo
1962–1973	Nigerian pound	20 shillings
	shilling	12 pence
1913–1962	West African pound	20 shillings
	shilling	12 pence
–1913	pound sterling	20 shillings
	shilling	12 pence

ORTHOGRAPHY AND NUMBER

Singular	Plural	Known Abbreviations and Symbols	Examples
kobo	kobo	k	10k
naira	naira	₦	₦10
penny	pence	d	10d
pound	pounds	£ N£	£10 N£10
shilling	shillings	/	10/-

Norway (NOK)

From about 1350 until 1814, Norway was in a union with Denmark, and its monetary system followed Denmark's rigsdaler and krone. With Napoleon's defeat in 1814,

Denmark — an ally of France — was compelled to cede Norway to the king of Sweden. That union would last until 1905, when Norway gained its independence. Until 1875, Norway's monetary system was based on Sweden's speciedaler (i.e., a daler "coin"), divided into 120 skillings rather than the rigsdaler's 96 skillings.

The year 1873 marked the formation of the Scandinavian Monetary Union, which initially included only Denmark and Sweden. Norway joined in 1875 and replaced its speciedaler with the Norwegian krone, divided into 100 øre and 30 skilling. Coincidentally, the monetary units of these three countries are very similar: krone (Denmark and Norway) and krona (Sweden). Whatever its spelling or language, the name means "crown." The øre, like the Swedish öre, is derived from the Latin *aureus* ("gold").

CHRONOLOGY

Year	Denomination	Equivalent
1875–present	Norwegian krone	100 øre
	krone	30 skilling
ca. 1813–1875	speciedaler	120 skilling

ORTHOGRAPHY AND NUMBER

Singular	Plural	Known Abbreviations and Symbols	Examples
krone	kroner	kr Nkr	10 kr
øre	øre		
skilling	skilling	Sk skill	10 Sk
speciedaler	speciedalers	Sp Sps	10 Sp

Oman (OMR)

Once known as Muscat and Oman, the country was separated from Zanzibar in 1861 and was made a British protectorate in 1891. Because of its location and its control by Great Britain, its monetary system closely followed British India's: rupees, anna, and pies were its legal tender. In 1959 a special currency unit, the Persian Gulf rupee, officially known as the "external rupee," was issued; it was equal to 100 naye paise ("new pice"). In 1966 the rupee was divided into 16 anna, with each anna equal to four baisa. The baisa, also spelled baiza, is the Arabic equivalent of the Indian paisa. Its plural can be spelled both with and without a final *s*.

The sultanate of Oman was created in 1970, and the rupee was replaced with the rial Saidi, divisible into 1,000 baisa. The rial Saidi was named in honor of the al-Bu Sa'id ruling family. In 1972, the rial Saidi was renamed the rial Omani.

Although Oman primarily uses the Latin alphabet for its abbreviations, it also uses the Arabic spellings for rial (ريال) and baisa (بيسة) with the Arabic-language numerals shown:

0	1	2	3	4	5	6	7	8	9	10	50	100	500	1000
٠	١	٢	٣	٤	٥	٦	٧	٨	٩	١٠	٥٠	١٠٠	٥٠٠	١٠٠٠

CHRONOLOGY

Year	Denomination	Equivalent
1972–present	rial Omani	1,000 baisa
1970–1972	rial Saidi	1,000 baisa
1966–1970	rupee	16 anna
	anna	4 baisa
1959–1966	Persian Gulf rupee	100 naye paise
ca. 1891–1959	Indian rupee	16 anna
	anna	12 pies

ORTHOGRAPHY AND NUMBER

Singular	Plural	Known Abbreviations and Symbols	Examples
anna	anna(s)*	A	10A
baisa	baisa(s)*		
naya paisa	naye paise	NP	10NP
pie	pies		
rial	rials	RO OR	RO10
rupee	rupees	R Rs	1R 10Rs

*Optional final s.

Pakistan (PKR)

Present-day Pakistan was part of British India from 1756 to 1947, and its monetary system was based on the Indian rupee, divisible into 16 anna, 64 pice, and 192 pies. When India achieved independence in 1947, Pakistan was divided into two non-contiguous provinces, West Pakistan and East Bengal — the latter renamed East Pakistan in 1955. The Indian rupee was replaced in 1948 at par with the Pakistani rupee, also divisible into 16 anna. In 1971, the rupee was decimalized, now being divided into 100 paise (also pice). In 1971 East Pakistan seceded and was renamed Bangladesh, while West Pakistan became simply Pakistan.

It should be noted that the abbreviations A and Re are for one anna and one rupee respectively, while As and Rs are the corresponding plural abbreviations. The following Eastern Arabic-language numerals are often used with the Urdu-language equivalents of Pakistan's monetary units:

0	1	2	3	4	5	6	7	8	9	10	50	100	500	1000
٠	١	٢	٣	۴	۵	۶	٧	٨	٩	١٠	۵٠	١٠٠	۵٠٠	١٠٠٠

CHRONOLOGY

Year	Denomination	Equivalent
1961–present	Pakistani rupee	100 paisa (*pice*)
1948–1961	Pakistani rupee	16 anna
ca. 1850–1948	Indian rupee	16 anna
	anna	4 pice
	pice	3 pies

ORTHOGRAPHY AND NUMBER

Singular	Plural	Known Abbreviations and Symbols	Examples
anna	anna(s)*	A As	1A 10As
paisa (*pice*)	paise (*pice*)	P Ps	10P 10Ps
pie	pies	Ps	10Ps
rupee	rupees	R Re Rs	Re1 Rs10

*Optional final s̲.

Palau (USD)

Palau is part of the western section of the Caroline Islands. Germany purchased the islands from Spain in 1899 and became the first nation to establish effective foreign rule. In 1914 Germany lost the islands to Japan during World War I; they were later captured by the United States in 1944 during World War II. In 1947 the islands became part of the United Nations Trust Territory of the Pacific Islands. They were administered by the United States, and the monetary system was based on the United States dollar. Palau became a self-governing nation in 1994 and now manages its own affairs, except for defense, which is overseen by the United States.

CHRONOLOGY

Year	Denomination	Equivalent
1944–present	U.S. dollar	100 cents
1914–1944	Japanese yen	100 sen
1899–1914	German mark	100 pfennig

ORTHOGRAPHY AND NUMBER

Singular	Plural	Known Abbreviations and Symbols	Examples
cent	cents	c ¢	10c 10¢
dollar	dollars	$	$10
mark	marks	m	10m

Singular	Plural	Known Abbreviations and Symbols	Examples
pfennig	pfennig	pf	10pf
sen	sen	Sn 銭	10 銭
yen	yen	¥ 円	¥10 10 円

Panama (PAB; also USD)

Panama was a Colombian province when Colombia, then part of what was known as Nueva Granada ("New Grenada"), completely gained its independence from Spain in 1821. Until 1847, the escudo was divisible into two pesos, and each peso in turn was equal to 8 reales. In that year the peso was decimalized, divided into 10 reales and 100 decimos. In 1853, the peso was divided into only 10 decimos. Twenty years later, however, the peso was divided into 100 centavos.

In 1903, Panama, aided by the United States, seceded from Colombia and became an independent nation. Monetary reforms in 1904 replaced the peso with the balboa, in honor of the Spanish explorer Vasco Nuñez de Balboa, who "discovered" the Pacific Ocean in 1513.

It is interesting to note that, since 1941, Panama has had no banknotes of its own. Panama's money, denominated in balboas and centesimos, consists only of coins; United States banknotes serve as its paper currency.

CHRONOLOGY

Year	Denomination	Equivalent
1904–present	balboa	100 centesimos
1872–1904	peso	100 centavos
1853–1872	peso	10 decimos
	decimo	10 centavos
1847–1853	peso	10 reales
	real	10 decimos
1819–1847	escudo	2 pesos
	peso	8 reales

ORTHOGRAPHY AND NUMBER

Singular	Plural	Known Abbreviations and Symbols	Examples
balboa	balboas	B/	B/10
centavo	centavos	c	10c
centesimo	centesimos	c ct cts ¢	10c 10¢
decimo	decimos		
escudo	escudos	$	10$
peso	pesos	$	$10
real	reales	R	10R

Papua New Guinea (PGK)

In 1884, Great Britain established a protectorate over the southeastern part of New Guinea. Germany had claimed northeastern New Guinea, also known in German as either Neu Guinea or Kaiser-Wilhelmsland. British New Guinea became part of the Sterling Zone, while German New Guinea's monetary system was based on the mark, divisible into 100 pfennig. In 1906, administrative control of British New Guinea was transferred to nearby Australia, now an independent commonwealth, and the territory was renamed Papua.

At the start of World War I, Germany lost its part of New Guinea to Australian troops; both territories were now members of the Sterling Zone and used the Australian pound. In 1946 the United Nations granted Australia a trusteeship over the territory of New Guinea. Papua and New Guinea merged in 1949. When Australia converted to a decimalized monetary system based on the Australian dollar in 1966, Papua New Guinea did also.

Full independence from Australia was granted in 1975, and the Australian pound was replaced with the kina, divisible into 100 toeas. The name kina is taken from the native pidgin language for the shell money that represented the means of monetary exchange of the coastal natives prior to the introduction of coinage by Great Britain and Germany. The toea is a valuable shell traditionally used by the natives inhabiting the coastal villages for bride-price ceremonies.

CHRONOLOGY

Year	Denomination	Equivalent
1975–present	kina	100 toeas
1966–1975	Australian dollar	100 cents
1906–1966	Australian pound	20 shillings
	shilling	12 pence
1884–1906	pound sterling	20 shillings
	shilling	12 pence
1884–1914	New Guinea mark	100 pfennig

ORTHOGRAPHY

Singular	Plural	Known Abbreviations and Symbols	Examples
cent	cents	c	10c
dollar	dollars	$	$10
kina	kina	K	K10
mark	marks	M	10M
penny	pence	d	10d
pfennig	pfennig	pf	10pf
pound	pounds	£ (or £)	£10
shilling	shillings	s /	10s 10/-
toea	toeas	t	10t

Paraguay (PYG)

Paraguay won its independence from Spain in 1811 and thereupon adopted the peso, divisible into 8 reales, as the basis of its monetary system. A monetary reform in 1870 divided the peso, also known as the *peso fuerte* ("strong peso"), into 100 centesimos until 1881, when it was divided into 100 centavos. In 1943 the peso was replaced with the guarani (named after the native Paraguayan Indian tribe and one of the country's two official languages), which was divided into 100 centimos. However, the peso and centavo continued to be in effect until 1944. Currently, the guarani is the sole monetary unit, as high inflation has rendered the centimo worthless.

CHRONOLOGY

Year	Denomination	Equivalent
1943–present	guarani	100 centimos
1881–1943	Paraguay peso	100 centavos
1870–1881	Paraguay peso	100 centesimos
–1870	Paraguay peso	8 reales

ORTHOGRAPHY AND NUMBER

Singular	Plural	Known Abbreviations and Symbols	Examples
centavo	centavos		
centesimo	centesimos		
centimo	centimos		
guaraní	guaranis	G Gs G/.	G10 Gs10 G/.10
peso	pesos	$	$10
real	reales	R	

Peru (PEN)

Peru was once a Spanish colony and used the escudo, peso, and real of its colonial ruler. Even though it gained its independence in 1821, Peru continued using the escudo until 1863, when the monetary system was decimalized, based on the sol. The sol, named in honor of the Spanish navigator Juan Diaz de Solis (ca. 1470–1516), was divided into 100 centavos. Inflation required a monetary reform in 1985 in which the sol was replaced with the inti, at an exchange of one inti per 1,000 soles. The inti, which was divisible into 100 centimos, was named after the Incas' Quechua-language word for "sun." Another devaluation, in 1991, replaced the inti with the nuevo sol, equal to one million inti.

CHRONOLOGY

Year	Denomination	Equivalent
1991–present	nuevo sol	100 centimos
1985–1991	inti	100 centimos
1863–1985	Peruvian sol	10 dineros
–1863	escudo	2 pesos
	peso	8 reales

ORTHOGRAPHY AND NUMBER

Singular	Plural	Known Abbreviations and Symbols	Examples
centavo	centavos	cts ctvs S/.	10 cts S/.0.10
centimo	centimos		
inti	intis	I/.	I/.10
peso	pesos		
real	reales	R Rs	10R 10 Rs
(nuevo) sol	(nuevos) soles	S/.	S/.10

Philippines (PHP)

The Philippines was claimed for Spain by Ferdinand Magellan in 1521, and its monetary system was essentially the same as that used by Spain. In 1859, the Spanish real was replaced by the peso, also referred to as the peso plata fuerte, divisible into 100 centimos. In Spanish, *peso* means weight, while *plata* and *fuerte* respectively mean "silver" and "strong"—hence, a "strong silver peso."

The escudo replaced the peso in 1871, but this lasted only one year; then the escudo was replaced by the peseta, a diminutive of "peso," divisible into 100 centimos. The peso was reinstituted in 1876 and divided into 100 centimos. With Spain's defeat in the Spanish-American War, the Philippines became a territory of the United States in 1898, and the U.S. dollar became legal tender. In 1903 the peso, equal to 100 centavos, was reinstituted.

After the Philippines gained independence in 1946 following World War II, the peso was retained until 1962. In that year it was renamed the piso, divisible into 100 sentimos. Piso and sentimo are the Tagalog-language equivalents of peso and centavo.

CHRONOLOGY

Year	Denomination	Equivalent
1962–present	piso	100 sentimos
1946–1962	peso	100 centavos
1903–1946	peso	100 centavos
1899–1903	U.S. dollar	100 centimos

Year	Denomination	Equivalent
1876–1899	peso	100 centimos
1872–1876	peseta	100 centimos
1871–1872	escudo	100 centimos
1859–1871	peso	100 centimos

ORTHOGRAPHY

Singular	Plural	Known Abbreviations and Symbols	Examples
centavo	centavos	c	10c
centimo	centimos	c cens	10c 10 cens
dollar	dollars	$	$10
escudo	escudos	$	10$
peso	pesos	$	$10
piso	piso	₱	₱10
sentimo	sentimos	s	10s

Poland (PLN; replaced PLZ)

By 1795, Poland had been partitioned three times and many of its provinces continued changing hands until 1815. In the eastern provinces taken by Russia, Russian rubles were in use from as early as 1842 until the end of World War I. The gulden and krone, divided into 100 halerzy, were used in the regions taken by Austria and the later Austro-Hungarian Empire. Groschen, thalers, guldens, and marks were used in the German-controlled areas of Prussia and Danzig (now Gdansk).

In the areas controlled by Germany during World War I, the German reichmark was replaced in 1916 with the Polish marka, divisible into 100 fenigow, the Polish equivalents of the German mark and pfennig. After the war's end, the Austrian krone remained until in use 1919, while the marka remained legal tender until 1924.

To fight the inflation that came after the end of World War I, the Polish zloty was reintroduced in 1922. It was divisible into 100 groszy, and equaled 1.8 million marka. The zloty, meaning "golden," was previously a coin used in the Polish duchy of the early eighteenth century. Grosz is simply the Polish variation of the Austro-Hungarian groschen and French gros coins.

Poland's monetary system often suffered from inflation. When the zloty was most recently devalued, the newest zloty replaced 10,000 older zlotys. In 2004, Poland joined the European Union, but it will be several years before it will participate in the European Union's monetary system (Eurozone) and adopt the euro. *See also* **European Union**.

The English plural spelling of zloty is generally zlotys, although it is sometimes spelled zloties. The Polish-language plural form of a monetary unit depends on the number it is associated with. The plural of zloty can be either złote or złotych, and of grosz either grosze or groszy.

CHRONOLOGY

Year	Denomination	Equivalent
1922–present	zloty	100 groszy
1916–1924	marka	100 fenigow
–1919	Austro-Hungarian krone	100 halerzy
–1917	Russian ruble	100 kopecks

ORTHOGRAPHY

Singular	Plural	Known Abbreviations and Symbols	Examples
fenig	fenigow	fen	10 fen
grosz	groszy	Gr	10Gr
halerze	halerzy	h hal	10h 10 hal
kopeck	kopecks	к коп	10к 10 коп
krone	kronen	K KR	10K 10KR
marka	marken	M Mk	10 M 10 Mk
ruble	rubles	P руб	10P 10 руб
zloty	zlotys	zł zło złot	10 zł 10 zło

Portugal (EUR; replaced PTE in 1999)

By the nineteenth century Portugal's monetary system was based on the real and the milréis, which was also known as the cruzado. When the monarchy was abolished in 1910, the escudo replaced the milréis at par, and was divisible into 100 centavos. In 1999 Portugal joined the European Union and adopted the euro, which became its sole legal tender in 2002. The dollar sign ($) has been used both as the symbol for the escudo and as a decimal point between escudos and the smaller centavos. As an example, 10$50 equals 10.50 escudos. *See also* **European Union**.

CHRONOLOGY

Year	Denomination	Equivalent
1999–present	euro	euro-cent
1910–2002	Portuguese escudo	100 centavos
–1910	milréis	1,000 réis

ORTHOGRAPHY

Singular	Plural	Known Abbreviations and Symbols	Examples
centavo	centavos	c cos cts ctv cent cvos $	10c $10
escudo	escudos	$ E	10$ 10E

Singular	Plural	Known Abbreviations and Symbols	Examples
euro	euro	€	€10
euro-cent	euro-cent	€	€0.10
réis	réis	Rs	Rs10

Qatar (QAR)

Present-day Qatar was once part of the Ottoman Empire; in 1916 it became a British protectorate. Because of the British influence and its proximity to the Indian subcontinent, its monetary system was then based on the Indian rupee, divided into 16 anna. In 1957 the rupee was decimalized and divided into 100 naye paise. In 1959 it was replaced with the Persian Gulf rupee, officially known as the "external rupee."

In 1966, Qatar refused to continue use of the Persian Gulf rupee and adopted a temporary monetary system based on the Saudi riyal, which was divided into 100 dirhams. Later that year the riyal was replaced with the Dubai and Qatar riyal. When Dubai and the other Trucial States formed the United Arab Emirates in 1971, Qatar issued its own riyal.

The transliteration of Arabic into English is not always a simple matter, and there are often variations in spelling; for example, dirham (درهم) is also found spelled "dirhem." Qatar's monetary units are sometimes expressed in combination with the Arabic-language numerals below:

0	1	2	3	4	5	6	7	8	9	10	50	100	500	1000
٠	١	٢	٣	٤	٥	٦	٧	٨	٩	١٠	٥٠	١٠٠	٥٠٠	١٠٠٠

It should be noted that the abbreviations R, Re, and Rp are for one rupee, while Rs is the plural abbreviation.

CHRONOLOGY

Year	Denomination	Equivalent
1971–present	Qatar riyal	100 dirhams
1966–1971	Dubai and Qatar riyal	100 dirhams
1966	Saudi riyal	100 dirhams
1959–1966	Persian Gulf rupee	100 naye paise
1957–1959	Indian rupee	100 naye paise
1916–1957	Indian rupee	16 anna

ORTHOGRAPHY AND NUMBER

Singular	Plural	Known Abbreviations and Symbols	Examples
anna	anna(s)*	A	10A
dirham	dirhams	DH	10DH

Singular	Plural	Known Abbreviations and Symbols	Examples
naya paisa	naye paise	NP	10NP
riyal	riyals	R QR	10R
rupee	rupee(s)*	R Re Rp Rs	R1 Re1 Rp1 Rs10

*Optional final s.

Romania (ROL)

Romania was ruled for hundreds of years by the Ottoman Turks and used its monetary system of the piastre and para. Before its independence in 1878, monetary system reforms in 1867 replaced the piastre with the leu, after the Romanian word for "lion." The leu is divided into 100 bani, a name from the Persian *ban*, meaning "lord."

CHRONOLOGY

Year	Denomination	Equivalent
1867–present	leu	100 bani
–1867	Turkish piastre	40 para (*parale*)

ORTHOGRAPHY AND NUMBER

Singular	Plural	Known Abbreviations and Symbols	Examples
ban	bani	b	10b
leu	lei	L	10L
para	parale	par	10 par
piastre	piastres		

Russia (RUB; replaced RUR in 1998)

Imperial Russia was created in 1547 when Ivan IV (Ivan the Terrible) was crowned czar. Russia's monetary system as it is known today was established as early as 1704 by Peter I (Peter the Great). He created the ruble (also rouble), derived from the Russian word *rubit* (рубить) — meaning "cut" or "cut down." The ruble was divided into 100 kopecks, from *kop'yio* (копьё) — meaning "lance."

Besides the ruble and kopeck, other monetary units were used from as early as the fourteenth century to the twentieth century. Some were coins created from units of account that were either multiples or fractions of the ruble and kopeck. Among these were the chervonetz (червонец), equal to 10 rubles; grivna (гривна), equal to 10 kopecks; denga (денга) or poludenga (полуоденга), equal to ½ kopeck; poltina (полтина), equal to 50 kopecks; polupoltina (полуополтина), equal to 25 kopecks; and polushka (полушка), equal to ¼ kopeck.

The transliteration of Russian into English is not always a simple matter, and one often finds variations in spelling for the monetary units, such as rouble for ruble, and kopec or kopek for kopeck. Russia's primary monetary units, with their Cyrillic spellings, are:

Unit	Singular	Plural*
kopeck (kopec, kopek)	копейка	копейки, копеек
ruble (rouble)	рубль	рублей, рубля

*Russian plural form is grammatically dependent

CHRONOLOGY

Year	Denomination	Equivalent
ca. 1704–present	ruble	100 kopecks

ORTHOGRAPHY AND NUMBER

Singular	Plural	Known Abbreviations and Symbols	Examples
kopeck	kopecks	к коп	10к 10 коп
ruble	rubles	р руб	10р 10 руб

Rwanda (RWF)

Present-day Rwanda was once part of German East Africa, and its monetary system was the German East African (Deutsch Ostafrika) rupie, divisible into 64 pesa, the German equivalent of India's paisa. During World War I, Belgium occupied German East Africa in 1916. Beginning in 1922, Belgium governed Ruanda-Urundi, first as a mandate from the League of Nations, and later (from 1946) as a trust territory under United Nations jurisdiction. In 1962, the trusteeship terminated, and the territory was divided into the two independent states of Rwanda and Burundi. Upon Rwanda's independence, the Rwanda-Urundi franc was on par with the Belgian franc; in 1964, Rwanda introduced its own franc, divided into 100 centimes.

CHRONOLOGY

Year	Denomination	Equivalent
1964–present	Rwandan franc	100 centimes
1916–1964	Ruanda-Urundi franc	100 centimes

Year	Denomination	Equivalent
1906–1917	German East African rupie	100 heller
–1906	German East African rupie	64 pesa

ORTHOGRAPHY AND NUMBER

Singular	Plural	Known Abbreviations and Symbols	Examples
centime	centimes	c ces	10c 10 ces
franc	francs	F Fr Frw	10F 10Fr
heller	heller		
pesa	pesa		
rupie	rupien		

St. Helena and Dependencies (SHP)

St. Helena has been a British dependency since 1834; it includes the neighboring islands of Ascension and Tristan de Cunha. In 1971 the imperial LSD system of pounds, shillings, and pence was replaced by a decimalized system based on the St. Helena pound, divisible into 100 new pence.

CHRONOLOGY

Year	Denomination	Equivalent
1971–present	St. Helena pound	100 new pence
–1971	pound sterling	20 shillings
	shilling	12 pence

ORTHOGRAPHY AND NUMBER

Singular	Plural	Known Abbreviations and Symbols	Examples
new penny	new pence	p	10p
penny	pence	d	10d
pound	pounds	£ (or ₤)	£10
shilling	shillings	/	10/-

St. Kitts and Nevis (XCD)

Until its independence in 1983, St. Kitts (St. Christopher) and Nevis had long been part of the British Empire and the Sterling Zone. In 1935 it changed its monetary system from the imperial LSD system to one based on the British West Indies dollar of the Eastern Caribbean Currency Authority. In 1965 the Eastern Caribbean Central Bank succeeded the Eastern Caribbean Currency Authority and replaced the West Indies dollar with the East Caribbean dollar. *See also* **East Caribbean States.**

CHRONOLOGY

Year	Denomination	Equivalent
1965–present	East Caribbean dollar	100 cents
1935–1965	British West Indies dollar	100 cents
–1935	pound sterling	20 shillings
	shilling	12 pence
	penny	4 farthings

ORTHOGRAPHY AND NUMBER

Singular	Plural	Known Abbreviations and Symbols	Examples
cent	cents	c	10c
dollar	dollars	$ EC$	$10
farthing	farthings	d	¼d ½d
penny	pence	d	10d
pound	pounds	£ (or £)	£10
shilling	shillings	/	10/-

St. Lucia (XCD)

Until its independence in 1979, St. Lucia was part of the British Empire and the Sterling Zone. Like several other Caribbean colonies, in 1935 it changed its monetary system from the imperial LSD system to one based on the British West Indies dollar of the Eastern Caribbean Currency Authority. In 1965 the Eastern Caribbean Central Bank succeeded the Eastern Caribbean Currency Authority and replaced the West Indies dollar with the East Caribbean dollar. *See also* **East Caribbean States.**

CHRONOLOGY

Year	Denomination	Equivalent
1965–present	East Caribbean dollar	100 cents
1935–1965	British West Indies dollar	100 cents
ca. 1860–1935	pound sterling	20 shillings
	shilling	12 pence
	penny	4 farthings

ORTHOGRAPHY AND NUMBER

Singular	Plural	Known Abbreviations and Symbols	Examples
cent	cents	c ¢	10c 10¢
dollar	dollars	$ EC$	$10
farthing	farthings	d	¼d ½d
penny	pence	d	10d
pound	pounds	£ (or £)	£10
shilling	shillings	/	10/-

St. Vincent and the Grenadines (XCD)

From 1763 until its independence in 1979, St. Vincent and the Grenadines island group had been part of the British Empire and the Sterling Zone. In 1949 it changed its monetary system from the imperial LSD system to one based on the British West Indies dollar of the Eastern Caribbean Currency Authority. In 1965, the Eastern Caribbean Central Bank succeeded the Eastern Caribbean Currency Authority and replaced the West Indies dollar with the East Caribbean dollar. *See also* **East Caribbean States.**

CHRONOLOGY

Year	Denomination	Equivalent
1965–present	East Caribbean dollar	100 cents
1949–1965	British West Indies dollar	100 cents
–1949	pound sterling	20 shillings
	shilling	12 pence
	penny	4 farthings

ORTHOGRAPHY AND NUMBER

Singular	Plural	Known Abbreviations and Symbols	Examples
cent	cents	c ¢	10c 10¢
dollar	dollars	$ EC$	$10
farthing	farthings	d	¼d ½d
penny	pence	d	10d
pound	pounds	£ (or £)	£10
shilling	shillings	/	10/-

Samoa (WST)

An 1899 treaty allowed Germany to annex a number of islands in the western part of an archipelago called Western Samoa, when Great Britain withdrew all its claims to these islands. The eastern islands of the archipelago, claimed by the United States, were to be known as American Samoa. In 1900, the German mark replaced the pound sterling, which had been the basis of the islands' monetary system since about 1820.

In 1914, near the start of World War I, New Zealand occupied Western Samoa. In 1915 the islands were again made part of the Sterling Zone, and the League of Nations gave New Zealand a mandate in 1920 to administer the islands. In 1946 the mandate was changed to a United Nations Trust Territory administered by New Zealand. When Western Samoa became independent in 1967, the New Zealand pound was replaced with a decimalized monetary system based on the tala, a native variation of the pronunciation of "dollar." The tala was divided into 100 sene, a native variation of "cent." The country's name was shortened to Samoa in 1997.

CHRONOLOGY

Year	Denomination	Equivalent
1967–present	tala	100 sene
1914–1967	New Zealand pound	20 shillings
	shilling	12 pence
	penny	4 farthings
1900–1915	mark	100 pfennig
ca. 1820–1900	pound sterling	20 shillings
	shilling	12 pence
	penny	4 farthings

ORTHOGRAPHY AND NUMBER

Singular	Plural	Known Abbreviations and Symbols	Examples
farthing	farthings	d	¼d ½d
mark	marks	M	10M
penny	pence	d	10d
pfennig	pfennig	pf	10pf
pound	pounds	Ł £ (or £)	£10
sene	sene	s	10s
shilling	shillings	/	10/-
tala	tala	$ WS$	$10 WS$10

San Marino (EUR; replaced ITL in 1999)

San Marino is one of only two countries that is completely surrounded by another country. In 1862 it entered into a customs union with Italy, which also guaranteed its defense. The monetary system was based on the Italian lira, and even though San Marino issued its own stamps and coins it relied on Italian banknotes. Because Italy joined the Eurozone in 1999, adopting the euro (which became its sole legal tender in 2002), San Marino's monetary system is now also based on the euro. *See also* **European Union.**

CHRONOLOGY

Year	Denomination	Equivalent
1999–present	euro	euro-cent
1862–2002	lira	100 centesimi

ORTHOGRAPHY AND NUMBER

Singular	Plural	Known Abbreviations and Symbols	Examples
centesimo	centesimi	cmi cen cent	10 cmi 10 cen
euro	euro	€	€10
euro-cent	euro-cent	€	€0.10
lira	lire	L. Lit. £	L.10 £10

São Tomé and Príncipe (STD)

Because São Tomé and Príncipe (whose name translates to St. Thomas and Prince) came under Portugal's control about 1485, its monetary system was the réis and escudo of its colonial ruler. In 1975 the island group gained its independence and reformed its monetary system, replacing the escudo with the dobra, which is named after a former gold coin of Portugal. The dollar sign ($) is used both as the symbol for the escudo and as a decimal point between escudos and the smaller centavos. As an example, 10$50 equals 10.50 escudos.

CHRONOLOGY

Year	Denomination	Equivalent
1975–present	dobra	100 centimos
1911–1975	Portuguese escudo	100 centavos
1870–1911	Portuguese milréis	100 réis

ORTHOGRAPHY AND NUMBER

Singular	Plural	Known Abbreviations and Symbols	Examples
centavo	centavos	c	10c
centimo	centimos	cent	10 cent
dobra	dobras	Db	Db 10
escudo	escudos	$	10$ 10$50
réis	réis	Rs	Rs10

Saudi Arabia (SAR)

The Ottoman Empire, in existence from 1517 until World War I, included all of present-day Saudi Arabia. By the late 1920s the area was divided into two major regions — Nejd and Hejaz, which would eventually be united in 1932 as Saudi Arabia. Neither the Nejd nor the Hejaz had a monetary system of it own, and both relied heavily on precious metal coins like the British gold sovereign, the silver Maria Theresa thaler, and the Ottoman piastre (colloquially known as a guerche), which was divided into 40 para.

In 1928, a monetary reform replaced the piastre with the riyal, on par with the Maria Theresa thaler and equal to 11 guerche. By the late 1950s the price of silver had increased to a level that required a devaluation of the riyal, so in 1960 a monetary reform divided the ryial into 20 guerche. In 1976, the riyal was redefined, divided into 100 halala, a term possibly taken from the Arabic *halal* (حلال), meaning "lawful."

Saudi Arabia uses both the Latin and Arabic alphabets for its monetary abbreviations. The Arabic letters *qaf* (ق) for querche (غروش), and *he* (ه) for halala (هللة) and riyal (ريال), are used with either the numerals 0 through 9 or the Arabic-language numerals shown below:

0	1	2	3	4	5	6	7	8	9	10	50	100	500	1000
٠	١	٢	٣	٤	٥	٦	٧	٨	٩	١٠	٥٠	١٠٠	٥٠٠	١٠٠٠

CHRONOLOGY

Year	Denomination	Equivalent
1976–present	Saudi riyal	100 halala
1960–1976	Saudi riyal	20 guerche
1928–1960	Saudi riyal	11 guerche
–1928	piastre	40 paras

ORTHOGRAPHY AND NUMBER

Singular	Plural	Known Abbreviations and Symbols	Examples
guerche	guerche		
halala	halala	H ه	10H ه١٠

Singular	Plural	Known Abbreviations and Symbols	Examples
para	para(s)*		
piastre	piastres	P ق	10P ١٠ق
riyal	riyals	SR SRls ريال	10SR ١٠ ريال

*Optional final s.

Senegal (XOF)

Senegal was established as a French colony in 1895, and until its independence in 1960 it was a member of the Franc Zone. The current monetary system is based on the Communauté Financière Africaine (African Financial Community, CFA) franc, a monetary union of former French colonies in Africa. *See also* **West African States**.

CHRONOLOGY

Year	Denomination	Equivalent
1960–present	CFA franc	100 centimes
1895–1960	French franc	100 centimes

ORTHOGRAPHY AND NUMBER

Singular	Plural	Known Abbreviations and Symbols	Examples
centime	centimes	c	10c
franc	francs	F Fr	10F 10Fr

Serbia and Montenegro
(YUM; replaced YUD, Serbia; EUR; replaced YUM which replaced YUD, Montenegro)

Serbia was once part of the Ottoman Empire, and used its monetary system of the piastre, divided into 40 para — a word from the Arabic *bara* (باره), meaning "silver." In 1815, Serbia became part of the Holy Roman Empire, and later of the Austro-Hungarian Empire. In 1866, a monetary reform introduced a decimalized system based on the dinar, the Arabic form of the ancient Roman denarius, which was divisible into 100 para. When Montenegro became an independent kingdom in 1910, the piastre was replaced with the perper, also divided into 100 para.

In 1918, after the end of World War I, Serbia and Montenegro, along with Bosnia-Herzegovina, Croatia, Macedonia, and Slovenia, united to form the Kingdom of the Serbs, Croats and Slovenes. At this time, a variety of currencies circulated throughout the new kingdom. The first reform aimed at creating a national monetary unit was based on the Austrian krone, divided into 100 heller. It was replaced in 1919 with the dinar used in Serbia, which was divided into 100 para and equal to four kronen. This new monetary system continued after the kingdom was renamed Yugoslavia in 1929.

In 1991 Yugoslavia began to break up — the federal republics of Croatia, Macedonia, and Slovenia seceded that year, while Bosnia-Herzegovina followed in 1992. The two remaining republics of Serbia and Montenegro formed a union that was still called Yugoslavia. Even though the two republics agreed to continue the union until at least 2005, Yugoslavia was renamed Serbia and Montenegro in 2003.

Despite their union, Serbia and Montenegro have separate monetary systems. Serbia kept its dinar, which has undergone a series of devaluations as a result of extreme hyperinflation. In 1992, the dinar was replaced by the "reformed" dinar; in 1993, the "October" dinar was instituted, and 1994 saw two more changes. The last of these dinars, called the *novi dinar* ("new dinar"), was often referred to as the "super dinar." The Serbian dinar issued before World War II was equal to 260,000,000,000,000,000,000,000,000,000 "super" dinars in 1994!

The same hyperinflation that affected Serbia also influenced Montenegro's monetary system. The German deutsche mark was introduced in 1999 as legal tender along with the dinar. However, in 2000 only the mark was considered legal tender, and when Germany fully adoped the euro in 2002, the euro then became the only legal tender in Montenegro.

Serbian and Montenegrin both use the Cyrillic alphabet. The letters д and дин serve as abbreviations for the dinar (динар); п for para (пара); х for heller (хелер); and н.д. for novi dinar (нови динар).

CHRONOLOGY—SERBIA

Year	Denomination	Equivalent
1994–present	new dinar (*novi dinar*)	100 para
1944–1994	Yugoslav dinar	100 para
1919–1944	Serbian dinar	100 para
1918–1919	krone	100 heller
1866–1918	Serbian dinar	100 para

CHRONOLOGY—MONTENEGRO

Year	Denomination	Equivalent
2001–present	euro	euro-cent
1999-2002	German mark	100 pfennig
1994–2000	new dinar	100 para
1944–1994	Yugoslav dinar	100 para
1919–1944	Serbian dinar	100 para
1918–1919	krone	100 heller
1910–1918	perper	100 para

ORTHOGRAPHY

Singular	Plural	Known Abbreviations and Symbols	Examples
dinar	dinars	D DIN д дин	10 д
euro	euro	€	€10
euro-cent	euro-cent	€	€0.10
heller	hellers	x.	10 x.
krone	kronen	Kr	10Kr
mark	marks	M DM	10 M
new dinar	new dinars	н.д.	10 н.д.
para	para(s)*	P par п	10 P 10 par 10 п
perper	perpera		
pfennig	pfennig	pf ₰	10pf 10₰

*Optional final s.

Seychelles (SCR)

The Seychelles were ceded to Great Britain in 1814 and were part of Mauritius until 1903. Early in the country's colonial history its monetary system was the pound sterling. By about 1878 the pound was replaced by the rupee, but divided into 100 cents instead of the customary 16 anna. In 1934 the Indian rupee was replaced with the Seychelles rupee, which continued in use after the Seychelles gained independence from Great Britain in 1976.

CHRONOLOGY

Year	Denomination	Equivalent
1934–present	Seychelles rupee	100 cents
1878–1934	rupee	100 cents

ORTHOGRAPHY

Singular	Plural	Known Abbreviations and Symbols	Examples
cent	cents	c	10c
rupee	rupees	R Sre	R10 Sre10

Sierra Leone (SLL)

Sierra Leone was established in 1808 as a British crown colony, and its monetary system was based on the imperial LSD system of pounds, shillings, and pence. The pound sterling was replaced at par with the West African pound in 1913. Following its independence in 1961, a 1964 monetary reform replaced the imperial system with a decimalized one based on the leone, meaning "lion," divisible into 100 cents.

CHRONOLOGY

Year	Denomination	Equivalent
1964–present	leone	100 cents
1913–1964	West African pound	20 shillings
	shilling	12 pence
–1913	pound sterling	20 shillings
	shilling	12 pence
	penny	4 farthings

ORTHOGRAPHY AND NUMBER

Singular	Plural	Known Abbreviations and Symbols	Examples
cent	cents	c ¢	10c 10¢
farthing	farthings	d	¼d ½d
leone	leones	Le.	Le. 10
penny	pence	d	10d
pound	pounds	£	£10
shilling	shillings	/	10/-

Singapore (SGD)

Singapore was part of the Straits Settlements, ruled by the British East India Company, from 1826 until 1858, when it became part of British India. In 1867, the Straits Settlements was made a separate crown colony, and its monetary system was based on the Straits Settlements dollar, divisible into 100 cents. In 1946, the Straits Settlements were broken up and Singapore became a crown colony. The Malayan dollar then replaced the Straits Settlements dollar at par. In 1963, Singapore became part of the Federation of Malaysia; it withdrew in 1965 and became an independent republic. In 1967, the Singaporean dollar replaced the Malayan dollar.

CHRONOLOGY

Year	Denomination	Equivalent
1967–present	Singaporean dollar	100 cents
1946–1967	Malayan dollar	100 cents
–1946	Straits Settlements dollar	100 cents

ORTHOGRAPHY AND NUMBER

Singular	Plural	Known Abbreviations and Symbols	Examples
cent	cents	c ¢	10c 10¢
dollar	dollar	$	$10

Slovakia (SKK; replaced CSK in 1993)

The former country of Czechoslovakia was formed in 1918 as a union of the Czech and Slovak regions of the Austro-Hungarian Empire. The monetary system was based on the koruna, divided into 100 halers. Koruna is both Czech and Slovak for "crown," while haler is related to the Austrian heller, whose name comes from the town now known as Schwäbisch Hall.

In 1939, Germany partitioned the Czechoslovak regions of Moravia and Bohemia as a protectorate. Slovakia declared itself independent, and the Czechoslovak koruna was replaced at par with the Slovak koruna, divisible into 100 halierov. After Germany's defeat in 1945, Slovakia was reunited with Moravia and Bohemia as Czechoslovakia, and its monetary system was again based on the Czechoslovak koruna.

In 1993, Czechoslovakia peacefully divided itself into the Czech Republic and Slovakia. In Slovakia, the Czechoslovak koruna was replaced with the Slovak koruna, divided into 100 haliers. In 2004, Slovakia joined the European Union, but it will not participate in the European Union's monetary system (Eurozone) and adopt the euro until about 2008.

The abbreviations Kč and Kčs (*korun Čsekoslovenkých*) were used in Czechoslovakia from 1918 to 1939 and from 1945 to 1993. The abbreviation Ks (*koruna Slovenska*) was used in Slovakia from 1939 to 1945, while Sk (*Slovenských korún*) has been used since 1993.

CHRONOLOGY

Year	Denomination	Equivalent
1993–present	Slovak koruna	100 halers
1945–1993	Czechoslovak koruna	100 halers
1939–1945	Slovak koruna	100 halierov
1918–1939	Czechoslovak koruna	100 halers

ORTHOGRAPHY AND NUMBER

Singular	Plural	Known Abbreviations and Symbols	Examples
halier	haliers	hal	10 hal
halier	halierov	h	10h
koruna	korun	K Kč Ks Kčs Sk	10K 10Kč 10Sk

Slovenia (SIT)

Except for a brief period from 1809 to 1814, when it was governed by France, Slovenia was part of Austria from 1335 until 1918. Slovenia's monetary system in the later half of the nineteenth century was based on the Austrian gulden and krone.

After the end of World War I, Slovenia united with Bosnia-Herzegovina, Croatia, Macedonia, Montenegro, and Serbia in 1918 to form the Kingdom of the Serbs, Croats and Slovenes. The first reform aimed at creating a national monetary unit was based on the Austrian krone, divided into 100 heller. However, it was replaced in 1919 by the dinar used in Serbia, which was divided into 100 para and equal to four kronen. This new monetary system continued after the kingdom was renamed Yugoslavia in 1929.

During World War II, Slovenian territory was split between Germany and Italy. Following the war, in 1945 Slovenia was again made part of Yugoslavia. It gained independence in 1991. In 1992, the tolar, a probable variation of the thaler (and hence "dollar"), replaced the dinar. The tolar was divided into 100 stotinov, taken from *sto*, meaning "one hundred." Although the English plural of tolar is tolars, the Slovene-language plural for the tolar can be either tolarja or tolarjev, depending on the number it is associated with. In 2004, Slovenia joined the European Union, but it will not participate in the European Union's monetary system (Eurozone) and adopt the euro until at least 2007.

CHRONOLOGY

Year	Denomination	Equivalent
1992-present	tolar	100 stotinov
1944-1992	Yugoslav dinar	100 para
1919-1944	Serbian dinar	100 para
1918-1919	krone	100 heller
1892-1918	Austrian krone	100 heller
-1892	Austrian gulden	100 kreuzer

ORTHOGRAPHY AND NUMBER

Singular	Plural	Known Abbreviations and Symbols	Examples
dinar	dinars	D DIN д дин	10D 10 дин
heller	heller		
krone	kronen	Kr	10Kr
para	para(s)*	P par п	10P 10 par 10 п
stotin	stotinov		
tolar	tolars	SIT	10 SIT

*Optional final s.

Solomon Islands (SBD)

Germany established control over the northern Solomons in 1885. In 1900 it transferred all but two islands to the British, who in 1893 had declared a protectorate over the central and southern Solomons. At the start of World War I in 1914, Australia occupied the remaining German Solomons; the League of Nations granted the area to Australia as a mandate in 1920.

The Solomons were part of the British Sterling Zone from 1893 until 1966, when they changed to a decimalized monetary system based on the Australian dollar, divisible into 100 cents. In 1975 the Australian-administered Solomons became independent as part of Papua New Guinea. In the British Solomons, the Australian dollar was replaced at par by the Solomon Islands dollar in 1977. One year later, those islands gained their independence.

CHRONOLOGY

Year	Denomination	Equivalent
1977–present	Solomon Islands dollar	100 cents
1966–1977	Australian dollar	100 cents
1920–1966	Australian pound	20 shillings
	shilling	12 pence
	penny	4 farthings
1893–1920	pound sterling	20 shillings
	shilling	12 pence
	penny	4 farthings

ORTHOGRAPHY AND NUMBER

Singular	Plural	Known Abbreviations and Symbols	Examples
cent	cents	c	10c
dollar	dollars	$ SI$	SI$10
farthing	farthings	d	¼d ½d
penny	pence	d	10d
pound	pounds	£	£10
shilling	shillings	/	10/-

South Africa (ZAR)

Since 1652, both the Dutch and the British have had strong influences in what is present-day South Africa. Dutch riksdaalders, guilders, stuivers, and duits circulated along with the British pound sterling, often called a pond — its Afrikaans equivalent. In 1910 the Boer- and British-controlled states were united, establishing the Union of South Africa. The pound sterling remained legal tender until 1920, when it was replaced at par with the South African pound, divisible into 20 shillings.

South Africa's monetary system was decimalized in 1961 when the pound was replaced with the rand, equal to 10 shillings and divisible into 100 cents. Rand means "ridge" or "margin," but probably owes its origin as a monetary unit to *Rand*, a shortened form of the Afrikaans word *Witwatersrand* ("white water's ridge"), the most productive gold-mining district in the world, which is located in the Transvaal.

CHRONOLOGY

Year	Denomination	Equivalent
1961–present	rand	100 cents
1920–1961	South African pound	20 shillings
	shilling	12 pence
	penny	4 farthings
ca. 1835–1920	pound sterling	20 shillings
	shilling	12 pence
	penny	4 farthings

ORTHOGRAPHY AND NUMBER

Singular	Plural	Known Abbreviations and Symbols	Examples
cent	cents	c	10c
farthing	farthings	d	¼d ½d
penny	pence	d	10d
pound	pounds	£ (or £)	£10
rand	rand	R	R10
shilling	shillings	s	/ 10s 10/-

Soviet Union *see* Russia

Spain (EUR; replaced ESP in 1999)

Before 1841, Spain had several monetary systems that coexisted throughout the country. There were over 130 different types of coins in circulation at the same time, by one estimation, and there had been several attempts to unify the chaos. The monetary reform instituted by Queen Isabella II in 1841 set the escudo equal to 2½ pesetas, 10 reales, and 100 decimos. When Spain joined the Latin Monetary Union in 1868, the peseta was divided into 100 centimos. In 1999 Spain joined the Euro-zone, adopting the euro, which became its sole legal tender in 2002. *See also* **European Union**.

CHRONOLOGY

Year	Denomination	Equivalent
1999–present	euro	100 euro-cent
1868–2002	peseta	100 centimos
1841–1868	escudo	2½ pesetas
	peseta	4 reales
	real	10 decimos

ORTHOGRAPHY AND NUMBER

Singular	Plural	Known Abbreviations and Symbols	Examples
centimo	centimos	c cs cto cts ctms cents	10c 10 cs 10 cts
escudo	escudos	$	10$
euro	euro	€	10€
euro-cent	euro-cent	€	0.10€
peseta	pesetas	Pta Ptas Pts	1 Pta 10 Ptas 10 Pts
real	reales	R Rs	10R 10 Rs

Sri Lanka (LKR)

Prior to 1796, Sri Lanka, formerly known as Ceylon, was ruled by the Portuguese beginning in 1505, and then by the Dutch beginning in 1658. Before it became a British crown colony in 1802, Ceylon's monetary system was based on the Dutch rijksdaalder. After 1802 the rijksdaalder was phased out, and Ceylon's monetary system was eventually based on the shilling, divisible into 12 pence and 48 farthings. In 1870, the Ceylonese rupee replaced the shilling; it was divided into 100 cents, instead of the 16 anna as in India. Ceylon gained its independence in 1948, and in 1972 the country was renamed Sri Lanka. The Ceylonese rupee was renamed the Sri Lankan rupee in 1978.

Although the solidus (/) is generally recognized as the symbol for the shilling, it has also been used to represent amounts less than one rupee, when it is preceded by either a hyphen or an equals sign. As an example, 10 cents would be written as either -/10 or =/10. It should also be noted that R and Re are the singular abbreviations for the rupee, while Rs is the plural abbreviation.

CHRONOLOGY

Year	Denomination	Equivalent
1978–present	Sri Lankan rupee	100 cents
1870–1978	Ceylonese rupee	100 cents
1802–1870	shilling	12 pence
	penny	4 farthings

ORTHOGRAPHY AND NUMBER

Singular	Plural	Known Abbreviations and Symbols	Examples
cent	cents	c /	10c -/10 =/10
farthing	farthings	d	¼d ½d
penny	pence	d	10d
rupee	rupees	R Re Rs	R1 Re1 Rs10
shilling	shillings	/	10/-

Sudan (SDD; replaced SDP in 1992)

In 1821, Egypt conquered the Sudan, then a province of the Ottoman Empire, and annexed it in 1822. In 1899, Sudan was brought under joint control, called a condominium, of Egypt and Great Britain. The monetary system was thereafter based on the Egyptian pound, divided into 100 piastres and 1,000 milliemes. In Egypt and other parts of the Arabic-speaking world, the pound is frequently referred to by its Arabic equivalent, *junyah* (جنيه).

Sudan gained its independence in 1956, but it was not until 1957 that the Sudanese pound replaced the Egyptian pound at par as the basis of its reformed monetary system. In 1992, the dinar, the Arabic form of the ancient Roman denarius, was added; it equalled 10 Sudanese pounds. In 1999, the pound was dropped as a monetary unit, keeping the dinar, equal to 100 piastres.

Sudan's modern monetary system primarily uses the Latin alphabet for its abbreviations, but it also frequently uses Arabic-language letters, such as *dal* (د) as the abbreviation for dinar (دينار); *qaf* (ق) for piastre or guerche (قروش); and *lam* (ل) for pound (i.e., libra), when combined with the Arabic-language numerals shown below:

0	1	2	3	4	5	6	7	8	9	10	50	100	500	1000
٠	١	٢	٣	٤	٥	٦	٧	٨	٩	١٠	٥٠	١٠٠	٥٠٠	١٠٠٠

CHRONOLOGY

Year	Denomination	Equivalent
1992–present	Sudanese dinar	100 piastres
1957–1999	Sudanese pound	100 piastres
	piastre	10 milliemes
ca. 1890–1957	Egyptian pound	100 piastres
	piastre	10 milliemes

ORTHOGRAPHY AND NUMBER

Singular	Plural	Known Abbreviations and Symbols	Examples
dinar	dinars	D SD د	10D 10SD د١٠
millieme	milliemes	M mms mills	10M 10mms 10 mills

Singular	Plural	Known Abbreviations and Symbols	Examples
piastre	piastres	P PT ق	10P 10PT ق۱۰
pound	pounds	LS ل	LS10 ل۱۰

Suriname (SRD; replaced SRG in 2004)

Present-day Suriname was settled by Great Britain as early as 1652. The settlement was transferred to the Dutch as a colony in 1667, and was then known as Dutch Guiana. From 1628 to 1648, Dutch Guiana, Aruba, Bonaire, Curaçao, Saba, St. Eustatius, and the southern half of St. Martin (known as St. Maarten; the northern half is French) constituted the Dutch West Indies. In 1815, the guilder, taken from the Dutch *gulden* and also known as the florin, was made divisible into 100 cents. Dutch Guiana was renamed Suriname in 1948, and the guilder was renamed the Surinamese guilder. In 2004 it was replaced with the Surinamese dollar at an exchange rate of 1,000 guilders to the dollar.

CHRONOLOGY

Year	Denomination	Equivalent
2004–present	Surinamese dollar	100 cents
1948–2004	Surinamese guilder (*gulden*) or florin	100 cents
1815–1948	Dutch West Indies guilder (*gulden*) or florin	100 cents

ORTHOGRAPHY AND NUMBER

Singular	Plural	Known Abbreviations and Symbols	Examples
cent	cents	c ct	10c 10ct
dollar	dollars	$	$10
florin	florins	F Sf *f*	F10 SF10 *f*10
guilder (*gulden*)	guilders (*gulden*)	G	10G

Swaziland (SZL)

From 1893 until its independence in 1968, Swaziland was under the administration of neighboring South Africa. During this time its monetary system was initially part of the Sterling Zone with its pound sterling, but was replaced with the South African pound in 1920. In 1961 South Africa converted its monetary system to a decimalized one, replacing the pound with the South African rand at the rate of 2 rand for every pound. In 1974, Swaziland replaced the rand at par with its own unit, the lilangeni, a word taken from the native Bantu *langeni*, meaning "money."

CHRONOLOGY

Year	Denomination	Equivalent
1974–present	lilangeni	100 cents
1961–1974	South African rand	100 cents
1920–1961	South African pound	20 shillings
	shilling	12 pence
	penny	4 farthings
1835–1920	pound sterling	20 shillings
	shilling	12 pence
	penny	4 farthings

ORTHOGRAPHY AND NUMBER

Singular	Plural	Known Abbreviations and Symbols	Examples
cent	cents	c	10c
farthing	farthings	d	¼d ½d
lilangeni	emalangeni	E	E1 E10
penny	pence	d	10d
pound	pounds	£ (or £)	£10
rand	rand	R	R10
shilling	shillings	s /	10s 10/-

Sweden (SEK)

Sweden was established as a kingdom in 1388. In 1396, the Union of Kalmar united Sweden, Denmark, and Norway under a single ruler. King Gustavus III reformed Sweden's monetary system in 1776, standardizing the riksdaler (national daler) as equal to 48 skillings and 192 öre. The daler is a variation of the German thaler and is thought by many to be the origin of the dollar, while the skilling was a variation of the British shilling. A monetary reform in 1855 introduced a decimalized system, with the riksdaler now divisible into 100 öre.

In 1873, the riksdaler was replaced with the krona, whose Swedish plural is kronor. In the same year Sweden adopted the gold standard as its requirement for joining the Scandinavian Monetary Union. The union initially included only Sweden and Denmark, with Norway joining in 1875.

Coincidentally, the monetary units of these three countries are very similar: krona (Sweden), krone (Denmark and Norway). Whatever the spelling or language, the name means "crown." The öre, like the Danish and Norwegian øre and the Icelandic eyrir, is derived from *aureus*, Latin for "gold."

CHRONOLOGY

Year	Denomination	Equivalent
1873–present	krona	100 öre
1855–1873	riksdaler	100 öre
1776–1855	riksdaler	48 skillings
	skilling	4 öre

ORTHOGRAPHY AND NUMBER

Singular	Plural	Known Abbreviations and Symbols	Examples
daler	daler		
krona	krona (*kronor*)	kr Sk SKr	10kr
öre	öre		
skilling	skillings	skill	10 skill

Switzerland (CHF)

From as early as 1291, Switzerland was a confederation of cantons with no real central government. Each canton had the right to its own monetary system. Eventually the mélange was reduced to about five systems that were based on geography. In general, the thaler was the common denominator, but the French-, German-, and Italian-speaking cantons generally adopted systems more in line with their closest neighbor. French-speaking cantons used the French sol; German-speaking cantons used the kreuzer; southern cantons bordering Italy used the soldi.

In 1803, Napoleon helped to re-establish the Swiss Federation and instituted the Swiss franc, divided into 100 centimes. Individual cantons, however, were still allowed to have their own systems. The federal constitution of 1848 reformed Switzerland's monetary system, and in 1850 the Swiss franc was the only system allowed. The franc was divisible into 10 batzen, a name thought to be derived from either bätz or betz—medieval German forerunners of *bär*, meaning "bear." The batzen was divided into 10 rappen, named after a medieval coin whose origin is thought to come from *raben*—"raven." In time, use of the batzen was avoided and the centime, also called a "cent," eventually became synonymous with the rappen.

In the German-speaking cantons, the franc is sometimes spelled frank, while residents of Italian-speaking cantons sometimes use the Italian equivalent, franco (plural, franchi).

CHRONOLOGY

Year	Denomination	Equivalent
1803–present	Swiss franc	100 centimes (rappen)
	batzen	10 centimes

ORTHOGRAPHY AND NUMBER

Singular	Plural	Known Abbreviations and Symbols	Examples
batzen	batzen	batz	10 batz
centime	centimes	c	10c
franc (*frank*)	francs (*franken*)	Fr Sfr	10Fr Sfr10
rappen	rappen	Rp	10Rp

Syria (SYP)

From 1516 to World War I, Syria was part of the Ottoman Empire. The country was occupied by French and British forces after the Ottomans' defeat. In 1920 the French instituted the Syrian pound, also referred to by its French equivalent, livre, to replace the Ottoman monetary system of the Turkish pound (also called lira), which was divided into 100 piastres or 1,000 milliemes. The piastre was also known by its colloquial name, guerche (or qirsh), and was equal to 40 para. From 1922 to its independence in 1946, Syria was a French mandate under the League of Nations. The Lebanese pound was also used as legal tender in Syria until 1948.

Letters of the Arabic alphabet often serve as abbreviations for certain monetary units. The letter *sin* (س) is the abbreviation for centime (سنتيم); *qaf* (ق or ق) or ghain (غ) for guerche or qirsh (غروش); *lam* (ل) for livre (ليرة) or pound; and the two-letter abbreviation *lam-sin* (ل.س) for the Syrian livre. These abbreviations are often used with the Arabic-language numerals below:

0	1	2	3	4	5	6	7	8	9	10	50	100	500	1000
٠	١	٢	٣	٤	٥	٦	٧	٨	٩	١٠	٥٠	١٠٠	٥٠٠	١٠٠٠

In addition to being the abbreviation for piastre, the letter p also serves as a decimal point between the piastre and the smaller centime.

CHRONOLOGY

Year	Denomination	Equivalent
1920–present	Syrian pound	100 piastres
	piastre	100 centimes
-1920	Turkish pound	100 piastres
	piastre	10 milliemes, 40 paras

ORTHOGRAPHY AND NUMBER

Singular	Plural	Known Abbreviations and Symbols	Examples
centime	centimes	c p س	0p10 س١٠
guerche	guerches	غ	غ١٠

Singular	Plural	Known Abbreviations and Symbols	Examples
millieme	milliemes		
para	paras		
piastre	piastres	ق ب p	١٠ق 10p
pound (*livre*)	pounds (*livres*)	ل.س £Syr. ل LS L	ل.س 10 .10ل 10L

Taiwan (TWD)

Prior 1949, Taiwan was part of mainland China. Monetary units during the reign of the emperors included the tael, cash, mace, and candareen — all based on specific weights of silver. In the late nineteenth and early twentieth centuries, the "Chinese dollar" was the popular English-language term for the yuan (圓), a larger silver-dollar-sized coin. Also spelled yüan, it means "round, a circle," i.e., a coin. Like the dollar, the yuan was divided into 100 fen (分), or cents. *See also* **China**.

In 1949, following the Communist revolution that drove the Nationalists to the nearby island of Taiwan, the yuan was replaced with the New Taiwan dollar, divisible into 100 cents. Undoubtedly this change was meant to underscore Taiwan's separation and independence from the Communist mainland.

Although Taiwan primarily uses the numerals 0 through 9 with Chinese ideographs of its monetary units, pre-Nationalist documents frequently combined the units with the Chinese numbers shown below:

	0	1	2	3	4	5	6	7	8	9	10	50	100	500	1000
Official Form		壹	貳	叁	肆	伍	陸	柒	捌	玖	拾	拾伍	佰	佰伍	仟壹
Common Form	零	一	二	三	四	五	六	七	八	九	十	十五	百	百五	千

CHRONOLOGY

Year	Denomination	Equivalent
1949–present	New Taiwan dollar	100 cents
1897–1949	Chinese dollar (*yuan*)	100 cents (*fen*)
–1897	tael	10 mace
	mace	10 candareen

ORTHOGRAPHY AND NUMBER

Singular	Plural	Known Abbreviations and Symbols	Examples
candareen	candareens	Cn	10 Cn
cent	cents	Ct	10 Ct

Singular	Plural	Known Abbreviations and Symbols	Examples
dollar	dollars	$ NT$	$10 NT$10
fen	fen	分	10分 分十
mace	mace		
tael	taels		
yuan	yuan	Y 圆	Y10 10圆 圆十

Tajikistan (TJS; replaced TJR in 2000)

From about 1868 Tajikistan was part of czarist Russia; from 1922 to 1929 it was part of the Uzbek Soviet Socialist Republic. In 1929, it was proclaimed the Tadzikh Soviet Socialist Republic, and its monetary system was based on the Russian ruble and kopeck.

Following its independence in 1991, like most of the former Soviet republics, Tajik-istan continued for a time the use of the Russian ruble. In 1995 it was replaced with the Tajikistani ruble, divided into 100 tenge. The tenge is the same as the monetary unit of Kazakhstan and Turkmenistan. The tenge was also used in the former emirate of Bukhara and the khanate of Khira (a.k.a. Kwarezm), which are now in Uzbek-istan.

To strengthen the country's banking system, in 2001 Tajikistan adopted the somoni, named in honor of Ismoili Somoni (847–907 A.D.), the first Tajikistani emperor and founder of the early Tajikistani nation. The somoni is divisible into 100 dirams, a pos-sible variant of the Arabic dirham. the somoni replaced the Tajikistani ruble at an exchange rate of one somoni for 1,000 rubles.

The transliteration of both Tajik and Russian into English is not always a simple matter, and one often finds variations in spelling for the monetary units, such as tenge and tange. Tajikistan's monetary units, with their Cyrillic spellings, are:

Unit	Singular	Plural
diram	дирам	дирам
kopeck	копейк	копейки
ruble	рубль[1]	рублей, рубля[3]
	рубл[2]	рубл
tenge	тенга	тенга
somoni	сомонй	сомонй

[1]Russian; [2]Tajiki; [3]Russian plural form is grammatically dependent

Although the Tajiki-language singular and plural spellings for diram (дирам) are the same, Tajikistan's central bank nonetheless gives the English plural as "dirams."

CHRONOLOGY

Year	Denomination	Equivalent
2001–present	somoni	100 dirams
1995–2000	Tajikistani ruble	100 tenge
–1995	Russian ruble	100 kopecks

ORTHOGRAPHY AND NUMBER

Singular	Plural	Known Abbreviations and Symbols	Examples
diram	dirams		
kopeck	kopecks	к коп	10к 10 коп
ruble	rubles	руб	10 руб
somoni	somoni	с	10с
tenge	tenge		

Tanzania (TZS)

Tanzania is the result of the 1964 merger of two British-controlled territories, Zanzibar and Tanganyika. Those territories, along with Kenya and Uganda, comprised an administrative region known as British East Africa.

Starting in 1885, present-day Tanzania was part of the German East Africa protectorate, and its monetary system was the German East African (Deutsch Ostafrika) rupie. The rupie, which was on par with the rupee of British India, was divisible into 16 anna and 64 pesa, the German equivalent of the Indian paisa. In 1906, a monetary reform decimalized the rupie, dividing it into 100 cents.

During World War I, Great Britain captured part of German East Africa, and incorporated its captured territory into British East Africa. The German East African rupie was then replaced at par with the British East African rupee, divisible into 100 cents. The rupee was replaced in 1920 with the florin, equal to two shillings and also divisible into 100 cents; the florin in turn was replaced by the East African shilling in 1921. In 1922 the League of Nations gave Britain a mandate over the region, which was then named Tanganyika.

Zanzibar had once been controlled by Portugal, but fell to Omani Arabs in the early eighteenth century. In time, Zanzibar broke away from Oman, and the area was made a British protectorate in 1890. In 1908, the monetary system was based on the Zanzibar rupee, divided into 100 cents and at par with the rupee of British India. In 1936, the rupee was replaced with the East African shilling.

In 1964, Zanzibar and Tanganyika formed a political union called the United Republic of Tanganyika and Zanzibar. The union was renamed the United Republic of Tanzania six months later. Tanzania continued to use the East African shilling until 1967, when it was replaced with the Tanzanian shilingi, divided into 100 senti. The shilingi and senti are Kiswahili (i.e., Swahili) equivalents of shilling and cent.

CHRONOLOGY—TANGANYIKA

Year	Denomination	Equivalent
1967–present	Tanzanian shilingi	100 senti
1921–1967	East African shilling	100 cents
1920–1921	British East African florin	2 shillings, 100 cents
1918–1920	British East African rupee	100 cents
1906–1918	German East African rupie	100 cents
1890–1906	German East African rupie	16 anna
	anna	4 pesa

CHRONOLOGY—ZANZIBAR

Year	Denomination	Equivalent
1967–present	Tanzanian shilingi	100 senti
1936–1967	East African shilling	100 cents
1908–1936	Zanzibar rupee	100 cents

ORTHOGRAPHY

Singular	Plural	Known Abbreviations and Symbols	Examples
anna	anna(s)*		
cent	cents	=/	=/05
florin	florins		
pesa	pesa		
rupie	rupien		
senti	senti		
shilingi	shilingi	TSh$	TSh$10
shilling	shillings	/= /-	10/= 10/-

*Optional final s.

Thailand (THB)

Before 1939, present-day Thailand was known as Siam. It is one of the few countries never colonized by any of the European powers. Siam's monetary system was long based on the tical, which was a weight equal to approximately 15 grams of silver. The tical, which was also referred to as the baht, was divided into four salung and 64 att (also spelled at), in addition to many other fractional units. The monetary system was decimalized in 1897, making the tical divisible into four salung and 100 satang. About 1926 the tical was officially renamed the baht.

Besides the numerals 0 through 9, Thailand often uses the Khmer numerals below:

0	1	2	3	4	5	6	7	8	9	10	50	100	500	1000
๐	๑	๒	๓	๔	๕	๖	๗	๘	๙	๑๐	๕๐	๑๐๐	๕๐๐	๑๐๐๐

when combined with the Thai-language units baht or tical (บาท), satang (ลตางด้), and their abbreviations.

CHRONOLOGY

Year	Denomination	Equivalent
ca. 1926–present	baht	100 satang
1897–c1926	tical (or *baht*)	4 salung
	salung	25 satang
–1897	tical (or *baht*)	4 salung
	salung	16 att

ORTHOGRAPHY

Singular	Plural	Known Abbreviations and Symbols	Examples
att (or at)	att (or at)		
baht	baht	B Bt Bht ฿ บท	๑๐ บท
salung	salung		
satang	satang	ST ลต	10 ST ๑๐ ลต
tical	ticals		

Timor Leste (USD; replaced codes IDR and TPE)

East Timor, also known Timor Leste, is one of the world's newest countries. It became a Portuguese colony in 1642, and its monetary system was based on the Portuguese milréis and the pataca. The pataca, a possible corruption of an Arabic word for the Spanish peso, was divided into 100 avos — meaning "fractional parts." In 1959, Portugal replaced the pataca at par with the escudo.

In 1975 East Timor unilaterally declared its independence but was immediately occupied by Indonesia and annexed by it several months later. The Indonesian rupiah, divided into 100 sen, replaced the Portuguese escudo. The annexation was rescinded in 1999, and East Timor became independent, adopting the name Timor Leste in 2002. The monetary system was changed in 2000 and is currently based on the U.S. dollar, even though the Indonesian rupiah and the Australian dollar also are used.

The dollar sign ($) is used as a decimal point between escudos and the smaller centavos, as well as between U.S. dollars and cents. As an example, 5$10 equals either 5.10 escudos or 5.10 dollars.

CHRONOLOGY

Year	Denomination	Equivalent
2000–present	United States dollar	100 cents
1975–1999	Indonesian rupiah	100 sen

Year	Denomination	Equivalent
1959–1975	Portuguese escudo	100 centavos
1894–1959	pataca	100 avos
–1894	Portuguese milréis	1,000 réis

ORTHOGRAPHY

Singular	Plural	Known Abbreviations and Symbols	Examples
avo	avos	A	10A
cent	cents	$	0$10
centavo	centavos	$	0$10
dollar	dollars	$	10$
escudo	escudos	$	10$
pataca	patacas	P ptc ptcs	10P 10 ptc
rupiah	rupiahs	Rp	Rp10
sen	sen		

Togo (XOF)

For much of its colonial history, Togo has been under the control of several European counties. From 1844 until 1914 it was under suzerainty as German Togoland, and its monetary system was based on the mark, which was divided into 100 pfennig. From 1914 to 1960 it was under the joint control of France and Great Britain, first as mandates authorized by the League of Nations in 1922, and from 1946 as UN trusteeships.

The British portion, participating in the Sterling Zone, was then known as British Togoland. This was part of an administrative area known as British West Africa, which was administered from the Gold Coast. In 1957 British Togoland merged with the Gold Coast and became the independent nation of Ghana.

French Togo, a member of the Franc Zone, achieved independence in 1960. Togo's current monetary system is based on the Communauté Financière Africaine (African Financial Community, CFA) franc, a monetary union of former French colonies in Africa. *See also* **West African States**.

CHRONOLOGY

Year	Denomination	Equivalent
1958–present	CFA franc	100 centimes
1916–1958	franc	100 centimes
1914–1916	shilling	12 pence
1897–1914	mark	100 pfennig

ORTHOGRAPHY AND NUMBER

Singular	Plural	Known Abbreviations and Symbols	Examples
centime	centimes	c	10c
franc	francs	F Fr CFA F	10F 10Fr
mark	marks	M	10M
penny	pence	d	10d
pfennig	pfennig	Pf	10 Pf
shilling	shillings	/	10/-

Tonga (TOP)

Once known as the Friendly Islands, Tonga was long part of the Sterling Zone and under British protection since 1900. It gained independence in 1970. In 1967, the monetary system was decimalized; the pa'anga, meaning "money," was divisible into 100 seniti (an alternative form of "cent").

CHRONOLOGY

Year	Denomination	Equivalent
1967–present	pa'anga	100 seniti
ca. 1880–1967	Tongan pound	20 shillings
	shilling	12 pence

ORTHOGRAPHY AND NUMBER

Singular	Plural	Known Abbreviations and Symbols	Examples
pa'anga	pa'anga	$ T$	$10 T$10
penny	pence	d	10d
pound	pounds	£	£10
seniti	seniti	s	10s
shilling	shillings	/ /s	10/- 10/s

Trinidad and Tobago (TTD)

Trinidad was originally claimed for Spain in 1498 by Christopher Columbus during his third voyage. It was established as a British colony in 1802, when Spain formally ceded it to Great Britain. Tobago was originally named "Bella Forma," but later became known as Tobago — a possible corruption of "tobacco." By 1814, it had been successively the colonial possession of Spain, Great Britain, Holland, and France. With

Napoleon's defeat, Tobago was ceded to Britain. As British colonies, the islands used the pound sterling.

The two colonies were unified in 1899 and the Trinidad and Tobago dollar, divisible into 100 cents, replaced the pound. However, the pound remained legal tender until 1935, when the British West Indies dollar replaced the Trinidad and Tobago dollar. From 1958 until 1962, when it gained its independence from Great Britain, Trinidad and Tobago was a member of the Federation of the West Indies, a self-governing federal state of 12 British colonial island territories whose capital was the Trinidadian city Port of Spain. In 1965 the British West Indies dollar was replaced with the re-issuance of the Trinidad and Tobago dollar. *See also* **East Caribbean States.**

CHRONOLOGY

Year	Denomination	Equivalent
1965–present	Trinidad and Tobago dollar	100 cents
1935–1965	British West Indies dollar	100 cents
1899–1935	Trinidad and Tobago dollar	100 cents
ca. 1838–1935	pound sterling	20 shillings
	shilling	12 pence

ORTHOGRAPHY AND NUMBER

Singular	Plural	Known Abbreviations and Symbols	Examples
cent	cents	c ¢	10c 10¢
dollar	dollars	$ TT$ BWI$	$10 BWI$10
penny	pence	d	10d
pound	pounds	£ (or £)	£10
shilling	shillings	/	10/-

Tunisia (TND)

Once part of the Ottoman Empire, Tunisia was established as a French protectorate in 1881. It became independent in 1956. During that time it was a member of the Franc Zone, with the Tunisian franc divided into 100 centimes. In 1958, the Tunisian dinar, an Arabic form of the ancient Roman denarius, replaced 1,000 francs; it was divided into 1,000 millimes.

Letters of the Arabic alphabet are often used as abbreviations of certain monetary units. The letter *dal* (د) is the abbreviation for dinar (دينار); *fey* for franc (فرنكا); and *mim* (م) for millim (مليم). They are used with either the numerals 0 through 9 or the Arabic-language numerals below:

0	1	2	3	4	5	6	7	8	9	10	50	100	500	1000
٠	١	٢	٣	٤	٥	٦	٧	٨	٩	١٠	٥٠	١٠٠	٥٠٠	١٠٠٠

CHRONOLOGY

Year	Denomination	Equivalent
1958–present	Tunisian dinar	1,000 millimes
1881–1958	Tunisian franc	100 centimes

ORTHOGRAPHY AND NUMBER

Singular	Plural	Known Abbreviations and Symbols	Examples
centime	centimes	c	10c
dinar	dinars	D TD د	10D 10د
franc	francs	F ف	10F 10Fف
millime	millimes	m م	10m 10م

Turkey (TRL)

Present-day Turkey was the center of the Ottoman Empire from 1473 until its 1917 defeat in World War I. Its monetary system was based on the lira, also referred to as the livre or pound. The lira was divided into 100 piastres, also called kurus (Turkish, kuruş). The piastre was divided into 40 para, derived from the Arabic *bara* (باره), meaning "silver," and the para was divided into three aspers (or akce). Besides the piastre, para, and asper, the lira was also divided into 16⅔ altilik, 20 beshlik, 30⅓ utuzlik, 40 yuzlik, and 50 ikilik, all of which were mostly used in other regions of the empire such as Albania.

The sultanate was abolished in 1922, and a 1926 monetary reform changed the Turkish lira to a decimalized system divided into 100 kurus. Because the lira has lost substantial purchasing power over the years, the kurus is essentially worthless today and is no longer used in everyday transactions.

CHRONOLOGY

Year	Denomination	Equivalent
1926–present	Turkish lira	100 kurus
–1926	Turkish pound (*lira*)	100 piastres
	piastre	40 para
	para	3 aspers

ORTHOGRAPHY AND NUMBER

Singular	Plural	Known Abbreviations and Symbols	Examples
asper	aspers		
kurus (*kuruş*)	kurus (*kuruş*)	K Kr Krs	10K 10Kr 10Krs

Singular	Plural	Known Abbreviations and Symbols	Examples
lira (*lirası*)	liras	TL	10TL
para	para(s)*	P Pa ب	10P 10Pa ب ١٠
piastre	piastres		

*Optional final s.

Turkmenistan (TMM)

From about 1863 Turkmenistan, then known as Turkistan, was part of czarist Russia. It became the Turkistan Autonomous Soviet Socialist Republic in 1922 and in 1924 was proclaimed the Turkmen Soviet Socialist Republic. Its monetary system was based on the ruble and kopeck.

Following its independence in 1991, like most of the former Soviet republics, Turkmenistan continued the use of the Russian ruble. In 1993 the ruble was replaced with the manat (also written as man'at), equal to 500 rubles and divisible into 100 tennesi.

The manat is also the major unit of Azerbaijan's monetary system, and is similar to "maneti," the Georgian term for the ruble. Manat was the name of the goddess of fate and destiny in pre-Islamic Arabia, and was also the name of the daughter of Allah.

CHRONOLOGY

Year	Denomination	Equivalent
1993–present	manat	100 tennesi
1991-1993	ruble	100 kopecks
–1991	Russian ruble	100 kopecks

ORTHOGRAPHY AND NUMBER

Singular	Plural	Known Abbreviations and Symbols	Examples
kopeck	kopecks	k коп	10k 10 коп
manat	manat	M	10M
ruble	rubles	R руб	10 руб
tennesi	tennesi		

Turks and Caicos Islands (USD)

Presently, the Turks and Caicos Islands are an overseas territory of Great Britain, but they were a Jamaican colony beginning in 1873. In 1920, the Jamaican pound replaced the pound sterling at par, and the British West Indies dollar was also legal tender beginning in 1951. In 1962, the Turks and Caicos Islands assumed the status of a separate crown colony, separating from Jamaica when that island gained its independence. The United States dollar became the official currency of the islands in 1969 though use of the pound sterling, which had been in effect since about 1850, continued until 1971.

CHRONOLOGY

Year	Denomination	Equivalent
1969–present	United States dollar	100 cents
1951–1971	British West Indies dollar	100 cents
1920–1969	Jamaican pound	20 shillings
	shilling	12 pence
	penny	4 farthings
ca. 1850–1919	pound sterling	20 shillings
	shilling	12 pence
	penny	4 farthings

ORTHOGRAPHY AND NUMBER

Singular	Plural	Known Abbreviations and Symbols	Examples
cent	cents	c ¢	10c 10¢
dollar	dollars	$	$10
farthing	farthings	d	¼d ½d
penny	pence	d	10d
pound	pounds	£ (or £)	£10
shilling	shillings	/	10/-

Tuvalu (AUD)

In 1892, Great Britain annexed the Gilbert Islands group as a protectorate, and in 1916 it became part of the Gilbert and Ellice Islands colony. As a British colony, it used the Australian pound until 1966, when the pound was replaced by the decimalized Australian dollar. In 1976 the Ellice Islands seceded from the colony and was renamed Tuvalu; it gained its independence in 1978. In 1979 the Gilbert Islands were given complete independence by Great Britain, and the country was renamed Kiribati.

CHRONOLOGY

Year	Denomination	Equivalent
1966–present	Australian dollar	100 cents
1892–1966	pound	20 shillings
	shilling	12 pence

ORTHOGRAPHY AND NUMBER

Singular	Plural	Known Abbreviations and Symbols	Examples
cent	cents	c	10c
dollar	dollars	$	$10
penny	pence	d	10d
pound	pounds	£ (or ₤)	£10
shilling	shillings	/	10/-

Uganda (UGX; replaced UGS in 1987)

Uganda was a British protectorate beginning in 1894. At the time much of Uganda's money consisted of cowrie shells. Because of the British influence and its proximity to the Indian subcontinent, in 1895 Uganda's monetary system became based on the Indian rupee, divided into 16 anna and 64 pice. In 1906, the rupee was decimalized and divided into 100 cents. The East African rupee was replaced with the East African florin in 1920. Two years later the florin was replaced by the East African shilling, also divisible into 100 cents.

Uganda gained its independence from Great Britain in 1962; in 1967 the East African shilling was renamed the Uganda shilling, which is known by its Swahili name, shilingi.

CHRONOLOGY

Year	Denomination	Equivalent
1967–present	Uganda shilling	100 cents
1921–1967	East African shilling	100 cents
1920–1921	East African florin	100 cents
1906–1920	East African rupee	100 cents
1895–1906	Indian rupee	16 anna
	anna	4 pice

ORTHOGRAPHY AND NUMBER

Singular	Plural	Known Abbreviations and Symbols	Examples
anna	anna(s)*	A As	1A 10As
cent	cents	c	10c
florin	florins		
penny	pence	d	10d
pice	pice		
rupee	rupees	R Rs	10R 10Rs
shilling	shillings	Shs /	10/-

*Optional final s.

Ukraine (UAH)

From the thirteenth century until 1918, different parts of Ukraine were subjugated by various foreign powers. The monetary system was the Russian ruble, divided into 100 kopecks. In 1918, a Bolshevik government was established in Ukraine; it introduced the karbovanets, equal to two grivna and 200 shahiv. In 1922, Ukraine was one of the four founding republics of the Soviet Union, and its monetary system again became based on the ruble, at par with the karbovanets — whose name probably comes from the Ukrainian *karb* (карб), meaning "notch, incision, or tally."

Ukraine unilaterally declared its independence from the Soviet Union in 1991 and introduced a transitional monetary system, a karbovanets coupon at par with the ruble. The transition ended in 1996, when Ukraine replaced the coupon with the hryvnia. The hryvnia, equal to 100,000 coupons, is divisible into 100 kopiykas.

The transliteration of Ukrainian into English is not always a simple matter, and one often finds variations in spelling for the monetary units; rouble for ruble, kopec or kopek for kopeck, and shagiv for shahiv. Ukraine's primary monetary units, with their Cyrillic spellings, are:

Unit	Singular	Plural
grivna, griven	гривна	гривень
hryvnia, hryvni	гривня	гривні, гривень[1]
karbovanets, karbovantsiv	карбованец	карбованців
kopeck (kopec, kopek)	копейка	копейки, копеек[1]
kopiyka, kopiyok	копійка	копійок
ruble (rouble), rublya	рубль	рублей, рубля[2]
shahiv (shagiv)	шагів	шагів

[1]Ukrainian plural form is grammatically dependent; [2]Russian plural form is grammatically dependent

CHRONOLOGY

Year	Denomination	Equivalent
1996–present	hryvnia	100 kopiykas
1992–1996	karbovanets coupon	none
1923–1992	Russian ruble	100 kopecks
1918–1923	karbovanets	2 grivna
	grivna	100 shahiv
–1917	Russian ruble	100 kopecks

ORTHOGRAPHY

Singular	Plural	Known Abbreviations and Symbols	Examples
grivna	grivna	грн	10 грн
hryvnia	hryvnia	грн	10 грн

Singular	Plural	Known Abbreviations and Symbols	Examples
karbovanets	karbovanets	крб	10 крб
kopeck	kopecks	к коп	10к 10 коп
kopiyka	kopiykas	к	10к
ruble	rubles	р руб	10р 10 руб
shahiv	shahiv	ш	10ш

United Arab Emirates (AED)

The United Arab Emirates (UAE) is a federation of seven independent states which were formerly known as either Trucial Oman or the Trucial States and were under the protection of Great Britain from 1892 to 1971. Its seven member states are Abu Dhabi, Ajman, Dubai, Fujairah, Ras al-Khaima, Sharjah, and Umm al-Qaiwain. Because of this British influence and their proximity to the Indian subcontinent, the Trucial States used the established Indian rupees, anna, and paise as legal tender. In 1959 a special currency unit, the Persian Gulf rupee, officially known as the "external rupee," was issued; it was equal to 100 naye paise. In 1966, the Persian Gulf rupee was replaced temporarily with the Saudi riyal, divided into 100 dirhams. However, Abu Dhabi refused this change and instead adopted the use of the Bahraini dinar, divided into 1,000 fils. Later that year the other six Trucial States completed their transition to the Dubai and Qatar riyal, divisible into 100 dirhams.

In 1971, the Trucial States joined with Bahrain and Qatar to attempt the formation of the Federation of Arab Emirates. The attempt failed, and Bahrain and Qatar then declared their independence. The six states of Abu Dhabi, Ajman, Dubai, Fujairah, Sharjah, and Umm al-Qaiwain formed the UAE in late December 1971. Ras al-Khaima joined the UAE two months later. The UAE dinar, divided into 1,000 fils, was then made the basis of the monetary system. In 1973, the UAE dirham, divided into 100 fils, replaced the dinar.

The former Trucial States and the UAE use both the Latin and Arabic alphabets for their monetary abbreviations. The Arabic letters *beh* (ب) for naya paisa and *dal* (د) for dirham (درهم), plus the Arabic words riyal (ريال) and fils (فلس), are used with either the numerals 0 through 9 or the Arabic-language numerals shown below:

0	1	2	3	4	5	6	7	8	9	10	50	100	500	1000
٠	١	٢	٣	٤	٥	٦	٧	٨	٩	١٠	٥٠	١٠٠	٥٠٠	١٠٠٠

CHRONOLOGY

Year	Denomination	Equivalent
1973–present	UAE dirham	100 fils
1971–1973	UAE dinar	1,000 fils
1966–1972	riyal (Ras al-Khaima only)	100 dirhams
1966–1971	riyal (Ajman, Dubai, Fujairah, Sharjah, and Umm al-Qaiwain)	100 dirhams

Year	Denomination	Equivalent
1966–1971	Bahraini dinar (Abu Dhabi only)	1,000 fils
1959–1966	Persian Gulf rupee	100 naye paise

ORTHOGRAPHY

Singular	Plural	Known Abbreviations and Symbols	Examples
dinars	dinars		
dirham	dirhams	Dhs dh د	10dh ١٠ د
fils	fils		
naya paisa	naye paise	NP ب	10 NP ١٠ب
rupee	rupees	R Rls	10R 10Rls
riyal	riyals	ريال	١٠ ريال

United Kingdom *see* Great Britain

United States (USD)

Before 1792, a variety of coins were legal tender in the United States and the earlier 13 colonies: Spanish dollars, Maria Theresa thalers, and British shillings. The dollar, divided into 100 cents, is perhaps one of the world's most recognized monetary units, along with the pound, franc, and now the euro. The United States dollar is the legal tender, not only in the 50 states but also in the various U.S.-controlled territories: American Samoa, Caroline Islands, Guam, Johnston Island, Marshall Islands, Midway Islands, Northern Mariana Islands, Puerto Rico, Virgin Islands, and Wake Island.

A number of countries with no real monetary systems of their own have declared the United States dollar as their sole legal tender. These include the British Virgin Islands, Micronesia, Palau, Panama, Timor Leste, and the Turks and Caicos Islands. In addition, countries such as Ecuador, El Salvador, Guatemala, and Haiti have adopted the dollar, abandoning their own systems.

The name "dollar" and the dollar sign ($) are not unique to the United States, and there are many stories about their origins. The most often quoted account for the origin of the dollar is that the name thaler came from the silver for coins mined at Joachimstal (or St. Joachim's Valley), now Jáchymov in Bohemia of the present-day Czech Republic. Other coins based on the thaler evolved, with variations on the name such as daalder (the Netherlands), dalar (Poland), and daler (Sweden). Pieces of eight, also known as the Spanish dollar, and the Maria Theresa thaler were legal tender during American colonial times. This common useage is probably the most logical reason for adopting the name as the basis of the United States' monetary system. In modern times there have been several variations used in other countries, such as the tala (Samoa), toea (Papua New Guinea), and tolar (Slovenia).

The well-known dollar sign symbol, the letter *S* with one or two vertical or sloping bars through it, has also been used in some countries, as the monetary symbol for the peso and escudo and for Ecuador's sucre. Countries that use the dollar sign to represent their own dollar generally place the sign before the dollar amount, e.g., $10, as is done in the United States. However, the dollar sign is sometimes used as the equivalent of a decimal point (e.g., 10$50) between pesos and centesimos or between escudos and centavos. One theory as to the symbol's origin is that it represents a contraction of the pieces of eight, a peso, which once might have been rendered as /8/.

There are also common nicknames given to a variety of U.S. coins that are multiples of its basic monetary units of dollar and cent. These include: trime (silver 3-cent piece), nickel (5 cents), dime (spelled disme in 1792, 10 cents), quarter (also "two bits," 25 cents), eagle ($10 gold piece), and double eagle ($20 gold piece).

CHRONOLOGY

Year	Denomination	Equivalent
1792–present	United States dollar	100 cents

ORTHOGRAPHY AND NUMBER

Singular	Plural	Known Abbreviations and Symbols	Examples
cent	cents	c ¢	10c 10¢
dollar	dollars	$	$10

Uruguay (UYU)

Uruguay was a Spanish colony until 1821, when it was conquered by the Portuguese of Brazil. Its monetary system was based on that of its colonial rulers — first the Spanish escudo and then the Portuguese milréis. Uruguay gained its independence from Brazil in 1825, but was then incorporated into the United Provinces of Rio de la Plata under Argentina's control. It seceded from the United Provinces in 1828 and declared itself a republic in 1830.

After independence, Uruguay used the Spanish peso as its monetary system until 1862, when it adopted the peso fuerte ("strong peso"), which was divisible into 100 centesimos. Inflation was common in South America, and a 1975 monetary reform replaced the peso fuerte with the nuevo peso, equal to 100 pesos fuertes. Further inflationary pressure caused the nuevo peso to be replaced in 1993 with the peso uruguayo, equal to 1,000 nuevos pesos.

CHRONOLOGY

Year	Denomination	Equivalent
1993–present	peso uruguayo	100 centesimos
1975–1993	new peso (*nuevo peso*)	100 centesimos
1862–1975	peso fuerte	100 centesimos

ORTHOGRAPHY

Singular	Plural	Known Abbreviations and Symbols	Examples
centesimo	centesimos	c cts	10c 10cts
new peso (*nuevo peso*)	new pesos (*nuevos pesos*)	N$	N$10
peso	pesos	$	$10

Uzbekistan (UZS)

Beginning about 1865, present-day Uzbekistan was part of czarist Russia; it became part of the Turkistan Autonomous Soviet Socialist Republic in 1921. In 1924, Turkistan was broken up, creating separate Turkmen and Uzbek Soviet Socialist Republics. The monetary system was based on the ruble and kopeck.

Following its independence in 1991, like most of the former Soviet republics, Uzbekistan temporarily continued the use of the Russian ruble. In 1993 it reformed its own system and introduced a transitional *kuponga kartchka* (Uzbek: купонга картчка), or "control coupon." In 1994, the transition was completed: the som was introduced, equal to 1,000 coupons and divided into 100 tiyin, a monetary unit of both Kazakhstan and Kyrgyzstan.

The transliteration of both Uzbek (or Uigur) and Russian into English is not always a simple matter, and one often finds variations in spelling for the monetary units: som, sum, or soum, and tiyin, tiyn, or tyjyn. Uzbekistan's monetary units, with their Cyrillic spellings, are:

Unit	Singular	Plural
kopeck	копей	копейки
ruble	рубль	рублей, рубля*
som	сўм	сўм
tiyin	тийин	тийин

*Russian plural form is grammatically dependent

Note that the Uzbek/Uigur Cyrillic spellings for som (сўм) and tiyin (тийин) are both different from the Kyrgyz spellings (сом; тыйын).

CHRONOLOGY

Year	Denomination	Equivalent
1994–present	som	100 tiyin
1993	som coupons	none
1924–1992	Russian ruble	100 kopecks

ORTHOGRAPHY AND NUMBER

Singular	Plural	Known Abbreviations and Symbols	Examples
kopeck	kopecks	к	10к
ruble	rubles	руб	10 руб
som	som	с	10с
tiyin	tiyin	т	10т

Vanuatu (VUV)

The New Hebrides, now known as Vanuatu, was established in 1824 as a British protectorate but was later governed by a joint British-French commission. After the Anglo-French New Hebrides Condominium was established in 1906, both the French franc and the pound sterling were legal tender until 1941 and 1940 respectively. The Australian pound was also legal tender from 1935 until 1941, when it and the French franc were replaced with the New Hebrides franc.

Beginning in 1945, the monetary system was on par with on the CFP franc, issued by the Communauté Financière Pacificienne (Pacific Financial Community), a monetary union of the New Hebrides, French Polynesia, New Caledonia, and Wallis & Futuna Islands — all French colonies in the Pacific. This was similar to the system of the CFA franc that is the basis of the monetary system of many former French colonies in central and western Africa. After Vanuatu gained its independence in 1980, a monetary reform replaced the franc in 1981 with the vatu, divisible into 100 centimes.

CHRONOLOGY

Year	Denomination	Equivalent
1981–present	vatu	100 centimes
1941–1981	New Hebrides franc	100 centimes
1935–1941	Australian pound	20 shillings
	shilling	12 pence
ca. 1906–1940	pound sterling	20 shillings
	shilling	12 pence
ca. 1906–1941	French franc	100 centimes

ORTHOGRAPHY AND NUMBER

Singular	Plural	Known Abbreviations and Symbols	Examples
centime	centimes	c	10c
franc	francs	F FNH	10F 10 FNH
penny	pence	d	10d
pound	pounds	£ (or ₤)	£10
shilling	shillings	/	10/-
vatu	vatu	VT	10VT

Vatican City (EUR; replaced ITL in 1999)

A large part of Italy, known as the States of the Church or Pontifical (i.e., Papal) States, was once under the direct rule of the pope. Prior to 1870, there were 18 papal states, many with their own monetary system. In 1870, nearly all the territory, including Rome, was annexed to a unified Italy. The monetary systems of these papal states, including the Vatican, were replaced with the Italian lira, divisible into 100 centesimi.

The 1929 Lateran Treaty recognized the full and independent sovereignty of the pope in Vatican City. In 1999 Italy joined the Eurozone, adopting the euro, which became its sole legal tender in 2002. The Vatican followed suit. *See also* **European Union.**

CHRONOLOGY

Year	Denomination	Equivalent
1999–present	euro	100 euro-cent
1870–2002	Italian lira	100 centesimi

ORTHOGRAPHY

Singular	Plural	Known Abbreviations and Symbols	Examples
centesimo	centesimi	c cent	10c 10 cent
euro	euro	€	€10
euro-cent	euro-cent	€	€0.10
lira	lire	L.	L.10

Venezuela (VEB)

After years as a Spanish colony, present-day Venezuela declared its independence in 1811 but did not fully secure it until 1821. Subsequently it was incorporated into a confederation known as Grand Granada or Greater Colombia until 1830. While a Spanish colony, and for a short period following independence, Venezuela retained the escudo, equal to 16 reales, of its colonial ruler. In 1843, the escudo was replaced by two pesos, divisible into 100 centavos.

In 1871, the venezolano, a name derived from that of the country, replaced the peso at par; it was divisible into 100 centavos. In 1879 the venezolano was replaced by the bolívar, named in honor of Simón Bolívar, known as El Liberator ("The Liberator"), who won independence for Bolivia, Panama, Colombia, Ecuador, Peru, and Venezuela. The bolívar is divided into 100 centimos.

CHRONOLOGY

Year	Denomination	Equivalent
1879–present	bolívar	100 centimos
1871–1879	venezolano	100 centavos
1843–1871	peso	100 centavos
–1843	escudo	16 reales

ORTHOGRAPHY AND NUMBER

Singular	Plural	Known Abbreviations and Symbols	Examples
bolívar	bolívares	B Bs	B10 Bs10
centavo	centavos		
centimo	centimos	c	10c
escudo	escudos		
peso	pesos		
real	reales	R Rs	10R 10 Rs
venezolano	venezolanos		

Vietnam (VND)

Present-day Vietnam, along with Cambodia and Laos, was once part of French Indochina, which was established in 1887. Its monetary system was based on the French Indochinese piastre, sometimes called the dong (Vietnamese: đồng) — meaning "coin." The piastre was divisible into 100 centimes, which were also called xu (also spelled sau and su) — meaning "pence" or "cents."

Following World War II, the country split in two. The northern part was the Democratic Republic of Vietnam, often referred to as North Vietnam, which declared its independence in 1945. The southern part, originally (1946) called the Autonomous Republic of Cochinchina, was renamed South Vietnam in 1947. Both countries replaced the piastre with their own monetary systems, each now officially using the Vietnamese-language equivalents of the former French piastre and centime — the dong, divided into 100 xu. However, the North Vietnamese dong was also divided into 10 hao (Vietnamese:

hào), the equivalent of "dime." When the North and South were reunified as the Socialist Republic of Vietnam in 1976, the South Vietnamese dong was demonetized. The
unified monetary system continued the same dong-hao-xu divisions that had been used
by the North since 1954. In 1985 a monetary reform replaced the dong with the new
dong, equal to 10 older dong.

CHRONOLOGY

Year	Denomination	Equivalent
1985–present	new dong	100 xu
1976–1985, unified	dong	10 hao
	hao	10 xu
1954–1976, North Vietnam	dong	10 hao
	hao	10 xu
1954–1976, South Vietnam	dong	100 xu
1878–1954	Indochinese piastre	100 centimes

ORTHOGRAPHY AND NUMBER

Singular	Plural	Known Abbreviations and Symbols	Examples
cent	cents	c	10c
dong (*đồng*)	dong (*đồng*)	đ D	10đ 10đ50 10D
hao (*hào*)	hao (*hào*)		
piastre	piastres	$	10$
xu	xu	c	10c

West African States (XOF)

The West African States is a confederation of eight former French colonial possessions of the administrative unit known as French West Africa. The federation currently consists of Benin, Burkina-Faso, Guinea-Bissau, Ivory Coast, Mali, Niger,
Senegal, and Togo. Mali left the monetary union in 1962 and issued its own currency
but rejoined the confederation in 1969. Mauritania, which had been an original member, left the confederation in 1973 and replaced the CFA franc with the ouguiya.

The monetary system of the West African Currency Union is based on the Communauté Financière Africaine (African Financial Community, CFA) franc, a union of
former French colonies in Africa. The CFA franc is guaranteed by the French treasury
and pegged to the French franc, into which it is freely convertible. *See also* **Central
African States**.

CHRONOLOGY

Year	Denomination	Equivalent
1958–present	CFA franc	100 centimes

ORTHOGRAPHY AND NUMBER

Singular	Plural	Known Abbreviations and Symbols	Examples
centime	centimes	c	10c
CFA franc	CFA francs	CFA F	10 F

Yemen (YER)

Today's Yemen was established with the 1990 merger of two Yemeni states — North and South. North Yemen, whose capital was Saana, gained its independence from the Ottoman Empire in 1918. It was renamed the Yemen Arab Republic in 1962. South Yemen, with Aden as its capital, had been occupied by the British since 1839. In the years that followed, Aden (as it was then known) was a protectorate, and in 1962 it became part of the Federation of South Arabia. In 1967, the Federation gained its independence from Great Britain and was renamed the People's Republic of South Yemen.

After gaining its independence from the Ottoman Turks, North Yemen replaced the Turkish piastre with the riyal, divisible into 40 buqshas. While a British protectorate, Aden, like many other Persian Gulf states, used the Indian rupee, divisible into 16 anna and 192 pies, as its monetary system. In 1951, the rupee was replaced with the East African shilling, divided into 100 cents. When the Federation of South Arabia was formed in 1962, the shilling was replaced by the South Arabian dinar, equal to 20 East African shillings and divisible into 1,000 fils. When the Federation of South Arabia was renamed the People's Republic of South Yemen in 1967, the South Arabian dinar was renamed the South Yemeni dinar. After unification in 1990, the dinar was demonetized.

The transliteration of Arabic into English is not always a simple matter, and one often finds variations in spelling for the monetary units. This especially true for buqsha (بغشة), which is also found spelled as bugacha and bogshah. Also, either the numerals 0 through 9 or the following Arabic-language numerals:

0	1	2	3	4	5	6	7	8	9	10	50	100	500	1000
٠	١	٢	٣	٤	٥	٦	٧	٨	٩	١٠	٥٠	١٠٠	٥٠٠	١٠٠٠

are used with the Arabic-language monetary units anna (انله), buqsha (نغشة), riyal (ريال), and rupee (رفبة). The Arabic letter *feh* (ف) is used as the abbreviation for fils (فاس, فلوس) — the Arabic spelling being dependent on the amount.

CHRONOLOGY—NORTH YEMEN

Year	Denomination	Equivalent
1978–present	Yemeni riyal	100 fils
1918–1978	riyal	40 buqshas

CHRONOLOGY—SOUTH YEMEN

Year	Denomination	Equivalent
1968–1990	South Yemeni dinar	1,000 fils
1965–1968	South Arabian dinar	1,000 fils
1951–1965	East African shilling	100 cents
1918–1951	Indian rupee	16 anna
	anna	12 pies

ORTHOGRAPHY AND NUMBER

Singular	Plural	Known Abbreviations and Symbols	Examples
anna	anna(s)*	A As	1A 10As
buqsha	buqshas	B	10B
cent	cents	c cts	10c 10cts
dinar	dinars		
fils	fils	F ف	F10 ٠اف
pie	pies		
riyal	riyals		
rupee	rupees	R Rs	
shilling	shillings	Sh	Sh 10/-

*Optional final s.

Zambia (ZMK)

From 1900 until its independence in 1964, Zambia, formerly known as Northern Rhodesia, was a British protectorate. There was a brief period from 1953 until 1963 when it was part of a federation with both Southern Rhodesia (now Zimbabwe) and Nyasaland (now Malawi) known as the Federation of Rhodesia and Nyasaland (or the Central African Federation). The monetary system of the federation was the Rhodesia and Nyasaland pound, divisible into the same proportions of shillings, pence, and farthings as the British pound sterling.

When Zambia gained its independence in 1964, the Rhodesian and Nyasaland pound was replaced at par with the Zambian pound. In 1968, a monetary reform replaced the pound with a decimalized system based on the kwacha, a Bantu word for "sunrise" or "dawn." The kwacha was equal to 10 shillings, and divisible into 100 ngwee — another native word, meaning "bright." The kwacha is also the major denomination of Malawi's monetary system, but there it is divided instead into 100 tambala.

CHRONOLOGY

Year	Denomination	Equivalent
1968–present	Zambian kwacha	100 ngwee
1964–1968	Zambian pound	20 shillings

Year	Denomination	Equivalent
1956–1964	Rhodesia and Nyasaland pound	20 shillings
	shilling	12 pence
1940–1956	Southern Rhodesian pound	20 shillings
	shilling	12 pence
1900–1940	pound sterling	20 shillings
	shilling	12 pence
	penny	4 farthings

ORTHOGRAPHY AND NUMBER

Singular	Plural	Known Abbreviations and Symbols	Examples
farthing	farthings	d	¼d ½d
kwacha	kwacha	K	K10
ngwee	ngwee	n	10n
penny	pence	d	10d
pound	pounds	£ (or £)	£10
shilling	shillings	/	10/-

Zimbabwe (ZWD)

Zimbabwe was known as Southern Rhodesia following the establishment of British influence in 1897. There was a brief period from 1953 to 1963 when Southern Rhodesia was in a federation with both Northern Rhodesia (now Zambia) and Nyasaland (now Malawi) known as the Federation of Rhodesia and Nyasaland (or the Central African Federation). The monetary system of the federation was the Rhodesia and Nyasaland pound, which was divided into the same proportions of shillings, pence, and farthings as the pound sterling.

After the federation was dissolved, the Rhodesia and Nyasaland pound was replaced with the Rhodesian pound in 1965. In 1970, Southern Rhodesia attained its independence from Great Britain and was renamed simply Rhodesia, not to be confused with Northern Rhodesia. The Rhodesian pound was replaced by a decimalized system based on the Rhodesian dollar, divisible into 100 new pence. The country's name was to change two more times. In 1979 it was renamed Zimbabwe Rhodesia, and in 1980 it took its present name of Zimbabwe, whereupon the Rhodesian dollar was renamed the Zimbabwe dollar.

CHRONOLOGY

Year	Denomination	Equivalent
1980–present	Zimbabwe dollar	100 cents
1970–1980	Rhodesian dollar	100 new pence
1965–1970	Rhodesian pound	20 shillings

Year	Denomination	Equivalent
	shilling	12 pence
1956–1965	Rhodesia and Nyasaland pound	20 shillings
	shilling	12 pence
1940–1956	Southern Rhodesian pound	20 shillings
	shilling	12 pence
1900–1940	pound sterling	20 shillings
	shilling	12 pence
	penny	4 farthings

ORTHOGRAPHY AND NUMBER

Singular	Plural	Known Abbreviations and Symbols	Examples
cent	cents	c	10c
dollar	dollars	$	$10
farthing	farthings	d	¼d ½d
penny	pence	d	10d
pound	pounds	£	£10
shilling	shillings	/	10/-

Glossary of Monetary Units

afghani (Pashto: افغانۍ) Afghanistan, since 1925. Divisible into 100 puls. It takes its name from that of the country.

agora (Hebrew: אגורה) Israel. Equal to one-hundredth of a pound from 1960 to 1980, and one-hundredth of a shekel from 1980 to 1985. Its origin is from the Hebrew, meaning "small coin." Both the English and the Hebrew plural is agorot (אגורית).

angolar Angola, from 1926 to 1958. Divisible into 100 centavos. It is named after the country as well as a Creole language spoken on the southern tip of São Tomé (St. Thomas) island.

anna (Arabic: انله; Hindi: आना) Bahrain, Bangladesh, Bhutan, Burma, India, Iraq, Kenya, Kuwait, Nepal, Oman, Pakistan, Qatar, Tanzania, Uganda, and Yemen. Its origin is thought to be the Hindi *ānā*— meaning "small."

argentino Argentina.

asper Turkey.

at *also* **att** Cambodia, Laos, Thailand.

auksinas Lithuania, in use from 1918 to 1923. Divisible into 100 skatiku. Both the English and the Lithuanian plural is auksinai.

aurar Plural of eyrir. *See* **eyrir**.

austral Argentina, in use from 1985 to 1992. Divisible into 100 centavos. Austral is a Spanish word meaning "southern"— primarily referring to the Southern Hemisphere.

avo The former Portuguese colonies of Macao and East Timor (now Timor Leste). Equal to one-hundredth of a pataca in Macao. The name avo means "fractional part."

baht (Thai: บาท) Thailand. Also used in place of the tical, and currently divisible into 100 satang. The name baht means "one-fourth" or "quarter."

baisa (Arabic: بيسة) *also* **baiza** Oman, since 1970. It is the Arabic version of the Indian paisa, meaning "quarter" or "one-fourth."

balboa Panama, since 1904. Divisible into 100 centesimos. It was named in honor of Vasco Nuñez de Balboa, the Spanish explorer who was first European to see the Pacific in 1513.

ban Moldova and Romania. Equal to one-hundredth of a leu. Its origin is from the Persian military title *ban*, meaning "lord." Both the English and the Romanian plural is bani.

batzen Switzerland (outdated). Divisible into 10 centimes, and thought to be derived from either *bätz* or *betz*— medieval German forerunners of *bär*, meaning "bear."

bipkwele Plural of epkwele. *See* **epkwele**.

birr (Amharic: ብር) *also* **bir** Eritrea and Ethiopia. Divisible into 100 cents. It is the Amharic word for "silver."

bolívar Venezuela, since 1879. Divisible into 100 centimos. It was named in honor of Simón Bolívar (1783–1830), the South American revolutionary leader known as El Liberator (The Liberator). Bolívar helped liberate Colombia, Ecuador, Peru, and Venezuela from Spain. Bolivia is named after him.

boliviano Bolivia, since 1863. Divisible into 100 centavos. It takes its name from that of the country, which was named in honor of Simón Bolívar. *See also* **bolívar**.

bob Slang name for the English shilling. Following decimalization of the pound in 1971, the term was also applied to the five-penny coin, which is 1/20 of a pound, just as a pound once equaled 20 shillings.

buqsha (Arabic: بقشة) *also* **bugacha, bogshah**

North Yemen, in use from 1918 to 1978. Equal to ¹⁄₄₀ of a riyal.

butut The Gambia, since 1970. Equal to one-hundredth of a dalasi.

candareen China, Taiwan.

cauri *also* **caury, cory** Guinea, in use from 1972 to 1986. Equal to one-hundredth of a syli. Its name comes from the cowrie shells that once served as a type of currency among the coastal tribes.

cedi *also* **sedi** Ghana, since 1965. Divisible into 100 pesewas. Its name is a word in Fanti, one of the Kwa languages, meaning "shell." Shells such as the cowrie once served as money among the coastal tribes.

cent Anguilla, Antigua and Barbuda, Aruba, Australia, Bahamas, Barbados, Belize, Bermuda, Botswana, Brunei, Canada, Cayman Islands, Cyprus, Dominica, Ecuador, El Salvador, Eritrea, Ethiopia, Fiji, Grenada, Guyana, Hong Kong, Indonesia, Jamaica, Kenya, Kiribati, Lesotho, Liberia, Malaysia, Maldives, Malta, Mauritius, Micronesia, Mongolia, Montserrat, Namibia, Nauru, The Netherlands, Netherlands Antilles, New Zealand, Palau, Papua New Guinea, Philippines, St. Kitts and Nevis, St. Lucia, St. Vincent and the Grenadines, Seychelles, Sierra Leone, Singapore, Solomon Islands, South Africa, Sri Lanka, Suriname, Swaziland, Taiwan, Tanzania, Timor Leste, Trinidad and Tobago, Turks and Caicos, Tuvalu, Uganda, United States, Vietnam, Yemen, Zimbabwe. The one-cent coin is often referred to as a "penny." The name is based on the Latin *centum*, meaning one hundred. Monetary variations of other countries are: centas, centavo, centesimo, centime, centimo, centisimo, santime, sene, seniti, sent, sente, senti, and sentimo.

centas The Lithuanian form of "cent" in use from 1923 to 1940 and reinstituted in 1993. It is equal to one-hundredth of a litas. *See also* **cent**.

centavo Angola, Argentina, Bolivia, Brazil, Cape Verde, Chile, Colombia, Costa Rica, Cuba, Dominican Republic, Ecuador, El Salvador, Guatemala, Guinea-Bissau, Honduras, Mexico, Mozambique, Nicaragua, Panama, Paraguay, Peru, Philippines, Portugal, São Tomé and Príncipe, Timor Leste, Venezuela. One of several Portuguese- or Spanish-language forms of "cent," used mostly by Central and South American counties. *See also* **cent**.

centesimo Chile, Cuba, Eritrea, Italy, Libya, Panama, Paraguay, San Marino, Uruguay, Vatican City. A form of "cent" used in Italy and several Spanish-speaking countries. *See also* **cent**.

centime Algeria, Andorra, Belgium, Benin, Bulgaria, Burkina Faso, Burundi, Cambodia, Cameroon, Central African Republic, Chad, Comoros, Congo (Democratic Republic of), Congo-Brazzaville (Republic of), Djibouti, Equatorial Guinea, Ethiopia, France, French Polynesia, Gabon, Guinea, Guinea-Bissau, Haiti, Ivory Coast, Laos, Lebanon, Luxembourg, Madagascar, Mali, Mauritania, Monaco, Morocco, Niger, Rwanda, Senegal, Switzerland, Syria, Togo, Tunisia, Vanuatu. The French form of "cent" in many Francophone countries. It is also spelled santime (سنتيم) in many Arabic-speaking countries that have the centime as a monetary unit. *See also* **cent**.

centimo Andorra, Costa Rica, Dominican Republic, Equatorial Guinea, Gibraltar, Morocco, Mozambique, Paraguay, Peru, Philippines, São Tomé and Príncipe, Spain, Venezuela. One of several Spanish-language forms of "cent." *See* **cent**.

chetrum *also* **chhetrum** Bhutan, since 1964. Equal to one-hundredth of a ngultrum. Its name comes from the combination of either the Tibetan or the Burmese word *che*, meaning "half," and *trum*, which is probably from the Hindi tramka, meaning "money." It is sometimes also referred to as naya paisa.

chon (Korean: 전) *also* **cheun, jeon, jun** North and South Korea. It means "coin" and is equal to one-hundredth of a won. Jun is used in North Korea, while jeon is used in South Korea.

colón Costa Rica, El Salvador. Named in honor of Christopher Columbus, whose name in Spanish is Cristóbal Colón.

córdoba Nicaragua, since 1912. Divisible into 100 centavos. It was named in honor of Hernández Gonzalo de Córdoba (1453–1515), a Spanish governor of Nicaragua during the early 16th century.

corona Austria from 1892 to 1924. Divisible into 100 heller and used as an alternative name for the korona. Corona is Latin for "crown"—the notable symbol of a ruler's sovereignty. Monetary variations of other countries are: korona, koruna, krona, króna, krone, and kroon.

coupon Georgia.

cruzado Brazil and Portugal. From the Portuguese *cruz*—"cross," or *cruzar*—"to cross or traverse."

cruzeiro Brazil. From the Portuguese *cruz*, meaning "cross."

daalder The Netherlands. Equal to to 2½ guilders. Named after the thaler, a forerunner of the dollar. *See also* **dollar**.

dalasi (Arabic: دلس) *also* **dalasy** The Gambia, since 1970. Divisible into 100 butut.

daler Denmark, Iceland, Norway, and Sweden. Based on the German thaler—the origin of the dollar and its variants. *See also* **dollar**.

decimo Colombia, Ecuador, Panama. From the Latin decimus, meaning "tenth."

den (Macedonian: дин) Macedonia, since 1992. Equal to one-hundredth of a denar. Both are from the Arabic form of the ancient Roman denarius. Both the English and the Macedonian plural is deni (дини).

denar (Macedonian: денар) Macedonia, since 1992. Divisible into 100 deni. It is similar to the dinar, the Arabic form of the ancient Roman denarius.

denga (Russian: динга) Nineteenth-century Russian coin equal to one-half kopeck. Its transliterated plural, den'gi (диньги), is Russian for "money."

deutsche mark West Germany, from 1948 to 1990; united Germany, until 2002. Divisible into 100 pfennig, it literally means "German mark" and was named to differentiate it from the ostmark of East Germany. Its origin is a Norse term from the third century for a unit of weight of precious metal; it was also used as a monetary unit by the Goths. *See also* **mark**.

dinar (Arabic: دينار; Serbian: динар) Algeria, Bahrain, Bosnia-Herzegovina, Croatia, Iran, Iraq, Jordan, Kuwait, Libya, Macedonia, Serbia and Montenegro, Slovenia, Sudan, Tunisia, United Arab Emirates, Yemen. The name is taken from both the ancient Roman denarius and Byzantium's denarius aureus. Its value was generally linked to another unit, the dirham. It is also from the denarius that we get the abbreviation for the British penny—the letter *D*.

diram (Tajiki: дирам) Tajikistan. Equal to one-hundredth of a somoni. It is a variation of the dirham. *See* **dirham**.

dirham (Arabic: دراهم) *also* **dirhem** Iraq, Jordan, Libya, Morocco, Qatar, United Arab Emirates. Thought to be the Arabic version of the Greek drachma, whose meaning is "handful" or "to grasp." It is generally equal to ⅒ of a dinar.

dobra São Tomé and Príncipe.

doit English spelling of the Dutch *duit*, meaning "small coin." It is thought to be derived from the old English word "whittle," because coins of this type, like the farthing, were used to make small change.

dollar Anguilla, Antigua and Barbuda, Australia, Bahamas, Barbados, Belize, Bermuda, Brunei, Canada, Cayman Islands, Dominica, Ecuador, El Salvador, Ethiopia, Fiji, Grenada, Guyana, Hong Kong, Jamaica, Kiribati, Liberia, Malaysia, Micronesia, Mongolia, Montserrat, Namibia, Nauru, New Zealand, Palau, Papua New Guinea, Philippines, St. Kitts and Nevis, St. Vincent and the Grenadines, Singapore, Solomon Islands, Suriname, Taiwan, Timor Leste, Trinidad and Tobago, Turks and Caicos, Tuvalu, United States, Zimbabwe. Although there are many stories about the dollar's origin, the most often quoted account is that dollar came from thaler, which came from the silver for coins mined at Joachimstal (or St. Joachim's Valley), now Jáchymov in Bohemia of the present-day Czech Republic. Other coins evolved with variations on the name thaler, such as the daalder (the Netherlands), the dalar (Poland), and the daler (Sweden). Pieces of eight, also known as the Spanish dollar, and the Maria Theresa thaler were legal tender during the colonial era, and this is probably the most logical reason for adopting the dollar as the basis of the United States' monetary system. Monetary variations of other countries are: daalder, dalar, daler, tala, talari, thaler, and tolar.

The well-known dollar-sign symbol ($), the letter *S* with one or two vertical or sloping bars through it, has also been used as the monetary symbol for the peso and escudo in some countries and for Ecuador's sucre. One theory as to the symbol's origin is that it represents a contraction of the pieces of eight, a peso, which might have been rendered as /8/.

dong (Vietnamese: đồng) Vietnam. It means "coin" and is currently divisible into 100 xu.

drachma (Greek: ΔΡΑΧΜΑΙ) Greece, until 2002. Divisible into 100 lepta. Its origin was the name of a standard weight, probably derived from the Greek drach (ΔΡΑΞ), meaning "handful," or drattomai (ΔΡΑΤΤΟΜΑΙ), "to grasp."

dram (Armenian: Դրամ) Armenia, since 1993. It means "money" and equals 100 lumas. It origin is probably from the ancient Greek drachma or drachm.

duit Indonesia, Netherlanads. *See* **doit.**

ekuele *see* **epkwele**

emalangeni Plural of lilangeni. *See* **lilangeni.**

epkwele Equatorial Guinea, in use from 1979 to 1985. Divisible into 100 centimos. The spelling was changed from ekuele in 1979, and the plural is bipkwele.

escudo Angola, Argentina, Bolivia, Cape Verde, Chile, Colombia, Costa Rica, Ecuador, El Salvador, Guatemala, Guinea-Bissau, Honduras, Mozambique, Panama, Philippines, Portugal, São Tomé and Príncipe, Spain, Timor Leste, Venezuela. The word is Spanish for "shield" (also from the Latin *scutum*— "shield"), referring to the coat of arms that appeared on the reverse of the Spanish real and escudo coins. The escudo is related to the Italian scudo coin.

euro, euro-cent European Union, since 1999. The official practice is to use the units "euro" and "euro-cent" as both singular and plural. Although the plurals "euros" and "cents" are also officially used in Spanish and Portuguese, it is surprising that in France, where the government tries very hard to keep its language from being modified with foreign words, "cent" is the official term; however, most people still use the older term, centime.

Greece was given an exception as its alphabet is the only one of the Eurozone countries not solely composed of Latin characters. The euro was allowed to be rendered by its Greek equivalent (ΕΥΡΩ), while the euro-cent was allowed to be replaced with the singular and plural forms for the lepto (ΛΕΠΤΟ, ΛΕΠΤΑ).

eyrir Iceland, since 1918. Equal to one-hundredth of a króna. Both the English and the Icelandic plural is aurar, a name from the Latin *aureus*, meaning "gold." The Danish and Norwegian øre and Swedish öre have a similar origin.

farthing Anguilla, Antigua and Barbuda, Australia, Bahamas, Barbados, Belize, Bermuda, Botswana, Gambia, Gibraltar, Great Britain, Grenada, Ireland, Jamaica, Malawi, Malta, Montserrat, Namibia, St.

Kitts and Nevis, St. Lucia, St. Vincent and the Grenadines, Samoa, Sierra Leone, Solomon Islands, South Africa, Sri Lanka, Swaziland, Turks aqnd Caicos, Zambia, Zimbabwe. The smallest monetary unit of all British coins until 1956, when the last coin was minted. Its name comes from the term "fourthling" — a term resulting from the practice of cutting the penny, which once was a silver coin, into four pieces. Silver farthings eventually gave way to copper and bronze coins, whose value became so small that if something was considered worthless, it was said to "not be worth a farthing."

fen (Chinese: 分) *also* **fyng** China and Taiwan. Smallest monetary unit of these countries, it equals ¹⁄₁₀ of a jiao and one-hundredth of a yuan renminbi. The name means "part."

fenig Poland, in use from 1916 to 1924. Equal to one-hundredth of a marka, and the equivalent of the German pfennig. In the areas of Poland controlled by Germany during World War I, the German reichmark was replaced in 1916 with the Polish marka, divisible into 100 fenigow.

fening (Bosnian: пфениг) Bosnia-Herzegovina, since 1998. It is the equivalent of the penny or German pfennig. Both the English and the transliterated Bosnian plural is feninga (пфенига).

filler (Hungarian: fillér) Croatia and Hungary. Corresponds to Austria's heller. It has the general of meaning of "penny" or "mite."

fils (Arabic: فلس) Bahrain, Iraq, Jordan, Kuwait, United Arab Emirates, Yemen. Equal to one-thousandth of a dinar. Its name derives from the Latin *follis*, meaning "money bag" — a large leather purse used for holding one's military pay. Its Arabic plural can be either falus (فلوس) or falsen (فالسا), depending on the number it is associated with.

florin Aruba, Austria, Ireland, Kenya, Netherlands, Netherlands Antilles, Suriname, Tanzania, Uganda. Also known as a guilder or *gulden* ("golden"), its origin goes back to Florence's fiorino d'oro (i.e., "gold florin") coin, which pictured a fleur-de-lis on the coin's reverse. *Fiorino* is the Italian diminutive, meaning "little florin," which comes from the florenus, a medieval coin. The British florin was equal to two shillings, and the name is also sometimes used for the 10-pence coin after the decimalization of the British monetary system.

forint Hungary, from 1857 to 1891 and reintroduced in 1946. Currently divisible into 100 filler, it is the Hungarian equivalent of the florin. *See also* **florin**.

franc (German: franken; Arabic: فرنكا) Algeria, Andorra, Belgium, Benin, Bulgaria, Burkina-Faso, Burundi, Cameroon, Central African Republic, Chad, Comoros, Congo (Democratic Republic of), Congo-Brazzaville (Republic of), Djibouti Equatorial Guinea, France, French Polynesia, Gabon, Guinea, Guinea-Bissau, Ivory Coast, Liechtenstein, Luxembourg, Madagascar, Mali, Mauritania, Monaco, Morocco, Niger, Rwanda, Senegal, Switzerland, Togo, Tunisia, Vanuatu. Origin is attributed to the Latin inscription *Francorum Rex* (King of the Franks) on a fourteenth-century gold coin issued under the reign of King John II, also known as Jean le Bon ("John the Good"). Monetary variations of other countries are: franco, frang, franga, and frank.

franco Dominican Republic, from 1883 to 1885. Spanish equivalent for the French franc. *See also* **franc**.

frang Colloquial name for the Luxembourgian franc, as used by its Dutch-speaking residents. *See also* **franc**.

franga Albania, from 1925 to 1946. Divisible into 100 qindarka. It was an Albanian equivalent of the French franc. *See also* **franc**.

frank German equivalent of the franc, as used in Switzerland; also the Flemish equivalent as used in Belgium. *See also* **franc**.

fuang Cambodia.

gourde Haiti. Divisible into 100 centimes. The name is from the Spanish word *gordo*, meaning "fat."

groat An English coin divisible into four pence. The name is taken from medieval English, meaning "great." This probably gave rise to the German groß , French gros, and Italian grosso coins — all of whose names mean "fat" or "thick."

grivna (Russian: гривна) Name for a monetary unit of medieval Russia which was later given to the 10-kopeck coin known as a grivennik (гривенникъ). Its name means "pendant," referring to an ornament worn by women. The transliterated Russian plural is griven (гривень). The grivna is the same as the Ukrainian hryvnia (гривня), but spelled with different final letters.

groschen Austria, from 1924 to 2002. Its name is a German diminutive of *groß*—

"large" — and is a variation of both the French gros and the Italian grosso coins. In today's German usage, it is taken to mean "penny" or "groat." A groschen was also used in The Holy Roman Empire.

grosz Poland, since 1922. Equal to one-hundredth of a zloty, and the equivalent of the groschen or groat. Its Polish plural, which can be either grosze or groszy, depends on the number it is associated with.

guaraní Paraguay, since 1943. Divisible into 100 centimos. It is named after the native Paraguayan Indian tribe and one of the country's two official languages.

guerche (Arabic: غروش) *also* **ghirsh, girsh, qirsh** Egypt, Ethiopia, Jordan, Saudi Arabia, Syria. Also the colloquial name for the piastre. Its origin appears to be the groschen or its variants.

guilder (Dutch: *gulden*) Aruba, Austria, Croatia, Guyana, Indonesia, Luxembourg, Netherlands, Netherlands Antilles, Suriname. The name means "golden." It was the name originally given to a golden coin that circulated widely throughout Europe. In the Netherlands, the guilder was also known as a florin. *See also* **florin**.

guinea An English gold coin, whose gold was mined from Guinea in Africa. It was originally divisible into 20 shillings, a pound, or a sovereign, but since 1717 its value has been equal to 21 shillings.

habibi Afghanistan. Divisible into 30 rupees. It was named after Habibullah Khan, an Afghan emir who ruled from 1901 to 1919, and is also taken from the Arabic word meaning "my darling."

halala (Arabic: هللة) Saudi Arabia, since 1976. Equal to one-hundredth of a riyal. Its name is possibly from the Arabic *halal* (حلال) meaning "lawful."

haler Czech Republic and the former Czechoslovakia. It is like the Slovak halier, and both are related to the Austrian heller. The English plural is halers, but the Czech plural depends on the number it is associated with — it can be either haléře or haléřů. *See also* **heller**.

halerzy Polish plural equivalent of the Austrian heller, equal to one-hundredth of a korona. The Polish singular is halerze.

halier Slovak-language equivalent of the Austrian heller and Czech haler. *See also* **heller**.

hao (Vietnamese: hào) Vietnam, since 1954. The meaning is essentially "dime."

heller (Bosnian: хелер) Austria from 1892 until 1925; Austria, Bosnia-Herzegovina, Burundi, Croatia, Liechtenstein, Macedonia, Rwanda, Serbia and Montenegro, Slovenia. It takes its name from the Austrian town now known as Schwäbisch Hall. The Czech haler and Slovak halier are monetary units derived from the heller.

hryvnia (Ukrainian: гривня) Ukraine, since 1996. It is the same as the Russian grivna (гривна) except for the spelling. The name is a monetary unit of medieval Russia, meaning "pendant"—referring to an ornament worn by women. Although the transliterated English singular and plural spellings are the same (*hryvnia*), the Ukrainian plural depends on the number it is associated with—it can be either hryvni (гривні) or hryven (гривень).

hwan (Korean: 환) North and South Korea, from 1953 to 1962. Divisible into 100 chon. "Hwan" was the official spelling until 1962, when it was changed to "won." *See also* **won**.

inti Peru, in use from 1985 to 1991. Divisible into 100 centimos. Its origin is from the Incas' Quechua language, meaning "sun."

jiao (Chinese: 角) China, since 1949, also called mao. It is ⅒ of a yuan renminbi and is divisible into 10 fen.

jeon (Korean: 전) *also* **jun** *see* **chon**

kak Cambodia, in use from 1975. It is equal to ⅒ of a new riel and divisible into 10 su.

kapeek Belarus, from 1992. It is the Belarusian equivalent of the Russian kopeck. *See also* **kopeck**.

kapeika Latvia, in use from 1919 to 1922 and again from 1992 until 1993. It is the Latvian equivalent of the Russian kopeck. *See also* **kopeck**.

karbovanets (Ukrainian: карбованец) Ukraine, from 1918 to 1919, and the denomination of a transitional coupon from 1992 to 1996. Its name probably comes from the Ukrainian *karb* (карб), meaning "notch, incision, or tally." The English plural is generally taken to be the same as the singular, but the transliterated Ukrainian plural is karbovanetsiv (карбованців).

khoums (Arabic: خمس) Mauritania. Equal to one-fifth of an ouguiya. It is no longer used.

kina Papua New Guinea, since 1975. Divisible into 100 toeas. Its name is taken from the native or pidgin language word for the shell money used by the coastal natives prior to the introduction of coinage by Great Britain and Germany.

kip (ກີບ) Laos, since 1955. Divisible into 100 at (also att).

kobo Nigeria, since 1973. Equal to one-hundredth of a naira. Its name is a native word for "copper."

kopeck (Russian: копейка) *also* **kopec, kopek** Armenia, Azerbaijan, Belarus, Estonia, Finland, Georgia, Kazakhstan, Kyrgyzstan, Latvia, Lithuania, Moldova, Poland, Russia, Tajikistan, Turkmenistan, Ukraine, Uzbekistan. Equal to one-hundredth of a ruble. The name is from *kop'yio* (копьё), meaning "lance." Because of changes in Russian orthography, an older form of the Russian spelling for kopeck is копѣйка. There also are foreign-language equivalents such as: kapeek (Belarus), kapeika (Latvia), and kopiyka (Ukraine). The transliterated Russian plural is either kopeyki (копейки) or kopeek (копеек), depending on the number it is associated with.

kopiyka (Ukrainian: копійка) Ukraine, since 1996. The equivalent of the Russian kopeck. The transliterated Ukrainian plural is kopiyok (копійок). *See also* **kopeck**.

korona Hungary, in use from 1892 to 1925. Divisible into 100 filler. It means "crown" and was also called corona, its Latin equivalent. *See also* **krone**.

koruna Czechoslovakia, 1918 to 1993; Czech Republic and Slovakia, since 1993. It means "crown" and is a derivation of the Austrian korona. The English plural is generally taken as korun—with or without a final *s*. However, both the Czech and Slovak plural depends on the number it is associated with—it can be either koruny or korún.

krajczár Hungary, in use from 1857 until 1891. Equal to one-hundredth of a forint. It is the Hungarian form of the Austrian kreuzer, probably from the Polish *krzyż*—"cross." *See also* **kreuzer**.

kreuzer Austria. The name means "cross." Other monetary equivalents are cruzado (Brazil, Portugal), cruzeiro (Brazil), and krajczár (Hungary).

krona Sweden, since 1873. Divisible into 100 öre. It means "crown," as does the Austrian krone. Both the English and the Swedish plural is kronor. *See also* **krone**.

króna Iceland, since 1918. Divisible into 100 aurar. It is a derivative of the Danish *krone*, meaning "crown." *See also* **krone**.

krone Austria, Bosnia-Herzegovina, Croatia, Denmark, Liechtenstein, Macedonia, Norway, Poland, Serbia and Montenegro, Slovenia. The name means "crown." Both the Danish and the Norwegian plural is kroner while the German plural is kronen. Other monetary equivalents are: corona, koruna, krona, króna, and kroon.

kroon Estonia. Divisible into 100 senti. It was used from 1928 to 1940 and reintroduced in 1992. It is a derivative of the Austrian *krone*, meaning "crown." Both the English and the Estonian plural is krooni. *See also* **krone**.

kuna Croatia, used from 1941 to 1945 and reintroduced in 1993. It is currently divisible into 100 lipa. Kuna is the Croatian word for "marten" (also Russian: куница, *kunitsa*), a mink-like animal whose fur was once a medium of monetary exchange.

kuponi (Georgian: კუპონი) Transitional currency used in Georgia from 1993 to 1995. Divisible into 100 kopecks.

kurus (Turkish: kuruş) Turkey, since 1926. Also referred to as a piastre. The origin is probably from the similar units of gros, groß, and grosso — meaning "fat, large, or thick."

kwacha Malawi, since 1971; of Zambia, since 1968. The name is a Chibemba word from the Bantu language family, meaning "sunrise" or "dawn," used by the Bemba natives of Malawi and northeast Zambia.

kwanza Angola, since 1977. Divisible into 100 lwei. It name is taken from the Kwanza (or Cuanza) River , one of the country's main rivers.

kyat Burma, since 1952. Divisible into 100 pyas. Its name is related to Thailand's tical, and its meaning is essentially "weight."

lari (Georgian: ლარი) Georgia, since 1995. Divisible into 100 tetri.

larin, also laari Maldives, since 1981. Equal to one-hundredth of a rufiyaa. It takes its name from Laristan, a subdivision of the ancient Persian province of Fars. The plural is lari.

lat Latvia, used from 1922 to 1941 and reinstituted in 1993. It takes its name from that of the country. Although the English plural is lats, the Latvian plural can be either lati or latu, depending on the number it is associated with.

lek Albania, since 1946. Divisible into 100 qindarka. It is derived from the abbreviation of the Albanian spelling of Alexander the Great. Although the English singular and plural forms for the lek are the same, the Albanian plural can be either lekë or leku, depending on the number it is associated with.

lempira Honduras since 1926. Divisible into 100 centavos. It is named in honor of the Lenca Indian chief Lempira (1497–1537), a national hero who fought against the Spanish colonists.

leone Sierra Leone, since 1964. Divisible into 100 cents. It takes its name from the country — Leone, meaning "lion."

lepton (Greek: ΛΕΠΤΟΝ) Greece, from 1828 until 2001. Equal to one-hundredth of a drachma. It comes from the Greek *leptos* (ΛΕΠΤΟΣ), meaning "slim" or "thin," and the transliterated plural is lepta (ΛΕΠΤΑ).

leu Moldova, used from 1918 to 1940 and reinstituted in 1994, and also of Romania since 1867. In both countries it is divisible into 100 bani. The name means "lion." Both the English and the Romanian plural is lei.

lev (Bulgarian: лев) Bulgaria, since 1880. Divisible into 100 stotinki. Like the leu, its name means "lion." The English plural is generally taken as lev, although the Bulgarian plural is transliterated as leva (лева).

licente, *also* lisente Plural of senti. *See* **senti**.

likuta The Democratic Republic of the Congo (formerly Zaire), from 1967 to 1993. Equal to one-hundredth of a zaire. Its name is derived from *kuta* ("stone") in the language of the Nupe, an ethnic group indigenous to several African countries. The plural is makuta.

lilangeni Swaziland, since 1974. Divisible into 100 cents. It is from a word in the native Bantu, *langeni*, meaning "money." The plural is emalangeni.

lipa Croatia, since 1993. Equal to one-hundredth of a kuna. It means "linden" — a lime tree.

lira Eritrea, Israel, Italy, Libya, Malta, San Marino, Turkey, Vatican City. The name is taken from the Latin *libra*, "scale," but also refers to a weight — a "pound," which in ancient Roman times equaled 327.5 grams. The French equivalent is livre. In Italy the plural is lire; in Malta it is liri. Elsewhere (including Turkey, where lira is the alternative name for the Turkish pound) the English plural spelling is liras. The Hebrew plural for the Israeli lira (לירה, or pound) is lirot (לירות).

lirası Turkish-language equivalent of lira.

lirot (Hebrew: לירות) The plural of the Israeli lira (לירה), or pound, used from 1948 to 1980. See also **lira**.

litas Lithuania used from 1923 to 1940 and reintroduced in 1993. Equal to 100 centu. Its name is probably taken from the short form of the country's name. The Lithuanian plural can be either litai or litų, depending on the number it is associated with.

livre (Arabic: ليرة) France, Lebanon, Syria. French equivalent of the lira, or pound. See also **lira**.

loti Lesotho, since 1980. Divisible into 100 lisente. The plural is maloti.

luma (Armenian: լումա) Armenia, since 1993. Equal to one-hundredth of a dram.

lwei also **lwee** Angola, since 1977. It takes its name from the Lwei River, a tributary of the Kwanza (also spelled Cuanza). Kwanza is also the name of a monetary unit worth 100 lwei. The plural has also been spelled lweys.

mace China, Taiwan.

macuta Angola.

makuta Plural of likuta. See **likuta**.

maloti Plural of loti. See **loti**.

manat (Turkmen: манат; Azeri: منات), also **man'at** Azerbaijan and Turkmenistan, since 1993. According to Islamic lore, Manat is the daughter of Allah. Manat is also the name of a female deity worshipped in pre-Islamic Arabia who was considered to be the goddess of fate and destiny. When the countries were Soviet republics, in Turkmenistan the Georgian language name for the ruble was maneti (მანეთი), in Azerbaijan, manat (منات) was the Azeri name for the ruble.

mark Bosnia-Herzegovina, Cameroon, Czech Republic, Estonia, Germany (also West and East), Micronesia, Montenegro, Nauru, Palau, Papua New Guinea, Samoa, Togo. Well-known German monetary unit whose name traces its origin to a medieval weight of precious metal. The reichmark (imperial mark) was introduced in 1873 following the establishment of the German Reich in 1871. The deutsche mark, or "German mark," was the monetary unit of West Germany from 1948 to 1990, and of the united Germany until

2002, when it was replaced by the euro. Its name differentiated it from the ostmark of East Germany. Other monetary derivations are the marka and markka.

marka Monetary unit, divisible into 100 fenigow, which is the Polish equivalent of the German mark. It was used from 1916 to 1924. See also **mark**.

markka Monetary unit, divisible into 100 penniä, which is the Finnish equivalent of the German mark. It was used from 1860 to 2002 and was frequently referred to as the "finnmark." Both the English and the Finnish plural is markkaa.

mehalek Ethiopia.

metical Mozambique, since 1980. Divisible into 100 centimos. Its name is taken from the Portuguese equivalent of the Arabic miskal, a one-time unit of weight. Its Portuguese plural is meticais.

mil (Hebrew: מיל; Arabic: مل) Israel, Jordan, Malta. The name represents the division of one-thousandth of a larger unit, such as a pound. Other monetary derivations are the milleme, millime, and millième. The English plural is most often given as mils, but the Hebrew milim (מילים) is also used; the Arabic plural is either milan (ملان) or millet (ملات), depending on the number it is associated with.

mill Cyprus.

millieme (French: millième) Egypt, Iraq, Jordan, Libya, Sudan, Syria, Tunisia. Its name is from the French, meaning "thousandth," and has the same meaning as the mil.

millime (Arabic: مليم) Arabic equivalent of the French millième. See **millieme**.

milréis Angola, Cape Verde, Guinea-Bissau, Macao, Mozambique, Portugal. Equivalent to 1,000 réis. See also **réis**.

mongo (Mongolian: мөнгө) also **mungu** Mongolia, since 1925. Equal to one-hundredth of a togrog. It takes its name from that of the country.

naira Nigeria, since 1973. Divisible into 100 kobo. It probably takes its name from that of the country.

nakfa Eritrea, since 1997. Divisible into 100 cents. It is named after Nak'fa, a town in the Sahel Mountains which served as the home of the Eritrean People's Liberation Front during its civil war with Ethiopia.

naya paisa (Hindi: नये पैसे) Bahrain, India (1957–1964), Duwait, Oman, Qatar, United Arab Emirates. Equal to one-hundredth of a rupee. It is Hindi for "new pice" (Hindi: *paisa*), taken from either the Sanskrit word *padikaha* (पादिक:) or the Hindi *padik* (पादिक), meaning "quarter," as the pice was one-fourth of an anna. Its English and transliterated Hindi plural is naye paise.

ngultrum Bhutan, since 1964. It is a derived word from *ngul*, a Dzongkha-language word meaning "silver," and *trum*, a loanword possibly from the Hindi word *tramka*, meaning "money."

ngwee Zambia, since 1968. A native word meaning "bright." It is equal to one-hundredth of a kwacha.

öre Sweden. Currently equal to one-hundredth of a krona. Its name is derived from the Latin *aureus*, meaning "gold," as are the Danish and Norwegian øre and the Icelandic eyrir.

øre Denmark and Norway. From the same root as the Swedish öre and the Icelandic eyrir: the Latin *aureus*, meaning "gold."

ouguiya (Arabic: أوقية) Mauritania, since 1973. Divisible into five khoums. The transliterated Arabic plural is ouguiyat (أوقيات).

pa'anga Tonga, since 1967. The name means "money." Divisible into 100 seniti.

paisa (Hindi: पैसे; Arabic: فيذة) *also* **poisha** Afghanistan, Bangladesh, Bhutan, Burma, India, Nepal, Pakistan. It is now equal to one-hundredth of a rupee, but in earlier times was equal to one-fourth of an anna or ¹⁄₆₄ of a rupee. It is taken from either the Sanskrit word *padikaha* (पादिक:) or the Hindi *padik* (पादिक), meaning "quarter." Its English equivalent is pice and the English plural is paise.

para (Serbian, Bosnian: пара; Arabic: پاره) Albania, Bosnia-Herzegovina, Croatia, Egypt, Lebanon, Libya, Macedonia, Romania, Saudi Arabia, Serbia and Montenegro, Slovenia, Syria, Turkey (countries once part of the Ottoman Empire). The name means "piece." The English plural can be written with or without a final s. The Romanian plural is parale; the transliterated Montenegrin plural is pare (паре); and the transliterated Macedonian plural is pari (пари).

pataca Macao and East Timor (now Timor Leste). Divisible into 100 avos. Its name is thought to be a possible corruption of an Arabic word for the Spanish peso.

pengo (Hungarian: pengő) *also* **pengoe** Hungary, in use from 1925 to 1946. Divisible into 100 fillér.

penni Finland, in use from 1860 to 2002. Equal to one-hundredth of a markka. It is a loan word from "penny" or the German pfennig. The Finnish plural is penniä.

penny Anguilla, Antigua and Barbuda, Australia, Bahamas, Barbados, Belize, Bermuda, Botswana, Cameroon, Canada, Cayman Islands, Cyprus, Dominica, Falkland Islands, Fiji, Gambia, Ghana, Gibraltar, Great Britain, Grenada, Guyana, Ireland, Jamaica, Kiribati, Lesotho, Malawi, Malta, Mauritius, Montserrat, Namibia, Nauru, New Zealand, Nigeria, Papua New Guinea, St. Helena, St. Kitts and Nevis, St. Lucia, St. Vincent and the Grenadines, Samoa, Sierra Leone, Solomon Islands, South Africa, Sri Lanka, Swaziland, Togo, Tonga, Trinidad and Tobago, Turks and Caicos, Tuvalu, Uganda, Vanuatu, Zambia, Zimbabwe. Closely associated with the cent. The penny was originally which was a pennyweight of silver, equal to ¹⁄₂₄₀ of a troy pound, so that a pound was equal to 240 pence. The penny was divisible into four farthings. The coin originated in Great Britain, and was based on the ancient Roman denarius (hence the abbreviation *D* for the penny).

When referring to coins, the term "penny" or its plural "pennies" is used: "there are three pennies on the table." When referring to the monetary unit, "pence" is the correct plural: "your change is three pence." Monetary variations of other countries are: fen, fenig, fening, pengő, penni, penning, pfennig, and pingin.

perper (Montenegrin: перпера) Montenegro, in uses from 1910 to 1918. Divisible into 100 para.

pesa Burundi, Rwanda, Tanzania.

peseta Andorra, Cuba, Equatorial Guinea, Gibraltar, Morocco, Spain. Divisible into 100 centimos. It is a diminutive of the peso, therefore meaning "little weight."

pesewa Ghana, since 1967, equal to one-hundredth of a cedi. It is a native word for "penny." The pesewa is virtually worthless today because of inflation and is no longer used in daily commerce, such as for coins or stamps.

peso Argentina, Chile, Colombia, Costa Rica, Cuba, Dominican Republic, Ecuador, El Salvador, Guatemala, Guinea-Bissau, Honduras, Mexico, Nicaragua, Panama, Paraguay, Peru, Philippines, Uruguay, Venezuela. The name is Spanish for "weight" or "piece," owing to the weight of pieces, such as the famous "piece of eight" (*peso de ocho*) cut from silver bars. It has several variants, such as the peso fuerte ("strong peso" of Paraguay and Uruguay), nuevo peso ("new peso" of Mexico and Uruguay), and peso plata fuerte ("silver strong peso" of the Philippines). Peseta is a diminutive form of peso, and piso is its Tagalog equivalent.

pfennig Cameroon, Czech Republic, Germany (also West and East), Micronesia, Montenegro, Nauru, Palau, Papua New Guinea, Samoa, Togo. Equal to one-hundredth of a mark. The name is undoubtedly a Germanic variation of the British penny, as are other units: fen, fenig, fening, pengő, penni, penning, pfennig, and pingin. *See also* **penny**.

phoenix (Greek: ΦΟΙΝΙΞ) Greece, in use from 1828 to 1833. Divisible into 100 lepta.

piastre (Arabic: قرش) *also* **piaster** Usually equal to one-hundred of a pound. Piastre is the French spelling, whose origin is from the Italian *piastra*—meaning "plate."

pice Bangladesh, India, Kenya, Uganda. The English form of paisa. *See* **paisa**.

pie Bahrain, Bangladesh, India, Oman, Pakistan, Yemen. Equal to one-third of an anna.

pingin Ireland. Gaelic for "penny." The plural form (pence) is pingine.

piso Philippines since 1962. Divisible into 100 sentimos. Piso is the Tagalog-language equivalent of peso, meaning "weight."

poisha see **paisa**

pond Afrikaans for "pound."

pound Anguilla, Antigua and Barbuda, Australia, Bahamas, Barbados, Belize, Bermuda, Botswana, Cameroon, Canada, Cayman Islands, Cyprus, Dominica, Egypt, Falkland Islands, Fiji, Gambia, Ghana, Gibraltar, Great Britain, Grenada, Iraq, Ireland, Israel, Jamaica, Jordan, Kiribati, Lebanon, Lesotho, Liberia, Libya, Malawi, Malta, Mauritius, Montserrat, Namibia, Nauru, New Zealand, Nigeria, Papua New Guinea, St. Helena, St. Kitts and Nevis, St. Lucia, St. Vincent and the Grenadines, Samoa, Sierra Leone, Solomon Islands, South Africa, Sudan, Swaziland, Syria, Tonga, Trinidad and Tobago, Turks and Caicos, Tuvalu, Vanuatu, Zambia, Zimbabwe. Once divisible into 20 shillings and 240 pence but now decimalized.

The pound also goes by equivalent foreign-language names such as: livre (French), lira (Italian), lirası (Turkish), lira (Hebrew: לירה), liri (Maltese) and junyah (Arabic: جنيه). It is derived from the Latin *pondus*—"pound"—a unit of weight which corresponded to the ancient Roman libra. The penny was originally equal to a pennyweight of silver, or $\frac{1}{240}$ of a troy pound, so that a pound was equal to 240 pence.

The symbol for the pound is taken from the initial letter of libra, written using a cursive capital letter *L* having either a single cross stroke (£) or double cross strokes (£) through it. Prior to Great Britain's change to a decimalized pound in 1971, the double cross stroke symbol (£) was primarily used. That is also the symbol for the Italian lira. Since 1971 the single cross stroke symbol has been preferred, so that it is not likely to be confused with the Italian lira. In other countries where the pound is the monetary unit, the simple capital letter *L* is often used.

pruta (Hebrew: פרוטה) Israel, in use from 1949 to 1960. Equal to one-hundredth of an Israeli lira. The plural is prutot (פרוטות).

pul (Pashto: پول) Afghanistan, since 1925. Currently equal to one-hundredth of an afghani.

pula Botswana, since 1976. Divisible into 100 thebe. It is a native word meaning "rain" or "blessings."

punt Ireland. Divisible into 100 pingine. It is Gaelic for "pound."

pya Burma, since 1952. Equal to one-hundredth of a kyat. It is said to be derived from the same root as the Indian paisa—either the Sanskrit *padikaha* (पादिक:) or the Hindi *padik* (पादिक), meaning "quarter."

qapik, (Azeri: qəpik) *also* **qepiq** Azerbaijan, since 1993. Equal to one-hundredth of a manat.

qindar *also* **qintar** Albania, since 1925. Currently equal to one-hundredth of a lek. It is derived from the Albanian word *njëqind*, meaning "one hundred." The plural is qindarka.

qindarka Plural of qindar. *See* qindar.

qirsh (Arabic: غروش) *also* **qursh, kurush** Alternate English spelling for guerche or ghirsh. *See* **guerche**.

quetzal Guatemala, since 1925. Divisible into 100 centavos. It is named after the country's national bird, an endangered species which is prominent in Meso-American mythology. The quetzal has never been successfully bred or held for any long time in captivity and soon dies after being captured or caged. For this reason it is considered a symbol of liberty or freedom.

quid The colloquial term for the English pound sterling.

qursh *see* **guerche**

rand South Africa since 1961. Divisible into 100 cents. *Rand* means "ridge" or "margin," and the currency unit probably takes its name from a shortened form of the Afrikaans *Witwatersrand* ("white water's ridge"), the most productive gold-mining district in the world, located in the Transvaal. The rand replaced the pound when the monetary system was decimalized.

rappen Liechtenstein, Switzerland. Synonomous with the centime of Switzerland since 1803, and equal to one-hundredth of a franc. It was named after a medieval coin whose origin is thought to be the German *raben*, meaning "raven."

real Argentina, Bolivia, Brazil, Chile, Colombia, Costa Rica, Cuba, Dominican Republic, Ecuador, El Salvador, Guatemala, Honduras, Mexico, Morocco, Nicaragua, Panama, Paraguay, Peru, Spain, Venezuela. The name means "royal." Monetary variations of other countries are réis, rial, and riyal. Its Spanish plural is reales.

réis Angola, Brazil, Cape Verde, Guinea-Bissau, Macao, Mozambique, Portugal, São Tomé and *Pricipe*. The Portuguese equivalent of real.

renminbi *see* **yuan renminbi**.

rial (Arabic: ريال) Iran and Oman. The name is an English spelling variation of riyal, meaning "royal." *See also* **real**, **riyal**.

riel Cambodia, since 1954. Currently divisible into 10 kak and 100 su.

rijksdaalder Netherlands, Sri Lanka. The name means "national daalder" or "state daalder," a Dutch coin equal to to 2½ guilders. It is named after the thaler, which was a forerunner of the dollar. It is equivalent to the Swedish riksdaler.

riksdaler Sweden. Divisible into 100 öre. It is equivalent to the Dutch rijksdaalder.

rin (Japanese: 釐) Japan, since 1871. Equal to one-hundredth of a yen and one-tenth of a sen. Its value is so small that it has not been used in daily commerce, such as for coins, since 1954.

ringgit Brunei and Malaysia. Divisible into 100 sen, and synonymous with the dollar. Ringgit is a Malay word meaning "jagged," referring to the milled edge of the coin.

riyal (Arabic: ريال) Iraq, Qatar, Saudi Arabia, United Arab Emirates, Yemen. Derived from the Spanish real, meaning "royal." It is often confused with the rial of Iran and Oman, as both words sound the same and have the same Arabic spelling.

ruble (Russian: рубль) *also* **rouble** Armenia, Azerbaijan, Belarus, Estonia, Finland, Georgia, Kazakhstan, Kyrgyzstan, Latvia, Lithuania, Moldova, Poland, Russia, Tajikistan, Turkmenistan, Ukraine, Uzbekistan. Czarist Russia, the Soviet Union, and post–Soviet Russia. Divisible into 100 kopecks. Its name is derived from the Russian *rubit* (рубить), meaning "cut" or "cut down"— referring to pieces of silver bars, as with the peso. Although the English plural is rubles, the transliterated Russian plural can be either rublei (рублей) or rublya (рубля), depending on the number it is associated with. Monetary variations of other countries are the rublei (Belarus) and rublis (Latvia).

rublei Belarus. *See* **ruble**.

rublis Latvia. *See* **ruble**.

rufiyaa (Arabic: رفيه) Maldives, since 1981. Divisible into 100 lari. It is an Arabic variation of the rupee. *See also* **rupee**.

rupee (Hindi: रुपया; Arabic: رقيه) Afghanistan, Bahrain, Bangladesh, Bhutan, Burma, India, Iraq, Kenya, Kuwait, Maldives, Mauritius, Nepal, Oman, Pakistan, Qatar, Seychelles, Sri Lanka, Uganda, United Arab Emirates, Yemen. Currently divisible into 100 paise. Its name is taken from the Sanskrit *rupaya*, meaning "silver." Monetary variations of other countries are: rupie, rufiyaa, rupiyah, rupia, and rupiah.

rupie Burundi, Rwanda, Tanzania. German equivalent of the rupee, used in the former German East African colonies. *See also* **rupee**.

rupiyah *also* **rupia**, **rupiah** Indonesia, since 1945. Divisible into 100 sen, and a variation of the rupee. *See also* **rupee**.

salung Thailand.

santim Latvia, in use from 1922 to 1941 and reintroduced in 1993. It is equal to one-hundredth of a lat and is a variation of the French centime. Although its English plural is santims, its Latvian plural can be either santimi or santimu, depending on the number it is associated with.

santime (Arabic: سنتيم) Arabic-language equivalent of centime.

santimi Latvia.

satang (Thai: สตางค์) Thailand, since 1897. Currently equal to one-hundredth of a baht.

schilling Austria, in use from 1924 to 2002, divisible into 100 groschen. It is the German equivalent of the English shilling. See also shilling.

scudo Italian coin whose name means "shield." It is the equivalent of the Spanish and Portuguese escudo. *See also* **escudo**.

sen (Japanese: 銭) Brunei, Cambodia, Indonesia, Japan, Malaysia, Micronesia, Palau, Timor Leste. In Japan, the sen (a loan word from the Chinese *ch'ien*— meaning "coin") is one-hundredth of a yen. In Indonesia, it is one-hundredth of a rupiyah. In other countries, such as Brunei, Malaysia, and Palau, sen appears to be a variation of *cent*. Monetary variations of other countries are: sene, sente, seniti, sent, senti, and sentimo.

sene Samoa, since 1967. Equal to one-hundredth of a tala. It is a native variation of "cent." *See also* **cent**.

sengi Democratic Republic of Congo (formerly Zaire). Equal to one-hundredth of a likuta.

seniti Tonga, since 1967. Equal to one-hundredth of a pa'anga. It is a native variation of "cent." *See also* **cent**.

sent Estonia, in use from 1928 to 1940 and reintroduced in 1992. It is equal to one-hundredth of a kroon and is the Estonian equivalent of "cent." Its Estonian plural is senti. *See also* **cent**.

sente Lesotho, since 1980. Equal to one-hundredth of a loti. The word is probably a native name for cent. The plural is lisente.

senti Tanzania, since 1967. Equal to one-hundredth of a shilingi (shilling). It is the Swahili equivalent of "cent." *See also* **cent**.

sentimo Philippines, since 1962. Equal to one-hundredth of a piso. Sentimo is the Tagalog-language equivalent of the Spanish centimo.

sertum Bhutan, since 1957. Currently divisible into 100 ngultrum.

shahi Iran. The name is derived from the Farsi (Persian) word *shah* (شاه), meaning "king."

shahiv Ukraine.

shekel (Hebrew: שקל) *also* **sheqal, sheqel** Israel, since 1980. One of the best-known biblical monies, the modern shekel is currently divisible into 100 agorot. The shekel was a biblical unit of weight: 3,000 talents equaled one shekel, a coin used for the annual tax payment to the ancient temple. The origin of the word is the Hebrew *shakal* (שקל), meaning "to weigh." The plural can be either the English form shekels or the transliterated Hebrew shekalim (שקלים).

shilingi Swahili equivalent of the British shilling in Kenya, Tanzania, and Uganda. *See* **shilling**.

shilling Anguilla, Antigua and Barbuda, Australia, Bahamas, Barbados, Belize, Bermuda, Botswana, Cameroon, Canada, Cayman Islands, Cyprus, Dominica, Eritrea, Ethiopia, Falkland Islands, Fiji, The Gambia, Ghana, Gibraltar, Great Britain, Grenada, Ireland, Jamaica, Kenya, Kiribati, Lesotho, Liberia, Malawi, Malta, Mauritius, Montserrat, Namibia, Nauru, New Zealand, Nigeria, Papua New Guinea, St. Helena, St. Kitts and Nevis, St. Lucia, St. Vincent and the Grenadines, Samoa, Sierra Leone, Solomon Islands, South Africa, Sri Lanka, Swaziland, Tanzania, Togo, Tonga, Trinidad and Tobago, Turks and Caicos, Tuvalu, Uganda, Vanuatu, Yemen, Zambia, Zimbabwe. British monetary unit also used by almost 60 countries, including colonial America. It was originally an English unit of account from as early as the eighth or ninth century, equal to $\frac{1}{20}$ of a pound, and divisible into 12 pence. In England, it was also divisible into four farthings. Multiples and divisions of the shilling also had names: a crown equaled 5 shillings; a half-crown equaled 2½ shillings, or "two and six" (two shillings and sixpence); a florin was equal to 2 shillings. A half-shilling was a sixpence, also known as as a "tanner," and a third of a shilling was a fourpence, or "groat." The shilling itself was a "bob."

Many feel that these monetary divisions were based on the ancient Roman system in which 12 denarii (silver pennies) equaled one solidus, meaning "solid." The abbreviation for the shilling — the letter *S*— is from the solidus, just as the letter *D* (for the denarius) is the abbreviation for the penny/pence. The forward slash symbol (/) often used for the shilling is called a solidus. Monetary variations of other countries are: schilling, shilingi, and skilling.

skatikas Lithuania, in use from 1918 to 1923. Equal to one-hundredth of an auksinas. The word is Lithuanian for "penny." Its Lithuanian plural is either skatikai or skatiku, depending on the number it is associated with.

skilling Norwegian equivalent of the British shilling. *See* **shilling**.

sol Argentina, Bolivia, Peru. Named in honor of the Spanish navigator Juan Diaz de Solis (ca. 1470–1516), who discovered Peru and the Rio de la Plata ("Silver River") estuary between Argentina and Uruguay. The Spanish plural is soles.

The sol is also a coin of pre- and post-revolutionary France. It was renamed sou and was equal to one-twentieth of a livre.

som (Kyrgyz: сом; Uzbek: сўм) Kyrgyzstan and Uzbekistan, since 1993. Divisible into 100 tyjyn.

somoni (Tajiki: сомонй) Tajikistan, since 2001. Divisible into 100 dirams. It is named in honor of Ismoili Somoni (A.D. 847–907), the first Tajik emperor and founder of the early Tajik nation.

sou France. Originally called a sol, and equal to five centimes or ¹⁄₂₀ of a livre.

stiver *see* **stuiver**

stotin Slovenia, since 1992. Equal to one-hundredth of a tolar. It is derived from *sto*, meaning "one hundred." Its Slovenian plural is stotinov.

stotinka (Bulgarian: стотинка) Bulgaria, since 1880. Equal to one-hundredth of a lev. It is derived from *sto* (Bulgarian: сто), meaning "one hundred." The Bulgarian plural is stotinki (стотинки).

stuiver *also* **stiver** Guyana, Netherlands. Dutch monetary unit equal to ¹⁄₂₀ of a guilder (*gulden*) or florin. One theory is that its name is derived from the Dutch word *stuiven*, meaning "gush" or "spurt." On the reverse of the bezemstuiver ("broom stuiver") coin there were seven arrows, symbolizing the seven provinces of the general states.

su Cambodia, since 1975. Equal to one-hundredth of a riel.

sucre Ecuador, in use from 1884 to 2000. Divisible into 100 centavos. It is named in honor of the South American liberator and general, Antonio José de Sucre (1795–1830). Strangely enough, although Sucre is the judi-

cial capital of Bolivia, that country has no monetary unit by that name.

syli Guinea, in use from 1972 to 1986. Divisible into 100 cauris. It comes from a native language (probably Susa) term for "elephant."

tael China, Taiwan

taka Bangladesh, since 1972. Divisible into 100 paisas (poishas). Its origin is from the Sanskrit *tanka*, meaning "coin."

tala Samoa, since 1967. Divisible into 100 sene. The name is a native variation of the pronunciation of "dollar."

talonas Lithuania, in use from 1991 to 1993. Its Lithuanian plural is talonu.

tambala Malawi, since 1971. Equal to one-hundredth of a kwacha. It is a native word for "cockerel."

tenge (Kazakh: теңге; Tajiki: тенге) *also* **tange** Kazakhstan (from 1993) and Tajikistan from (1995 to 2000). The Kazakh tenge is divisible into 100 tiyn; the Tajiki tenge is equal to one-hundredth of a Tajiki ruble. Its origin is a word meaning "scales," as on a fish.

tennesi (Turkmen: теннеси) Turkmenistan, since 1993. Equal to one-hundredth of a manat.

tetri (Georgian: თეთრი) Georgia since 1995. Equal to one-hundredth of a lari.

thaler Ethiopia. *See* **dollar**.

thebe Botswana, since 1976. Equal to one-hundredth of a pula. The name is a native word meaning "shield" — a symbol that appeared on some of the country's first coins.

tical *also* **tikal** Cambodia, until 1863; Siam (now Thailand), until 1926. The Cambodian tical was divisible into eight fuang or 64 att, the Siamese tical into four salung.

tiyn (Kazakh: тиын; Kyrgyz: тыйын; Uzbek: тийин) *also* **tiyin**, **tyjyn** Kazakhstan, Kyrgyzstan, and Uzbekistan, since 1993. The Kazakh tiyn equals one-hundredth of a tenge; both the Kyrgyz and the Uzbek tiyn equal one-hundredth of a som.

toea Papua New Guinea, since 1975. Equal to one-hundredth of a kina. The toea is a valuable shell traditionally used by the natives inhabiting the coastal villages for bride-price ceremonies.

togrog (Mongolian: төгрөг) *also* **tugrik**, **tughrik** Mongolia, since 1925. Divisible into 100 mongo. The name means "round," similar in meaning to the Chinese yuan.

tolar Slovenia, since 1992. Divisible into 100 stotinov. Although the English plural is tolars, the Slovenian plural can be either tolarja or tolarjev, depending on the amount.

toman Iran, in use from 1825 to 1932. Divisible into 10 krans and 200 shahis.

tugrik *see* **togrog**

vatu Vanuatu, since 1981. Divisible into 100 centimes. The name is derived from that of the country.

venezolano Venezuela, in use from 1853 to 1879. Divisible into 100 centavos. The name venezolano is taken from the name of the country.

won (Korean: 원) North and South Korea. Divisible into 100 chon (North Korea) and 100 jeon (South Korea). Prior to 1962, the official name of the won was "hwan." The word won, like the Chinese yuan, means "round."

xu *also* **sau, su** Vietnam, since 1954. Currently equal to one-hundredth of a dong. When Vietnam was part of French Indochina, xu was an alternate name for the centime; thus the xu had the meaning of "pence" or "cents."

yen (Japanese: 円) One of the world's major currencies, the yen has been the monetary unit of Japan since 1871; it is divisible into 100 sen. Yen (pronounced "en" in Japanese) is the Japanese-language equivalent of the Chinese yuan, meaning "round" or "cir-

cle." In addition, the Japanese ideograph for yen (y) is an abbreviation for yuan (圆).

yuan (Chinese: 圆) *also* yuan renminbi China (since 1949), Mongolia and Taiwan. Divisible into 100 fen or 10 jiao. In the late nineteenth and early twentieth centuries, the Chinese dollar (a larger silver-dollar-sized coin) was the popular English-language term for the yuan. Also spelled yüan, the word means "round, a circle," i.e., a coin. Yuan is also the name of a river in southeast-central China, a tributary of the Yangtze, as well as the name of a Mongol dynasty. In 1949, following the revolution that drove the Nationalists to the nearby island of Taiwan, the monetary system was reformed to a more egalitarian one. The yuan was renamed the yuan renminbi, or "people's currency." Often the yuan simply goes by "renminbi."

zaire *also* **zaïre** Democratic Republic of the Congo (formerly Zaire), in use from 1967 to 1998. Divisible into 100 makuta. It takes its name from that of the country.

zloty (Polish: złoty) Poland, since 1922. Divisible into 100 groszy. In Polish, it means "golden." Although the English plural is zlotys, the Polish plural can be either złote or złotych, depending on the number it is associated with.

Appendix A:
Foreign Language
Number Systems

	0	1	2	3	4	5	6	7	8	9	10	50	100	500	1000
Amharic	።	፩	፪	፫	፬	፭		፯	፰	፱	፲	፶	፻	፭፻	፲፻
Arabic	٠	١	٢	٣	٤	٥	٦	٧	٨	٩	١٠	٥٠	١٠٠	٥٠٠	١٠٠٠
Bangla	০	১	২	৩	৪	৫	৬	৭	৮	৯	১০	৫০	১০০	৫০০	১০০০
Burmese	၀	၁	၂	၃	၄	၅	၆	၇	၈	၉	၁၀	၅၀	၁၀၀	၅၀၀	၁၀၀၀
Chinese, official	零	壹	貳	叁	肆	伍	陸	柒	捌	玖	拾	拾伍	佰壹	佰伍	仟壹
Chinese, common	〇	一	二	三	四	五	六	七	八	九	十	十五	百	百五	千
Farsi	٠	١	٢	٣	۴	۵	۶	٧	٨	٩	١٠	۵٠	١٠٠	۵٠٠	١٠٠٠
Georgian		ა	ბ	გ	დ	ე	ვ	ზ	ჱ	თ	ი	ნ	რ	ჶ	ჩ
Korean		일	이	삼	사	오	육	칠	팔	구	십	오십	백	오백	천
Khmer/Lao/Thai	០	១	២	៣	៤	៥	៦	៧	៨	៩	១០	៥០	១០០	៥០០	១០០០
Sanskrit/Hindi	०	१	२	३	४	५	६	७	८	९	१०	५०	१००	५००	१०००

Appendix B:
Families of Monetary Units

cent	centas, centavo, centesimo, centime, centimo, centisimo, santime, sene, seniti, sent, sente, senti, sentimo
cross	cruzado, cruzeiro, krajczár, kreuzer
crown	corona, korona, koruna, króna, krone, kroon
denarius	decimo, den, denar, dinar, dinero, dirham, diram
dollar	daalder, dalar, daler, tala, talari, thaler, tolar
florin	forint
franc	franco, franga
gold, golden	aureus, aurar, eyrir, öre, øre
gross	groschen, grosz, guerche, kurus, qirsh
Hall*	haler, halier, heller
lion	leone, leu, lev
mark	marka, markka
mil	mill, millieme, millime, milréis
paisa	baiza, besa, pesa, pice, pie, poisha, pya
penny	fen, fenig, fening, pengő, penni, penning, pfennig, pingin
pound	libra, lira, livre, pond, punt
royal	real, réis, rial, riyal
ruble	rublei, rublis
rupee	rufiyaa, rupiah, rupie
solidus	shilingi, shilling, skilling, sol, sou
weight	peseta, peso, piso

---

* or Schwäbisch-Hall

Appendix C: Monetary Abbreviations and Symbols

The following tables list over 340 abbreviations and symbols for the monetary units given in this book. Unless indicated otherwise, the English singular form is given and the abbreviation or symbol applies to both the singular and plural unit (e.g., Fr is the abbreviation for both franc and francs). Latin letters that either have one or more lines through them (e.g., ฿, ₭, ₮, ¥) or are preceded by a symbol (e.g., £F, $b, /s) are listed as symbols rather than abbreviations, and some letters that appear to be Latin are listed under the Cyrillic alphabet.

Abbreviations Using Latin Letters

A, a	anna, avo, eyrir		BF	franc (Belgium)
A$	dollar (Australia)		bht	baht
Af	afghani		BK	bipkwele
Afg	afghani		BR	ruble (Belarus)
Afl	florin (Netherlands Antilles)		Bs	bolivar, boliviano
Afs	afghanis,* florin (Netherlands Antilles)		bt	baht
			BWI$	dollar (British West Indies)
Ag	angolar		Bz$	dollar (Belize)
Ags	angolares*		C, c	cedi, cent, centas, centavo, centesimo, centime, centimo, colón, sen, xu
AMD	dram			
An	anna			
Ans	anna		C$	dollar (Canada), cordoba
As	anna*		c/.	centavo
aur	aurer*		cen	centime, centesimo
B, b	baht, ban, bolivar, buqsha, butut		cens	centimos*
B$	dollar (Bahamas)		ces	centimes
B/	balboa		cent	centas, centavo, centime, centesimo, centimo
batz	batzen			
BD	dinar, dollar (Bahrain)		CF	franc (Comoros)
Bd$	dollar (Bermuda)		CH	chetrum
Bds$	dollar (Barbados)		Ch$	peso (Chile)

CI$	dollar (Cayman Islands)	G, g	guinea,† gourde, groschen, guarani, guilder (*gulden*)
cme	centime	G$	dollar (Guyana)
cmes	centimes*	G/	guarani
cmi	centesimi*	Gi	guilder (*gulden*)
Cn	candareen, chon	gn	guinea†
cnt	centas, centavo	gns	guineas*
COP	kopeck	Gr	grosz
COR	corona	Gs, gs	guaranis, guineas*
cos	centavos*	H, h	halala, haler, halerze, halier, heller
CR	colon	Hal, hal	halerze, halier, haller
cs	centavos, cents, cordoba	HK$	dollar (Hong Kong)
Cs$	cruzeiro	I/.	inti
ct	cent, centas, centavo, centimo	IL	pound (Israel)
ctms	centimos*	IR£	pound (Ireland)
cto	centavo, centimo	IS	shekel
cts	cents,* centavos,* centesimos,* centimes,* centimos*	JD	dinar (Jordan)
ctv	centavo	K, k	kina, kip, kobo, kopeck, koruna, krone, kurus, kwacha, kyat, makuta
ctvos	centavos*	KAP	kapeikas
ctvs	centavos*	Kč	koruna (Czech Republic, Slovakia)
cv	centavo	Kčs	koruna (Czech Republic, Slovakia)
cvos	centavos*	KD	dinar (Kuwait)
cvs	centavos*	KM	mark (Bosnia-Herzegovina)
Cz$	cruzado	KN	kip, kuna
D, d	dalasi, dinar, pence, penny	KOP	kopeek
DA	dinars (Algeria)	KR	korona
Db	dobra	Kr, kr	kreuzer, krona, krone, kroon, kurus
Dh	dirham	Krs	kurus
Dhs	dirhams*	Ks	koruna (Slovakia)
din	dinar	Kshs	shilling (Kenya)
Dkr	krone (Denmark)	kz	kwanza
DM	deutsche mark	KZr	kwanza reajustado
drs	dinars*	L	larin, lek, lempira, leu, lira (Italian), litas
E	escudo, lilangeni	L£	pound (Lebanon)
E$	dollar (Ethiopia)	LD	dinar (Libya)
EC$	dollar (East Caribbean)	LE	pound (Egypt)
ESC	escudo	Le	leone
Eth$	birr	Lit	lira (San Marino), litas
F, f	fillér, fils, florin, franc	LL	pound (Lebanon)
F$	dollar (Fiji)	Lm	lira (Malta)
FBu	franc (Burundi)	lp	lipa
fc	franc	LS	pound (Sudan, Syria)
fcs	francs*	Ls	lat
FD	franc (Djibouti)	Lt	litas
fen	fenig	LuxF	franc (Luxembourg)
FG	franc (Guinea)	Lv	lev
fl, Fl	florin	lw	lwei
FNH	franc (New Hebrides, now Vanuatu)		
Fr, fr	franc, franga		
Frs	francs*		
Frw	franc (Rwanda)		
Ft	forint		

M, m	maloti,* mark, marka, markka, manat, mil, millieme, millime
MAN	manat
mills	milliemes*
mk	mark, marka, markka
mms	milliemes*
MT	metical
N, n	ngwee
N$	dollar (Namibia), new peso
N£	pound (Nigeria)
Na	naira
Naf	florin (Netherlands Antilles)
NF	new franc (*nouveau franc*)
Nfa	nakfa
NIS	new Israel shekel
NK	new makuta
Nkr	krone (Norway)
NKz	new kwanza (*novo kwanza*)
NP, np	naya paisa, new pence, new penny, new pesewa
NT$	dollar (Taiwan)
NU	ngultrum
NZ	new zaire (*nouveau zaïre*)
NZ$	dollar (New Zealand)
OR	rial (Oman)
P, p	centime, new penny, paisa, para, pataca, pengő, penni, penny, pesewa, peso, piastre, pice, pul, pula
P$	paisa
Pa, pa	para
par	para
pen	penni
Pf, pf	pfennig
PG	peso (Guinea-Bissau)
Ps	paisa, pies,* puls*
pt	pataca, piastre
pta	peseta
ptas	pesetas*
ptc	pataca
ptcs	patacas*
Pts	peseta, patacas*
Q, q	qapik, qindar, quetzal
QD, qd	qindar
qind	qindar
qint	qindar
QR	riyal (Qatar)
R	rand, real, reís, rial, riel, riyal, ruble (Armenia, Turkmenistan), rufiyaa, rupee
R$	real (Brazil)
Ra	real
RBL	ruble, rublei
RBS	rigsbank skilling

RD$	peso (Dominican Republic)
Re	rupee†
Rf	rufiyaa
Rl	rial†
Rls	rials*
RM	reichmark, ringgit
RO	rial (Oman)
Rp	rappen, rupee, rupiah
Rs	rupee,* real,* réis
RUB	rublei, rublis
s	santimi, sene, sengi, seniti, sent, sente, sentimo, shilling, skilling
S	schilling, sol, stiver (*stuiver*), syli
S/.	sol, sucre
sant	santimi
SD	dinar (Sudan)
Sf	florin (Suriname)
SFr	franc (Switzerland)
Sh, sh	shilling
Shs	shillings*
SI$	dollar (Solomon Islands)
Sk, sk	koruna (Slovakia), skatikas, skilling
skill	skilling
Skr	krona
SlT	tolar
Sn, sn	sen
Sp	speciedaler
Sps	speciedalers*
SR	riyal (Saudi Arabia)
Sre	rupee (Seychelles)
SRls	riyals (Saudi Arabia)
St	stiver (*stuiver*)
ST	stotinka (Macedonia), satang
Sy	syli
t	tambala, thebe, toea
T$	pa'anga
TD	dinar (Tunisia)
Tg	togrog (tughrik, tughik)
TL	lira (Turkish)
Tө	togrog (tughrik, tughik)
TSh$	shilingi (Tanzania)
TT$	dollar (Trinidad and Tobago)
VT	vatu
UM	ouguiya
Wn	won
WS$	dollar (Samoa)
Y	yuan
Z, z	zaire
Zł, zł	zloty
Zło, zło	zloty
Złot, złot	zloty

†Singular abbreviation
*Plural abbreviation

Abbreviations Using Non-Latin Alphabets

AMHARIC

ብ	dollar, talari, birr (ብር)
ሳ	cent, santime (ሳንቲም)
ግ	piastre, guerche (ግርሽ)

ARABIC

ب	naya paisa, para (باره), piastre (قرش)
پ	para (باره), pul (پول)
د	dinar (دينار), dirham (دراهم)
دن	dinar (دينار)
س	cent (سنتات), santime (سنتيم)
غ	piastre, also guerche or qirsh (غروش)
ف	fils (فاس), franc (فرنكا)
ق	piastre, also guerche or qirsh (غروش)
ي	piastre, also guerche or qirsh (قرش)
ل	pound, also livre, lira (ليرة)
م	mil (مل), millieme, millime (مليم)
ه	halala (هللة)

BURMESE

`	anna
၈	paise
၌	pya
၀	rupee

CYRILLIC

гри	hryvnia (гривня)
д	dinar (динар)
дин	dinar (динар)
к	kopeck (копейка), kopiyka (копійка)
коп	kopeck (копейка)
крб	karbovanets (карбованец)
л	lev (лев)
лв	lev (лев)
н.д.	novi (new) dinar (нови динар)
п	para (пара)
р	ruble (рубль)
руб	ruble (рубль)
с	som (сом, сӱм), somoni (сомонй), stotinka (стотинка)
ст	stotinka (стотинка)
стот	stotinka (стотинка)
т	tyjyn, also tiyin and tiyn (тыйын, тийин)
тө	togrog, also tughrik and tughik (төгрөг)

(continued)

x	heller (хелер)
ш	shahiv, also shagiv (шагів)

CHINESE

分	fen
角	jiao
圓	yuan

DEVANĀGARĪ

आ	anna (आना)
न पै	naya paisa (नये पैसे)
पै	pice, paisa (पैसे)
पा	pie (पा)
रू	rupee (रुपया)

GREEK

δρ, 𝔇ρ, ΔΡ, ΔΡΑΧ	drachma (δραχμαι, ΔΡΑΧΜΑΙ)
Λ	lepton (ΛΕΠΤΟΝ)
ΛΕΠ	lepton (ΛΕΠΤΟΝ)

HEBREW

אג	agora (אגורה)
ש	shekel (שקל)
ש ח	new Israel shekel (שקל חדש)

JAPANESE

厘	rin
銭	sen
円	yen

KOREAN

전	chon (also cheun, jeon, jun)
환	hwan
원	won

MONGOLIAN

ᠮᠥᠩᠭᠥ	mongo (also mung, mungu)
ᠲᠥᠭᠥᠷᠢᠭ	togrog (also tughrik, tughik)

MISCELLANEOUS

₫	dong (đồng)	჻ჰრ	Georgian ruble (჻ჰრჳჃჲჲ)
₧	kip (ກີບ)	บาท	baht (บาท)
Ռ, Ռ.Բ., Ռ.ԲԼ	Armenian ruble (Ռ.ՈՒԲԼԻ)	ลต	satang (ลตางด์)

Symbols

₳	austral	₪	new Israel shekel
฿	baht	₱	piso
$Eth	birr	₱	peso
$b	peso boliviano	$a	peso (Argentina)
¢	cedi, cent, centavo, centimo, colon, sen	₰	pfennig
ċ	cent	£C	pound (Cyprus)
$	centavo, colon, dollar, escudo, pa'anga, peso, piastre, ringgit, sucre, tala	£E	pound (Egypt)
		£F	pound (Falkland Islands)
		£G	pound (Gibraltar)
		£L	pound (Libya)
₡	colon	£P	pound (Palestine)
₢	cordoba	£Syr	pound (Syria)
₢	cruziero	Ł	pound (Samoa)
₫	dong	£, £	pound, lira
E°	escudo (Chile)	៛	riel (Cambodia)
€	euro	৳	rupee (Bengali)
ƒ	florin	/s	seniti, shilling
₣	franc	/	shilling
₭	kip	₮	togrog (also tughrik, tughik)
£M, £m	lira (Malta)	₩	won
₦	naira	¥	yen

Unicode Symbols

The Unicode Standard is a character coding system for computers designed to support the worldwide interchange, processing, and display of written text in languages of the modern world. There is an assigned code point or address — a hexadecimal number that is used to represent that character or form defined in Unicode. Even though a given Unicode font potentially has 65,536 characters that can cover more than 48 alphabet systems, not all fonts that support the Unicode standard have every one of the assigned symbols.

Symbol	Monetary Unit	Unicode*
$	dollar, peso	0024
/	shilling	002F
¢	cent	00A2
£	pound, lira	00A3
¥	yen	00A5
৳	rupee (Bengali)	09F3
฿	baht	0E3F
៛	riel (Khmer)	17DF
€	euro	20A0
₡	colon	20A1
₢	cruziero	20A2
₣	franc	20A3
₦	naira	20A6
Pts	peseta	20A7
Rs	rupee	20A8
₩	won	20A9
₪	new Israel shekel	20AA
₫	dong	20AB
₭	kip	20AD
₮	togrog	20AE
₯	drachma	20AF
₰	pfennig	20B0
₱	peso	20B1
₤	pound, lira	22A4
﷼	riyal	FDFC

*4.0 Standard Code Point

Appendix D:
ISO-4217 Currency Codes

The International Organization for Standardization (ISO) has defined three-letter currency codes for international monetary units according to the ISO-4217 standard. In most cases the three-letter code is composed of the country's two-letter Internet code (ISO-3166 standard) and a letter to represent the currency unit. For example, the code for Canadian dollars is simply Canada's two-character Internet code (CA) plus a one-character currency designator (D). Besides monetary units, the ISO-4217 standard also defines codes for precious metals, entities used in international finance (such as SDRs — special drawing rights), and multinational confederations, such as the CFA franc, whose codes generally begin with the letter X.

By Country

Country	Monetary Unit	Currency Code
Afghanistan	afghani	AFA
Albania	lek	ALL
Algeria	dinar	DZD
American Samoa	U.S. dollar	USD
Andorra	Andorran peseta	ADP*
	euro	EUR
	Spanish peseta	ESP*
	French franc	FRF*
Angola	kwanza	AOA
	new kwanza	AON*
	new kwanza readjustado	AOR*
Anguilla	East Caribbean dollar	XCD
Antigua and Barbuda	East Caribbean dollar	XCD
Argentina	austral	ARA*
	peso	ARS
Armenia	dram	AMD

Country	Monetary Unit	Currency Code
Aruba	guilder	AWG
Australia	dollar	AUD
Austria	schilling	ATS*
	euro	EUR
Azerbaijan	manta	AZM
Bahamas	dollar	BSD
Bahrain	dinar	BHD
Bangladesh	taka	BDT
Barbados	dollar	BBD
Belarus	ruble	BYB, BYR*
Belgium	euro	EUR
	franc	BEF*
Belize	dollar	BZD
Benin	CFA franc†	XOF
Bermuda	dollar	BMD
Bhutan	Indian rupee	INR*
	ngultrum	BTN
Bolivia	boliviano	BOB
Bosnia and Herzegovina	convertible mark	BAM
Botswana	pula	BWP
Bouvet Island	krone	NOK
Brazil	cruzeiro	BRE*
	real	BRL
	cruzeiro real	BRR*
British Indian Ocean Territory	U.S. dollar	USD
Brunei	dollar	BND
Bulgaria	lev	BGL*
	Bulgarian lev	BGN
Burkina-Faso	CFA franc†	XOF
Burma	kyat	MNK
Burundi	franc	BIF
Cambodia (Khmer)	riel	KHR
Cameroon	CFA franc‡	XAF
Canada	dollar	CAD
Cape Verde	escudo	CVE
Cayman Islands	dollar	KYD
Central African Republic	CFA franc‡	XAF
Chad	CFA franc‡	XAF
Chile	Chilean peso	CLP
China	yuan renminbi	CNY
Christmas Island	Australian dollar	AUD
Cocos-Keeling Islands	Australian dollar	AUD
Colombia	peso	COP
Comoros	franc	KMF
Congo (Democratic Republic of)	franc congolais	CDF
	new zaire	ZRN*
	zaire	ZRZ*
Congo-Brazzaville	CFA franc‡	XAF
Cook Islands	New Zealand dollar	NZD
Costa Rica	colon	CRC

Country	Monetary Unit	Currency Code
Croatia	kuna	HRK
Cuba	peso	CUP
Cyprus	pound	CYP
Czech Republic	koruna	CSK,* CZK
Denmark	krone	DKK
Djibouti	franc	DJF
Dominica	East Caribbean dollar	XCD
Dominican Republic	peso	DOP
Ecuador	U.S. dollar	USD
	sucre	ECS*
Egypt	pound	EGP
El Salvador	colon	SVC*
	U.S. dollar	USD
Equatorial Guinea	epkwele	GQE*
	CFA franc‡	XAF
Eritrea	nakfa	ERN
Estonia	kroon	EEK
Ethiopia	birr	ETB
Falkland Islands	pound	FKP
Faroe Islands	krone	DKK
Fiji	dollar	FJD
Finland	euro	EUR
	markka	FIM*
France	euro	EUR
	franc	FRF*
French Guiana	euro	EUR
	French franc	FRF*
French Polynesia	CFP franc	XPF
Gabon	CFA franc‡	XAF
Gambia	dalasi	GMD
Georgia	lari	GEL
Germany	ostmark	DDM*
	deutsche mark	DEM*
	euro	EUR
Ghana	cedi	GHC
Gibraltar	pound	GIP
Great Britain	pound sterling	GBP
Greece	euro	EUR
	drachma	GRD*
Greenland	krone	DKK
Grenada	East Caribbean dollar	XCD
Guadeloupe	euro	EUR
	French franc	FRF*
Guam	U.S. dollar	USD
Guatemala	quetzal	GTQ
Guinea	franc	GNF
	syli	GNS*
Guinea-Bissau	peso	GWP*
	CFA franc†	XOF
Guyana	dollar	GYD

Country	Monetary Unit	Currency Code
Haiti	gourde	HTG
	U.S. dollar	USD
Heard Islands	Australian dollar	AUD
Honduras	lempira	HNL
Hong Kong	Hong Kong dollar	HKD
Hungary	forint	HUF
Iceland	krona	ISK
India	Indian rupee	INR
Indonesia	rupiah	IDR
Iran	rial	IRR
Iraq	dinar	IQD
Ireland	euro	EUR
	pound	IEP*
Israel	new Israel shekel	ILS
Italy	euro	EUR
	lira	ITL*
Ivory Coast	CFA franc†	XOF
Jamaica	dollar	JMD
Japan	yen	JPY
Jordan	dinar	JOD
Kazakhstan	tenge	KZT
Kenya	shilling	KES
Kiribati	Australian dollar	AUD
Kuwait	dinar	KWD
Kyrgyzstan	som	KGS
Laos	kip	LAK
Latvia	lat	LVL
Lebanon	pound	LBP
Lesotho	loti	LSL
	South African rand	ZAR*
Liberia	dollar	LRD
Libya	dinar	LYD
Liechtenstein	Swiss franc	CHF
Lithuania	litas	LTL
Luxembourg	euro	EUR
	franc	LUF*
Macao	pataca	MOP
Macedonia	denar	MKD
Madagascar	franc	MGF
Malawi	kwacha	MWK
Malaysia	ringgit	MYR
Maldives	rufiyaa	MVR
Mali	CFA franc†	XOF
Malta	lira	MTL
Marshall Islands	U.S. dollar	USD
Martinique	euro	EUR
	French franc	FRF*
Mauritania	ouguiya	MRO
Mauritius	rupee	MUR
Mayotte	euro	EUR

Country	Monetary Unit	Currency Code
Mayotte (continued)	French franc	FRF*
McDonald Islands	Australian dollar	AUD
Mexico	peso	MXN, MXP*
Micronesia	U.S. dollar	USD
Moldova	leu	MDL
Monaco	euro	EUR
	French franc	FRF*
Mongolia	tugrik	MNT
Montenegro	euro	EUR
	dinar	YUD,* YUM*
Montserrat	East Caribbean dollar	XCD
Morocco	dirham	MAD
Mozambique	metical	MZM
Namibia	dollar	NAD
	South African rand	ZAR*
Nauru	Australian dollar	AUD
Nepal	rupee	NPR
Netherlands	euro	EUR
	guilder	NLG*
Netherlands Antilles	guilder	ANG
New Caledonia	CFP franc	XPF
New Zealand	dollar	NZD
Nicaragua	cordoba oro	NIO
Niger	CFA franc†	XOF
Nigeria	naira	NGN
Niue	New Zealand dollar	NZD
Norfolk Island	Australian dollar	AUD
North Korea	won	KPW
Northern Mariana Islands	U.S. dollar	USD
Norway	krone	NOK
Oman	rial	OMR
Pakistan	rupee	PKR
Palau	U.S. dollar	USD
Panama	balboa	PAB
	U.S. dollar	USD
Papua New Guinea	kina	PGK
Paraguay	guarani	PYG
Peru	nuevo sol	PEN
Philippines	peso	PHP
Pitcairn	New Zealand dollar	NZD
Poland	zloty	PLN, PLZ*
Portugal	euro	EUR
	escudo	PTE*
Puerto Rico	U.S. dollar	USD
Qatar	rial	QAR
Reunion	euro	EUR
	French franc	FRF*
Romania	leu	ROL
Russia	ruble	RUB, RUR*
Rwanda	franc	RWF

Country	Monetary Unit	Currency Code
St. Helena	pound	SHP
St. Kitts and Nevis	East Caribbean dollar	XCD
St. Lucia	East Caribbean dollar	XCD
St. Pierre and Miquelon	euro	EUR
	French franc	FRF*
St. Vincent and the Grenadines	East Caribbean dollar	XCD
Samoa	tala	WST
San Marino	euro	EUR
	Italian lira	ITL*
São Tomé and Príncipe	dobra	STD
Saudi Arabia	riyal	SAR
Senegal	CFA franc†	XOF
Serbia	dinar	YUD,* YUM
Seychelles	rupee	SCR
Sierra Leone	leone	SLL
Singapore	dollar	SGD
Slovakia	koruna	CSK,* SKK
Slovenia	tolar	SIT
Solomon Islands	dollar	SBD
Somalia	shilling	SOS
South Africa	rand	ZAR
South Korea	won	KRW
Spain	peseta	ESP*
	euro	EUR
Sri Lanka	rupee	LKR
Sudan	dinar	SDD
	pound	SDP*
Suriname	dollar	SRD
	guilder	SRG*
Svalbard and Jan Mayen	krone	NOK
Swaziland	lilangeni	SZL
Sweden	krona	SEK
Switzerland	franc	CHF
Syria	pound	SYP
Taiwan	new Taiwan dollar	TWD
Tajikistan	ruble	TJR*
	somoni	TJS
Tanzania	shilling	TZS
Thailand	baht	THB
Timor Liste	escudo	TPE*
	rupiah	IDR*
	U.S. dollar	USD
Togo	CFA franc†	XOF
Tokelau	New Zealand dollar	NZD
Tonga	pa'anga	TOP
Trinidad and Tobago	dollar	TTD
Tunisia	dinar	TND
Turkey	lira	TRL
Turkmenistan	manat	TMM
Turks and Caicos Islands	U.S. dollar	USD

Country	Monetary Unit	Currency Code
Tuvalu	Australian dollar	AUD
Uganda	shilling	UGS,* UGX
Ukraine	hryvnia	UAH
United Arab Emirates	dirham	AED
United States	U.S. dollar	USD
Uruguay	peso uruguayo	UYU
Uzbekistan	sum	UZS
Vanuatu	vatu	VUV
Vatican City	euro	EUR
	Italian lira	ITL*
Venezuela	bolivar	VEB
Vietnam	dong	VND
Virgin Islands (British)	U.S. dollar	USD
Virgin Islands (U.S.)	U.S. dollar	USD
Wallis and Futuna	CFP franc	XPF
Western Sahara	dirham	MAD
Yemen	rial	YER
Zambia	kwacha	ZMK
Zimbabwe	dollar	ZWD

*Obsolete code. †Responsible authority: Banque Centrale des États de l'Afrique de l'Ouest (BCEAO).
‡Responsible authority: Banque des États de l'Afrique Centrale (BEAC).

By Currency Code

Currency Code	Country	Monetary Unit
ADP*	Andorra	peseta
AED	United Arab Emirates	dirham
AFA	Afghanistan	afghani
ALL	Albania	lek
AMD	Armenia	dram
ANG*	Netherlands Antilles	guilder
AOA	Angola	kwanza
AON*	Angola	new kwanza
AOR*	Angola	new kwanza readjustado
ARA*	Argentina	austral
ARS	Argentina	peso
ATS*	Austria	schilling
AUD	Australia	dollar
	Christmas Island	
	Cocos-Keeling Islands	
	Heard Islands	
	Kiribati	
	McDonald Islands	
	Nauru	
	Norfolk Island	
	Tuvalu	

Currency Code	Country	Monetary Unit
AWG	Aruba	guilder
AZM	Azerbaijan	manta
BAM	Bosnia and Herzegovina	convertible mark
BBD	Barbados	dollar
BDT	Bangladesh	taka
BEF*	Belgium	franc
BGL*	Bulgaria	lev
BGN	Bulgaria	lev
BHD	Bahrain	dinar
BIF	Burundi	franc
BMD	Bermuda	dollar
BND	Brunei	dollar
BOB	Bolivia	boliviano
BRE*	Brazil	cruzeiro
BRL	Brazil	real
BRR*	Brazil	cruzeiro real
BSD	Bahamas	dollar
BTN	Bhutan	ngultrum
BWP	Botswana	pula
BYB	Belarus	ruble
BYR*	Belarus	ruble
BZD	Belize	dollar
CAD	Canada	dollar
CDF	Democratic Republic of Congo	franc congolais
CHF	Liechtenstein	franc
	Switzerland	
CLP	Chile	peso
CNY	China	yuan renminbi
COP	Colombia	peso
CRC	Costa Rica	colon
CSK*	Czechoslovakia	koruna
CUP	Cuba	peso
CVE	Cape Verde	escudo
CYP	Cyprus	pound
CZK	Czech Republic	koruna
DDM*	East Germany	ostmark
DEM*	Germany	deutsche mark
DJF	Djibouti	franc
DKK	Denmark	krone
	Faroe Islands	
	Greenland	
DOP	Dominican Republic	peso
DZD	Algeria	dinar
ECS	Ecuador	sucre
EEK	Estonia	kroon
EGP	Egypt	pound
ERN	Eritrea	nakfa
ESP*	Andorra	peseta
	Spain	peseta
ETB	Ethiopia	birr

Currency Code	Country	Monetary Unit
EUR	Andorra	euro
	Austria	
	Belgium	
	Finland	
	France	
	French Guiana	
	Germany	
	Greece	
	Guadeloupe	
	Ireland	
	Italy	
	Luxembourg	
	Martinique	
	Mayotte	
	Monaco	
	Montenegro	
	Netherlands	
	Portugal	
	Réunion	
	St. Pierre and Miquelon	
	San Marino	
	Spain	
	Vatican City	
FIM*	Finland	markka
FJD	Fiji	dollar
FKP	Falkland Islands	pound
FRF*	Andorra	franc
	France	
	French Guiana	
	Guadeloupe	
	Martinique	
	Mayotte	
	Monaco	
	Réunion	
	St. Pierre and Miquelon	
GBP	Great Britain	pound
GEL	Georgia	lari
GHC	Ghana	cedi
GIP	Gibraltar	pound
GMD	Gambia	dalasi
GNF	Guinea	franc
GNS*	Guinea	syli
GQE*	Equatorial Guinea	epkwele
GRD*	Greece	drachma
GTQ	Guatemala	quetzal
GWP*	Guinea-Bissau	peso
GYD	Guyana	dollar
HKD	Hong Kong	dollar
HNL	Honduras	lempira
HRK	Croatia	kuna

Currency Code	Country	Monetary Unit
HTG	Haiti	gourde
HUF	Hungary	forint
IDR	Indonesia	rupiah
	Timor Leste	
IEP*	Ireland	pound
ILS	Israel	new Israel shekel
INR	Bhutan	rupee
	India	
IQD	Iraq	dinar
IRR	Iran	rial
ISK	Iceland	krona
ITL*	Italy	lira
	San Marino	
	Vatican City	
JMD	Jamaica	dollar
JOD	Jordan	dinar
JPY	Japan	yen
KES	Kenya	shilling
KGS	Kyrgyzstan	som
KHR	Cambodia	riel
KMF	Comoros	franc
KPW	North Korea	won
KRW	South Korea	won
KWD	Kuwait	dinar
KYD	Cayman Islands	dollar
KZT	Kazakhstan	tenge
LAK	Laos	kip
LBP	Lebanon	pound
LKR	Sri Lanka	rupee
LRD	Liberia	dollar
LSL	Lesotho	loti
LTL	Lithuania	litas
LUF*	Luxembourg	franc
LVL	Latvia	lat
LYD	Libya	dinar
MAD	Morocco	dirham
	Western Sahara	
MDL	Moldova	leu
MGF	Madagascar	franc
MKD	Macedonia	denar
MNK	Burma	kyat
MNT	Mongolia	tugrik
MOP	Macao	pataca
MRO	Mauritania	ouguiya
MTL	Malta	lira
MUR	Mauritius	rupee
MVR	Maldives	rufiyaa
MWK	Malawi	kwacha
MXN	Mexico	peso
MXP*	Mexico	peso

Currency Code	Country	Monetary Unit
MYR	Malaysia	ringgit
MZM	Mozambique	metical
NAD	Namibia	dollar
NGN	Nigeria	naira
NIO	Nicaragua	cordoba oro
NLG*	Netherlands	guilder
NOK	Bouvet Island	krone
	Norway	
	Svalbard and Jan Mayen	
NPR	Nepal	rupee
NZD	Cook Islands	New Zealand dollar
	New Zealand	
	Niue	
	Pitcairn	
	Tokelau	
OMR	Oman	rial
PAB	Panama	balboa
PEN	Peru	nuevo sol
PGK	Papua New Guinea	kina
PHP	Philippines	peso
PKR	Pakistan	rupee
PLN	Poland	zloty
PLZ*	Poland	zloty
PTE*	Portugal	escudo
PYG	Paraguay	guarani
QAR	Qatar	rial
ROL	Romania	leu
RUB	Russia/Soviet Union	ruble
RUR*	Russia/Soviet Union	ruble
RWF	Rwanda	franc
SAR	Saudi Arabia	riyal
SBD	Solomon Islands	dollar
SCR	Seychelles	rupee
SDD	Sudan	dinar
SDP*	Sudan	pound
SEK	Sweden	krona
SGD	Singapore	dollar
SHP	St. Helena	pound
SIT	Slovenia	tolar
SKK	Slovakia	koruna
SLL	Sierra Leone	leone
SOS	Somalia	shilling
SRD	Suriname	dollar
SRG*	Suriname	guilder
STD	São Tomé and Príncipe	dobra
SVC	El Salvador	colon
SYP	Syria	pound
SZL	Swaziland	lilangeni
THB	Thailand	baht
TJR*	Tajikistan	ruble

Currency Code	Country	Monetary Unit
TJS	Tajikistan	somoni
TMM	Turkmenistan	manat
TND	Tunisia	dinar
TOP	Tonga	pa'anga
TPE*	Timor Leste	escudo
TRL	Turkey	lira
TTD	Trinidad and Tobago	dollar
TWD	Taiwan	new Taiwan dollar
TZS	Tanzania	shilling
UAH	Ukraine	hryvnia
UGS*	Uganda	shilling
UGX	Uganda	shilling
USD	American Samoa	dollar
	British Indian Ocean Territory	
	Ecuador	
	El Salvador	
	Guam	
	Haiti	
	Marshall Islands	
	Micronesia	
	Northern Mariana Islands	
	Palau	
	Panama	
	Puerto Rico	
	Timor Leste	
	Turks and Caicos Islands	
	United States	
	Virgin Islands (British)	
	Virgin Islands (U.S.)	
UYU	Uruguay	peso uruguayo
UZS	Uzbekistan	sum
VEB	Venezuela	bolivar
VND	Vietnam	dong
VUV	Vanuatu	vatu
WST	Samoa	tala
XAF	Cameroon	CFA franc‡
	Central African Republic	
	Chad	
	Congo–Brazzaville	
	Equatorial Guinea	
	Gabon	
XCD	Anguilla	East Caribbean dollar
	Antigua and Barbuda	
	Dominica	
	Grenada	
	Montserrat	
	St. Kitts and Nevis	
	St. Lucia	
	St. Vincent and the Grenadines	
XOF	Benin	CFA franc†

Currency Code	Country	Monetary Unit
XOF (continued)	Burkina-Faso	
	Guinea-Bissau	
	Ivory Coast	
	Mali	
	Niger	
	Senegal	
	Togo	
XPF	French Polynesia	CFP franc
	New Caledonia	
	Wallis and Futuna	
YER	Yemen	rial
YUD*	Serbia	dinar
YUM	Serbia	dinar
ZAR	Lesotho	rand
	Namibia	
	South Africa	
ZMK	Zambia	kwacha
ZRN*	Congo (Democratic Republic of)	new zaire
ZRZ*	Congo (Democratic Republic of)	zaire
ZWD	Zimbabwe	dollar

*Obsolete code. †Responsible authority: Banque Centrale des États de l'Afrique de l'Ouest (BCEAO).
‡Responsible authority: Banque des États de l'Afrique Centrale (BEAC).

Appendix E:
Central Banks

All listed web sites for the following central banks provide English-language information, except where noted. All Internet addresses are subject to change without notice.

Country	Central Bank	Web Site
Afghanistan	Central Bank of Afghanistan	none
Albania	Bank of Albania	www.bankofalbania.org
Algeria	Central Bank of Algeria	www.bank-of-algeria.dz
Andorra	Institut Nacional Andorrà de Finances	www.inaf.ad
Angola	National Bank of Angola	www.bna.ebonet.net1
Anguilla	Eastern Caribbean Central Bank	www.eccb-centralbank.org
Antigua & Barbuda	Eastern Caribbean Central Bank	www.eccb-centralbank.org
Argentina	Central Bank of the Republic of Argentina	www.bcra.gov.ar
Armenia	Central Bank of the Republic of Armenia	www.cba.am
Aruba	Central Bank of Aruba	www.cbaruba.org
Australia	Reserve Bank of Australia	www.rba.gov.au
Austria	National Bank of Austria	www.oenb.co.at
Azerbaijan	National Bank of Azerbaijan	www.nba.az
Bahamas	Central Bank of the Bahamas	centralbankbahamas.com
Bahrain	Bahrain Monetary Agency	www.bma.gov.bh
Bangladesh	Bangladesh Bank	www.bangladesh-bank.org
Barbados	Central Bank of Barbados	www.centralbank.org.bb
Belarus	National Bank of the Republic of Belarus	www.nbrb.by
Belgium	National Bank of Belgium	www.bnb.be
Belize	Central Bank of Belize	www.centralbank.org.bz
Benin	Central Bank of West African States	www.bceao.int
Bermuda	Bermuda Monetary Authority	www.bma.bm
Bhutan	Royal Monetary Authority of Bhutan	www.rma.org.bt
Bolivia	Central Bank of Bolivia	www.bcb.gov.bo[2]
Bosnia-Herzegovina	National Bank of Bosnia and Herzegovina	www.cbbh.gov.ba
Botswana	Bank of Botswana	bankofbotswana.bw
Brazil	Central Bank of Brazil	www.bcb.gov.br
Brunei	Brunei Currency Board	www.finance.gov.bn/bcb/bcb_index.htm

Country	Central Bank	Web Site
Bulgaria	Bulgarian National Bank	www.bnb.bg
Burkina-Faso	Central Bank of West African States	www.bceao.int
Burma	Central Bank of Myanmar	none
Burundi	Bank of the Republic of Burundi	none
Cambodia	National Bank of Cambodia	none
Cameroon	Bank of Central African States	www.beac.int[3]
Canada	Bank of Canada	www.bankofcanada.ca
Cape Verde	Bank of Cape Verde	www.bcv.cv
Cayman Islands	Cayman Islands Currency Board	www.cimoney.com.ky
Central African Republic	Bank of Central African States	www.beac.int[3]
Chad	Bank of Central African States	www.beac.int[3]
Chile	Central Bank of Chile	www.bcentral.cl
China	People's Bank of China	www.pbc.gov.cn
Colombia	Bank of the Republic of Colombia	www.banrep.gov.co
Comoros	Central Bank of the Comoros	none
Congo (Democratic Republic of)	Central Bank of the Congo	www.bcc.cd/go.html[3]
Congo–Brazzaville	Bank of Central African States	www.beac.int[3]
Costa Rica	Central Bank of Costa Rica	www.bccr.fi.cr[2]
Croatia	Croatian National Bank	www.hnb.hr
Cuba	National Bank of Cuba	www.bc.gov.cu
Cyprus	Central Bank of Cyprus	www.centralbank.gov.cy
Czech Republic	Czech National Bank	www.cnb.cz
Denmark	National Bank of Denmark	www.nationalbanken.dk
Djibouti	National Bank of Djibouti	www.banque-centrale.dj
Dominica	East Caribbean Central Bank	www.eccb-centralbank.org
Dominican Republic	Central Bank of the Dominican Republic	www.bancentral.gov.do[2]
Ecuador	Central Bank of Ecuador	www.bce.fin.ec[2]
Egypt	Central Bank of Egypt	www.cbe.org.eg
El Salvador	Central Reserve Bank of El Salvador	www.bcr.gob.sv/ebcr.htm
Equatorial Guinea	Bank of Central African States	www.beac.int[3]
Eritrea	National Bank of Eritrea	none
Estonia	Bank of Estonia	www.bankofestonia.info
Ethiopia	National Bank of Ethiopia	www.telecom.net.et
Falkland Islands	Bank of England	www.bankofengland.co.uk
Fiji	Reserve Bank of Fiji	www.reservebank.gov.fj
Finland	Bank of Finland	www.bof.fi
France	Bank of France	www.banque-france.fr
French Polynesia	Institut d'Émission d'Outre-mer	www.iedom.fr[3]
Gabon	Bank of Central African States	www.beac.int[3]
Gambia	Central Bank of the Gambia	none
Georgia	National Bank of Georgia	www.nbg.gov.ge
Germany	Central Bank of the Federal Republic of Germany (Deutsche Bundesbank)	www.bundesbank.de
Ghana	Bank of Ghana	www.bog.gov.gh
Gibraltar	Bank of England	www.bankofengland.co.uk
Great Britain	Bank of England	www.bankofengland.co.uk
Greece	Bank of Greece	www.bankofgreece.gr
Grenada	Eastern Caribbean Central Bank	www.eccb-centralbank.org

Country	Central Bank	Web Site
Guatemala	Bank of Guatemala	www.banguat.gob.gt
Guinea	Central Bank of the Republic of Guinea	www.bcrg.gov.gn³
Guinea-Bissau	Central Bank of West African States	www.bceao.int
Guyana	Bank of Guyana	www.bankofguyana.org.gy
Haiti	National Bank of the Republic of Haiti	www.brh.net³
Honduras	Central Bank of Honduras	www.bch.hn²
Hong Kong	Hong Kong Monetary Authority	www.info.gov.hk/hkma
Hungary	National Bank of Hungary	www.mnb.hu
Iceland	Central Bank of Iceland	www.sedlabanki.is
India	Reserve Bank of India	www.rbi.org.in
Indonesia	Bank Indonesia	www.bi.go.id
Iran	Central Bank of the Islamic Republic of Iran	www.cbi.ir
Iraq	Central Bank of Iraq	none
Ireland	Central Bank of Ireland	www.centralbank.ie
Israel	Bank of Israel	www.bankisrael.gov.il
Italy	Bank of Italy	www.bancaditalia.it
Ivory Coast	Central Bank of West African States	www.bceao.int
Jamaica	Bank of Jamaica	www.boj.org.jm
Japan	Bank of Japan	www.boj.or.jp
Jordan	Central Bank of Jordan	www.cbj.gov.jo
Kazakhstan	National Bank of Kazakhstan	www.nationalbank.kz
Kenya	Central Bank of Kenya	www.centralbank.go.ke
Kiribati	Reserve Bank of Australia	www.rba.gov.au
Korea, North	Central Bank of the Democratic People's Republic of Korea	none
Korea, South	Bank of Korea	www.bok.or.kr/svc/ frame_eng.html
Kuwait	Central Bank of Kuwait	www.cbk.gov.kw
Kyrgyzstan	National Bank of the Kyrgyz Republic	www.nbkr.kg
Laos	Bank of the Lao People's Democratic Republic	none
Latvia	Bank of Latvia	www.bank.lv
Lebanon	Bank of Lebanon	www.bdliban.com
Lesotho	Central Bank of Lesotho	www.centralbank.org.ls
Liberia	Central Bank of Liberia	none
Libya	Central Bank of Libya	www.cbl-ly.com
Liechtenstein	Swiss National Bank	ww.snb.ch
Lithuania	Bank of Lithuania	www.lb.lt
Luxembourg	Central Bank of Luxembourg	www.bcl.lu
Macao	Monetary Authority of Macao	www.amcm.gov.mo
Macedonia	National Bank of the Republic of Macedonia	www.nbrm.gov.mk
Madagascar	Central Bank of Madagascar	none
Malawi	Reserve Bank of Malawi	www.rbm.malawi.net
Malaysia	Central Bank of Malaysia	www.bnm.gov.my
Maldives	Maldives Monetary Authority	www.mma.gov.mv
Mali	Bank of Central African States	www.beac.int³
Malta	Central Bank of Malta	www.centralbank malta.com

Country	Central Bank	Web Site
Mauritania	Central Bank of Mauritania	none
Mauritius	Bank of Mauritius	www.intnet.mu
Mexico	Bank of Mexico	www.banxico.org.mx
Moldova	National Bank of Moldova	www.bnm.org
Monaco	European Central Bank	www.ecb.int
Mongolia	Bank of Mongolia	www.mongolbank.mn
Montenegro	Central Bank of Montenegro	www.cb-mn.org/ indexE.htm
Montserrat	Eastern Caribbean Central Bank	www.eccb-centralbank.org
Morocco	Bank al-Maghrib	www.bkam.ma
Mozambique	Bank of Mozambique	www.bancomoc.mz
Namibia	Bank of Namibia	www.bon.com.na
Nauru	Reserve Bank of Australia	www.rba.gov.au
Nepal	State Bank of Nepal	www.nrb.org.np
Netherlands	The Netherlands Bank	www.dnb.nl
Netherlands Antilles	Bank of the Netherlands Antilles	www.centralbank.an
New Zealand	Reserve Bank of New Zealand	www.rbnz.govt.nz
Nicaragua	Central Bank of Nicaragua	www.bcn.gob.ni
Niger	Central Bank of West African States	www.bceao.int
Nigeria	Central Bank of Nigeria	www.cenbank.org
Norway	Bank of Norway	www.norges-bank.no
Oman	Central Bank of Oman	www.cbo-oman.org
Pakistan	State Bank of Pakistan	www.sbp.org.pk
Palau	none	none
Panama	National Bank of Panama	www.banconal.com.pa[2]
Papua New Guinea	Bank of Papua New Guinea	www.bankpng.gov.pg
Paraguay	Central Bank of Paraguay	www.bcp.gov.py[2]
Peru	Central Reserve Bank of Peru	www.bcrp.gob.pe
Philippines	Central Bank of the Philippines	www.bsp.gov.ph
Poland	National Bank of Poland	www.nbp.pl
Portugal	Bank of Portugal	www.bportugal.pt
Qatar	Qatar Central Bank	www.qcb.gov.qa
Romania	National Bank of Romania	www.bnro.ro
Russia	Central Bank of Russia	www.cbr.ru
Rwanda	National Bank of Rwanda	www.bnr.rw[3]
St. Helena and Dependencies	Bank of England	www.bankofengland.co.uk
St. Kitts and Nevis	Eastern Caribbean Central Bank	www.eccb-centralbank.org
St. Lucia	Eastern Caribbean Central Bank	www.eccb-centralbank.org
St. Vincent and the Grenadines	Eastern Caribbean Central Bank	www.eccb-centralbank.org
Samoa	Central Bank of Samoa	www.cbs.gov.ws
San Marino	Istituto di Credito Sammarinese	www.ics.sm
São Tomé & Príncipe	Central Bank of São Tomé & Príncipe	www.bcstp.st
Saudi Arabia	Saudi Arabian Monetary Agency	www.sama-ksa.org
Senegal	Central Bank of West African States	www.bceao.int
Serbia	National Bank of Serbia	www.nbs.co.yu/english/ index.htm
Seychelles	Central Bank of the Seychelles	www.cbs.sc
Sierra Leone	Bank of Sierra Leone	www.bankofsierraleone.org

Country	Central Bank	Web Site
Singapore	Monetary Authority of Singapore	www.mas.gov.sg
Slovakia	National Bank of Slovakia	www.nbs.sk
Slovenia	Bank of Slovenia	www.bsi.si
Solomon Islands	Central Bank of the Solomon Islands	www.cbsi.com.sb
Somalia	Central Bank of Somalia	none
South Africa	South African Reserve Bank	www.reservebank.co.za
Spain	Bank of Spain	www.bde.es
Sri Lanka	Central Bank of Sri Lanka	www.lanka.net/centralbank
Sudan	Bank of Sudan	www.bankofsudan.org
Suriname	Central Bank of Suriname	www.cbvs.sr
Swaziland	Central Bank of Swaziland	www.centralbank.sz/ cbs.html
Sweden	Bank of Sweden	www.riksbank.se
Switzerland	Swiss National Bank	www.snb.ch
Syria	Central Bank of Syria	www.syrecon.org/ establishments1a1.html
Taiwan	Central Bank of China	www.cbc.gov.tw
Tajikistan	National Bank of the Republic of Tajikistan	www.nbtj.org[4]
Tanzania	Bank of Tanzania	www.bot-tz.org
Thailand	Bank of Thailand	www.bot.or.th
Timor Liste	none	none
Togo	Bank of Central African States	www.beac.int[3]
Tonga	National Reserve Bank of Tonga	www.reservebank.to
Trinidad and Tobago	Central Bank of Trinidad and Tobago	www.central-bank.org.tt
Tunisia	Central Bank of Tunisia	www.bct.gov.tn
Turkey	Central Bank of the Republic of Turkey	www.tcmb.gov.tr
Turkmenistan	State Central Bank of Turkmenistan	none
Turks & Caicos	none	none
Tuvalu	Reserve Bank of Australia	www.rba.gov.au
Uganda	Bank of Uganda	www.bou.or.ug
Ukraine	National Bank of Ukraine	www.bank.gov.ua
United Arab Emirates	Central Bank of the United Arab Emirates	www.cbuae.gov.ae
United States	Federal Reserve Bank	www.federalreserve.gov
Uruguay	Central Bank of Uruguay	www.bcu.gub.uy
Uzbekistan	Central Bank of Uzbekistan	www.gov.uz/government/ cbu/cbu_0.htm
Vanuatu	Reserve Bank of Vanuatu	www.rbv.gov.vu
Vatican City	Vatican Bank (a.k.a. Institute for Religious Works)	none
Venezuela	Central Bank of Venezuela	www.bcv.org.ve[2]
Vietnam	State Bank of Vietnam	asemconnectvietnam.gov. vn/ministries/state_ bank.htm
Yemen	Central Bank of Yemen	www.centralbank.gov.ye
Zambia	Bank of Zambia	www.boz.zm
Zimbabwe	Reserve Bank of Zimbabwe	www.rbz.co.zw

1. In Portuguese only
2. In Spanish only
3. In French only
4. In Russian only

References

Numismatic and Philatelic Sources

Cowitt, Philip P. *1988–1989 World Currency Yearbook*. Brooklyn, NY: International Currency Analysis Inc., 1991.

Dunkling, Leslie, and Adrian Room. *The Guinness Book of Money*. London: Guinness Publishing, 1990.

Kloetzel, James E., ed. *2004 Scott Standard Postage Stamp Catalogue*. 160th ed. 6 vols. Sidney, OH: Scott Publishing Co., 2003.

Krause, Chester L., and Clifford Mishler. *Standard Catalog of World Coins*. Iola, WI: Krause Publications, 1979.

_____, _____, and Colin R. Bruce II. *1999 Standard Catalog of World Coins*. 26th ed. Iola, WI: Krause Publications, 1999.

_____, _____, and _____, eds. *2003 Standard Catalog of World Coins, 1901–Present*. 30th ed. Iola, WI: Krause Publications, 2002.

Pick, Albert. *Standard Catalog of World Paper Money*. 3rd ed. Iola, WI: Krause Publications, 1980.

_____, Colin R. Bruce II, and Neil Shafer, eds. *Standard Catalog of World Paper Money. Vol. 2, General Issues: 1650–1960*. 8th ed. Iola, WI: Krause Publications, 1996.

Room, Adrian. *Dictionary of Coin Names*. London: Routledge & Kegan Paul, 1987.

Shafer, Neil, and George S. Cuhaj, eds. *Standard Catalog of World Paper Money. Vol. 3, Modern Issues 1961–Date*. 8th ed. Iola, WI: Krause Publications, 2002.

Yalcinkaya, Orner. "The Meaning of World Currencies." *IBNS Journal*. 42, no. 4, 2004: 25–26.

Foreign Languages

Alderson, A. D., and Fahir İz. *The Oxford Turkish Dictionary*. 3rd ed. Oxford: Oxford University Press, 1992.

Andrusyshen, C. H., and J. N. Krett. *Українсько-Англійськии Словник* (Ukrainian-English Dictionary). Toronto: University of Toronto, 1993.

Anglicko-Slovenský a Slovensko-Anglický Vreckový Slovník (English-Slovak and Slovak-English Pocket Dictionary). Bratislava: Slovenské Pedagogické Nakladatel'stvo, 1998.

Atkins, Beryl T., *et al. Collins Robert French-English English-French Dictionary*. 5th ed. Glasgow: HarperCollins, 1998.

Benson, Morton. *Englesko-Srpskohrvatski Rečnik* (Serbocroatian and English Dictionary). Cambridge, England: Cambridge University Press, 1990.

Boon, Thòm Boonyavong. *English-Lao Dictionary*. Vientiane: Lao-American Association, 1962.

Cambridge Klett Concise Polish-English Dictionary: Podręczny Słownik Angielsko-Polski, Polsko-Angielski. Cambridge, England: Cambridge University Press, 2003.

Cherkesi, E. *Georgian-English Dictionary*. Oxford: University of Oxford, 1950.

Cleasby, Richard, and Gudbrand Vigfusson.

An Icelandic-English Dictionary. Oxford: Oxford University Press, 1957.

Collins English-Greek Dictionary. Glasgow: HarperCollins, 1997.

Collins German-English, English-German Dictionary. Glasgow: HarperResource, 2003.

Dalby, Andrew. *A Guide to World Language Dictionaries.* London: Library Association Publishing, 1998.

Daniels, Peter T., and William Bright, eds. *The World's Writing Systems.* New York: Oxford University Press, 1996.

Danish Dictionary: English-Danish, Danish-English. London: Routledge, 1995.

Elias, Elias A. *Elias Modern Dictionary: Arabic-English.* Cairo: Elias Modern Publishing House, 1994.

_____, and Edward E. Elias. *Elias Modern Dictionary: English-Arabic.* Cairo: Elias Modern Publishing House, 1993.

Kirkeby, Willy A. *English-Swahili Dictionary.* Dar es Salaam, Tanzania: Kapela Publishing Co., 2000.

Komac, Daša. *English-Slovene/Slovene-English Modern Dictionary.* New York: Hippocrene Books, 1994.

Kromhout, Jan. *Afrikaans-English, English-Afrikaans Dictionary.* New York: Hippocrene Books, 2001.

Larousse Concise Dictionary: Portuguese-English, English-Portuguese. Paris: Larousse, 2003.

László, Országh, and Magay Tamás. *Angol Magyar Nagyszótár* (English-Hungarian Dictionary). Budapest: Akadémiai Kiadó, Klasszikus Nagyszótárak, 1998.

Lê, Bá Khanh. *Vietnamese-English, English-Vietnamese Dictionary: With a Supplement of New Words English-Vietnamese.* New York: Hippocrene Books, 1991.

Leslau, Wolf. *Concise Amharic Dictionary: Amharic-English, English-Amharic.* Wiesbaden: Otto Harrassowitz, 1976.

McGregor, R. S., ed. *The Oxford Hindi-English Dictionary.* Oxford: Oxford University Press, 1993.

Miroiu, Mihai. *Romanian-English, English-Romanian Dictionary.* New York: Hippocrene Books, 1996.

Newmark, Leonard, ed. *Albanian-English Dictionary.* Oxford: Oxford University Press, 1998.

Nguyen, Dinh-Hoa. *Vietnamese-English Dictionary.* Rutland, VT: C. E. Tuttle Company, 1966.

Norwegian Dictionary: Norwegian-English, English-Norwegian. London: Routledge, 1994.

Osselton, N. E., and R. M. Hempelman. *The New Routledge Dutch Dictionary: Dutch-English/English-Dutch.* London: Routledge, 2003.

The Oxford English-Hebrew Dictionary. Oxford: Oxford University Press, 1996.

The Oxford Italian Desk Dictionary: Italian-English, English-Italian. Oxford: Oxford University Press, 1997.

Piesarskas, Bronius, and Bronius Svecevičius. *Lithuanian Dictionary: English-Lithuanian, Lithuanian-English.* London: Routledge, 1995.

Prisma's Swedish-English and English-Swedish Dictionary. 3rd ed. Minneapolis: University of Minnesota Press, 1997.

Rusev, Rusi. *Bulgarian-English Dictionary.* New York: F. Ungar Publishing Co., 1953.

Saagpakk, Paul F. *Eesti-Inglise Sõnaraamat* (Estonian-English Dictionary). New Haven: Yale University Press, 1982.

Simpson, D. P. *Cassell's New Latin Dictionary: Latin/English, English/Latin.* New York: Funk & Wagnalls, 1968.

Trnka, Nina. *Czech/English, English/Czech Concise Dictionary.* New York: Hippocrene Books, 1991.

Turkina, E. *Latviešu-Angļu Vārdnīca* (Latvian-English Dictionary). København: Imanta, 1964.

von Osterman, George F. *Manual of Foreign Languages.* 4th ed. New York: Central Book Company, 1952.

Webster's New World Concise Spanish Dictionary. New York: Wiley, 2004.

Wheeler, Marcus, and Paul Falla, eds. *The Oxford Russian Dictionary: Russian-English.* Oxford: Oxford University Press, 1997.

Williams, M. Monier. *A Dictionary English and Sanskrit.* Delhi: Motilal Banarsidass, 1956.

Wuolle, Aino. *English-Finnish Dictionary.* Porvoo: Söderström, 1978.

_____. *Finnish-English Dictionary.* Porvoo: Söderström, 1979.

Yacoubian, Adour H. *English-Armenian and Armenian-English Concise Dictionary.* Los Angeles: Armenian Archives Press, 1944.

Zekaria, A., ed. *Dictionary Amharic-English, English-Amharic.* New Delhi: Languages-of-the World Publications, 1991.

Index